THE SECRET CODE OF
THE SUPERIOR INVESTOR

Also by

JAMES K. GLASSMAN AND KEVIN A. HASSETT

Dow 36,000 _____

THE·SECRET CODE·OF·THE SUPERIOR INVESTOR

HOW TO BE A LONG-TERM WINNER IN A SHORT-TERM WORLD

JAMES K. GLASSMAN

CROWN
BUSINESS
NEW YORK

To my grandfathers . . .
Bertram Schiff (1899–1971),
who bought me my first share of stock,
and
Herbert Glassman (1896–1972),
who taught me business was a kick

Published by Crown Business, New York, New York.
Member of the Crown Publishing Group.

Random House, Inc. New York, Toronto, London, Sydney, Auckland
www.randomhouse.com

CROWN BUSINESS is a trademark and the Rising Sun colophon is a
registered trademark of Random House, Inc.

Printed in the United States of America

DESIGN BY ELINA D. NUDELMAN

Library of Congress Cataloging-in-Publication Data

Glassman, James K.
The secret code of the superior investor : how to be a long-term
winner in a short-term world / James K. Glassman.—1st ed.
1. Stocks.   2. Securities.   3. Investments.   4. Portfolio management.
5. Finance, Personal.
I. Title.
HG6041.G54   2001

332.6—dc21   2001047281

ISBN 0-8129-9108-7

10 9 8 7 6 5 4 3 2 1

FIRST EDITION

CONTENTS

Preface ix

Introduction 3

PART 1: THE BASICS

1. Your Goals Determine Your Investments 31

2. The Longer Your Time Horizon, the More
   Shares You Need to Own 33

3. Don't Own Stocks and Bonds; Own a Portfolio 37

PART 2: PRINCIPLES OF THE SECRET CODE

4. Buy and Hold 49

5. Stocks Are Cheap 53

6. Be a Partaker, Not an Outsmarter 63

7.   Read the Gospel 67

8.   Buy Companies with a Moat to Protect Them 73

PART 3: PUTTING THE CODE INTO ACTION

9.   It's *Not* the Economy, Stupid 81

10.   Diversify, Diversify, Diversify 85

11.   P/E Ratios 93

12.   Count the Cash 105

13.   Find Companies with Solid Assets and Without
      Threatening Debt 115

14.   No One Can Time the Market. Don't Try It. 121

15.   Nix the Nasdaq. Do the Dow. 125

16.   Always Think Taxes 133

17.   Always Think Inflation 139

18.   Always Think Expenses 143

19.   Never Buy on Margin 149

20.   Never Short a Stock 153

21.   Steal This Fund 157

22.   Don't Watch CNBC in Broad Daylight 163

23.   Give Dividends the Respect They Deserve 169

24.   Make Your Children and Grandchildren
      Investors at Birth 175

25. If You Can't Sit Still, Set Up a "Fun-
    and-Games" Account 179

26. Systems Don't Work, but Use This One Anyway 183

PART 4: WHEN TO BUY, WHEN TO SELL

27. Bear Markets Are for Buying 191

28. Make a Wish List and Keep it Handy 195

29. Sell Almost Never 199

PART 5: WHAT TO BUY

30. Invest in People, Not Stocks 207

31. Invest with Your Heart as well as Your Mind 211

32. Value or Growth? Both 217

33. Some of the Best Stocks Are Right Under
    Your Nose 225

34. Own Companies, Not Countries 231

35. Don't Invest in Things. Invest in Brains. 239

36. Do Drugs 245

37. If You Could Buy Only One Stock 251

38. The Industry to Buy for the Next Generation 257

39. Boring Is Beautiful 265

40. Small-Caps Are Big Winners 269

41. Technology Is a Sector, Not a Retirement Plan 275

PART 6: BONDS AND CASH

42. Bonds for the Short-Term and
    Medium-Term Only 287

43. Build a Ladder for Your Bonds,
    and Hold Them to Maturity .295

44. Municipal Bonds Can Be Bargains 299

45. Forget Corporate Bonds 303

46. Hot TIPS: Buy the One Investment
    Guaranteed to Beat Inflation 307

47. Stash Your Cash 311

    Conclusion 315

    Index 319

LIKE MANY BOOKS, this one was accidental. A few years out of college, I started a weekly alternative newspaper in New Orleans. My main interest at the time was politics, not stocks. But in Louisiana, along with articles about gothic politicians, rock reviews and crayfish recipes, our readers, we found surprisingly, were interested in finance, so we decided to cover local stocks. The job fell to me, and since the newspaper had only three writers and we wanted the world to think there was a huge staff, I wrote under a pseudonym, Benjamin O'Connor—Benjamin, after the stock-market genius (see Chapter 7) and the newborn son of my stockbroker, and O'Connor because I liked the sound, I guess. O'Connor and I fell in love with the market.

The affair has continued for 30 years, in publications as varied as the *Reader's Digest* and the *International Herald Tribune.* Over this period, something big happened in finance: lots of Americans entered the stock market for the first time. When I started my New Orleans weekly, only one in 10 families owned stocks; in 1990, the figure was one in five; today, one in two. Many were reluctant investors, thrust into a baffling and frustrating world. They have to make their own decisions about where to put their 401(k) money, whether to buy stocks or bonds, high-tech or oil-service. They have had to cope with terrorist attacks and sudden economic slowdowns. They don't know where to turn.

Which is where this book, which I have wanted to write since my O'Connor days, comes in. It is a guide for the perplexed—for novices on up—and it offers readers the chance to gain the same mastery over the principles and practice of finance as superior investors. In fact, the closest analog is *Mastering the Art of French Cooking,* Julia Child's 1961 book that clearly and elegantly demystified a subject that fascinated and intimidated millions. Investing also fascinates and intimidates, but, unlike French cooking, it can't be ignored in favor of hamburgers. There's nowhere to hide. If you stick your money under the mattress, you are certain to lose. For most Americans—whether we like it or not—stocks offer the *only* route to the kind of wealth necessary for a comfortable life. Not investing is not an option.

Throughout, I use examples of real stocks, and, while I preach long-term investing, it's important to understand that businesses can change between the time a manuscript is finished and a book is in your hands. So check out current conditions yourself; don't buy merely on a tip—not even mine.

Read *The Secret Code of the Superior Investor* more than once: first, straight through; then, dip into it as you need to remind yourself about education stocks, Treasury bonds, P/E ratios and the hundreds of other details the book covers. It will bring you profit, comfort and joy.

The author, using his actual name, has thanks to distribute as well. First, to the financial giants on whose shoulders I am standing: Benjamin Graham, Philip Fisher, Burton Malkiel and, above all, Warren Buffett. To my editor John Mahaney, my agent Rafe Sagalyn, and my mentors in journalism and finance and life in general, including Ian Arnof, Max Boot, Seph Dupuy, Jill Dutt, David Fenstermaker, Neal Freeman, David Ignatius, Arthur Levitt, Jack Limpert, Phil Merrill, T. Nolan, Martin Peretz, Warren Poland, Tom Rapier and Jim Warren. Also, to my colleagues at the American Enterprise Institute, especially Kevin Hassett (with whom I wrote *Dow 36,000*), Christopher DeMuth and David Gerson, and at TechCentralStation.com, especially Charles Francis and Justin Peterson. Thanks, as well, to Sharon Utz of AEI and James Freeman, who helped me with the research on *The Secret Code of the Superior Investor*; to Jon Newlin, my guide in all things literary, to my daughters, Zoe and Kate, to Molly Lowe, to my parents, Elaine Garfield and Stanley Glassman, and to Nancy Hechinger, who has brought *me* comfort and joy—and is a great editor, to boot.

—Falls Village, Connecticut, September 2001

THE SECRET CODE OF
THE SUPERIOR INVESTOR

"As there are few subjects of conversation more general than the value of stocks, and hardly any thing so little understood, we shall here give account of them in as clear and concise a manner as possible."

—*Encyclopedia Britannica*, first edition (1768)

INTRODUCTION

TODAY, INVESTORS ARE DESPERATE for certainty in an uncertain financial world. They are looking for rigorous, practical, straightforward, tried-and-true advice that applies in both bear and bull markets. That is what this book provides—a set of principles that will give you ballast, helping you keep your investing equilibrium no matter which ways the winds blow. The catastrophic terror attacks on September 11, 2001 only underscored the importance of a bedrock financial creed, solid ground even in the worst earthquake. Now more than ever, investors need to turn to time-tested principles. I call the principles a "Secret Code." It's a code in two senses of the word: both as a group of rules to guide you and as a set of tools to decipher a mystery. The truth is, the advice most investors get is garbled, raw, confusing. This book helps you crack the secret code of investing.

It offers specific recommendations on what to buy (for example, pharmaceutical and for-profit education stocks) and what not to (semiconductor stocks, corporate bonds). It tells you how to build the best portfolio for retirement, how to accumulate what you need for your kids' tuition or your trip to Paris, how to find a broker, how to avoid being skewered by taxes, inflation and the stock market's wild volatility.

But, more important, this is a book built on a coherent philosophy of investing—a set of precepts that I have been developing over more than 20 years—by studying and analyzing financial history, by writing about investing as a columnist for such publications as the *Washington Post, Reader's Digest* and the *International Herald Tribune,* and by practicing what I preach. It's a code that works. During the debacle of 2000, the portfolio of stocks that my co-author, economist Kevin Hassett, and I recommended in our 1999 book, *Dow 36,000,* rose smartly. Our top pick, Tootsie Roll Industries—yes, chocolate lollipops in an age of microchips—shot up more than 50 percent. In *Dow 36,000,* we developed a sophisticated financial theory that led to an enthusiastic view of the stock market for the decade ahead, but we warned investors vigorously that they must follow a specific discipline and beware that shares would not go straight up. In this book I have developed that discipline fully and spell it out in clear detail in a Secret Code of 47 laws.

Throughout the late 1990s, investing was too easy. Toss a dart at the stock pages and you speared a winner. The market as a whole tripled, and the tech-heavy Nasdaq quintupled. A profitless company like Priceline.com, online seller of discounted airline tickets, soared from $10 a share to $100 in two months. You couldn't lose money in stocks if you tried.

The period was so lucrative that it taught investors bad habits. Any swing, no matter how uncoordinated, made a hit. The wind was so strong at your back in a year like 1998 that an infield pop-up blew over the fence for a home run. But, starting in March 2000, as headwinds began to blow, those bad habits suddenly put many of America's 50 million investing families—20 million of them new to the market since 1993—at a loss.

The way to make money today is not to ferret out the hottest stock and then buy and sell it at precisely the right moment. Instead, it is to become a partner in a good business for a long time, ignoring all the noise and keeping your eyes on the prize.

If that sounds easy, it is not. Unfortunately, investors are beset on all sides by exploiters and distracters. The media are interested, naturally, in selling advertising and subscriptions, so they constantly scream about the hottest mutual fund, the sizzling stock of the month (or the day), or they obsess about what the Federal Reserve will do at its next meeting. In this book, you will learn that *none* of that matters to the superior investor. You will also learn to turn off CNBC, CNNfn and any other network that emphasizes up-to-the-minute stock quotes. Watching prices bob up and down simply makes investors anxious. In fact, every newspaper in America should eliminate its stock pages and devote the space to articles about the actual *businesses* that investors buy when they purchase shares of stock.

Meanwhile, Wall Street analysts tout the same stocks that their firms are underwriting—a scandalous conflict of interest—or they show clients charts that profess to establish "support levels" and "takeoff points." Again, this book will encourage you to ignore all of this sound and fury and concentrate on the information that will really make you money—information about the *companies* whose shares you are buying. As super-investor Warren Buffett once put it: "Most of our large stock positions are going to be held for many years, and the scorecard on our investment decisions will be provided by business results over that period, and not by prices on any given day." In the short term, the price of a stock is determined by the emotions of investors, but in the long term it is determined by the operating results of the company. Those results are a lot easier to predict than the emotions.

Investing is hard, but it is not hard in the way most people think it is. It requires not the latest juicy tip or a brilliant intuition about when a stock is headed south but, instead, an appreciation of the wisdom of Benjamin Graham, the greatest financial mind of the twentieth century. Graham wrote more than 60 years ago: "The investor's chief problem—and even his worst enemy—is likely to be himself." This book will help you tame that enemy by becoming what I call a "superior investor"—more informed than the crowd, and above it. As a superior investor following the

Secret Code, you will understand why it is better to be calm than frenetic, and why day-trading—in fact, stock trading of *any* sort—is as old-fashioned and foolish as bell-bottoms.

Here, then, are the big, basic principles that inform the Code and form the core of this book:

1. **Get in touch with your inner investor.**

   Before you invest a penny, you need to know who you are and what you want. The best qualities for investors are the same ones Aristotle admired: moderation, common sense, restraint, modesty and integrity. It's rare to find a successful investor who isn't a solid citizen in the classical sense. Contrary to popular opinion, sharp-dealing and a gambler's lust for the main chance are *not* at the soul of good investing.

After all, investing begins with delayed gratification, with the abnegation of desire. Having earned $10, you really have only two choices. You can use it for consumption, getting pleasure or comfort right now—buying a movie ticket or a plate of sushi or a plaid tee-shirt—or you can put it away, that is, invest it. Actually, "put it away" is not the right phrase. When you invest, you actually give *someone else* the use of your money. It is still being used, turned into a factory or a ton of steel or the windows of a new school, but the full benefit doesn't go to you—at least not immediately.

Investing also rewards faith and trust. Since you are turning over your money to someone else, you can't be sure what will happen to it. For that reason, investing thrives in a society where the rule of law and a culture based on responsibility are well established.

The hope is that, if you put your money away, you will have a good deal more of it in the future, so that, having postponed your purchase, you will be able to buy two movie tickets, a plate of shushi *plus* some shrimp tempura and maybe a classier tee-shirt. The longer you hold your investments, the more valuable they become. Patience pays, literally.

Investors come in two varieties, as you will see in detail in

Chapter 6. **Outsmarters** think the way to make money in the market is to beat the system, buying on tips, selling (somehow) just before the market falls. They don't much care which companies they buy, only which *stocks*. **Partakers**, on the other hand, try to find good businesses and become partners, sharing in corporate fortunes over the long haul. The reason outsmarters don't win at investing is that it's not a game you can *beat*. Yes, exceptional investors can get returns that might be a few percentage points better than the market as a whole. You might be born this way, or you might decide to devote your life to becoming a professional investor as others become professional golfers or neurosurgeons. But why? As a partaker, you get nearly all the benefits with little of the sweat and anxiety.

You should also resign yourself to the fact that you cannot predict what stocks will do in the short term. Admitting ignorance can be the start of wisdom. Burton Malkiel, a Princeton University economist, famously said that stocks move in a "random walk"—that is, a pattern "in which future steps or directions cannot be predicted on the basis of past actions."

In other words, at any moment, all public information is reflected in a company's stock price. All possible knowledge about the firm has been "discounted" or priced into the stock. (Company insiders may have special information, but they are prohibited by law from acting on it.) It is *new* public information that changes a stock's price, and, by definition, what's new is not known, or knowable. Analysts may have a good idea that a pharmaceutical company will get federal approval for a blockbuster drug. The event has not happened yet, but it is anticipated and built into the price. Under such circumstances, if the drug is rejected by the feds, then the price will probably fall.

It should actually be a relief to learn that one of the most important laws of investing is that nobody can outsmart the market. But accepting that knowledge requires a kind of equanimity that many investors lack. Virtues like moderation and restraint aren't in big supply. Think of them as goals, and the Secret Code, by telling you the truth about stocks—including your limitations in picking and trading them—will help you at least approach these objectives.

The second part of knowing yourself is easier: decide what you want and when you want it. There are three kinds of investment assets you can choose, and the selection depends on your time horizon, a concept developed in the next few chapters. Stocks are for the long run (meaning you need to hold them for five years or more), bonds are for the medium term (one to five years), and cash is for the short term. Cash, by the way, is actually the same thing as a very short-term bond. When you open a checking account, for example, you're making a loan to a bank—a loan that you can withdraw any time you want by writing a check. The market generally rewards partnership more than it rewards lending. In other words, the market believes lending is safer and surer, in part because lenders stand in front of shareholders in a bankruptcy. But this age-old risk preference is not truly rational, not supported by history. For that reason, stocks present an excellent opportunity today—since they return *too much*.

But that's for a later chapter—5, to be exact. The point here is that, once you understand that assets are linked to time, you can look at your own needs and make matches. For most of your life, your retirement fund should be invested in stocks. If you have saved $50,000 for the down payment on a house you expect to buy within two years, then that money should be kept in bonds. Your emergency funds, which you could need any second, should be kept in cash, which is a technical term for certificates of deposit, bank accounts, Treasury bills or a money market fund—anything that retains its value from day to day and that is accessible.

Finally, before you invest, you need to assess your own level of risk aversion—how scared you are when stocks take a sharp fall. If owning stocks keeps you awake at night, then the extra gains probably aren't worth it. For your health and sanity, you are better off moving into the stock market slowly. The Secret Code, however, should help reduce your fear by showing you how the riskiness of stocks is modulated significantly by two things: diversification and time. . . .

2. Time is money.

Time is the single most important factor in investing—more important than the stocks or the bonds you pick, or your cleverness in buying or selling at just the right moment. The reason time is so powerful can be summed up in a phrase: the miracle of compounding, which Albert Einstein called the most powerful force in the universe. Each year, you earn a small return on your original investment—your principal. But as time goes by, you earn an additional return on your *returns,* or interest on interest. This idea is so important that I need to spell it out with a little math.

Say you invest $100 in a savings account that earns 6 percent interest, paid annually. Assume as well that you don't withdraw the principal or the interest but let it mount up over the years.

By the end of the first year, your $100 earns $6 in interest for a total of $106 ($100 × 1.06 = $106). But in the second year, the 6 percent interest applies not merely to the original $100 but to the extra $6 in interest. Thus: $106 × 1.06 = $112.36. After 10 years, the investment grows in this manner to $189.83 ($100 × 1.06 to the tenth power). If we had applied the 6 percent each year simply to the original principal, then the total would have been $160. Instead of earning $60 on your initial $100, you earn $89.83—or nearly half-again as much. That's the power of compounding in action, and, over long periods, the power is miraculous.

Since 1926, the broad U.S. stock market, as represented by the Standard & Poor's 500-Stock Index—roughly the 500 largest American companies listed on the three major stock exchanges—has returned an average of 11 percent a year. A stock's annual "return" is the rise in its price (its "capital appreciation") over the course of a year plus the dividends it paid (if any), compared with the stock's price at the beginning of the year. So if General Electric cost $50 a share on Jan. 1 and

$54.50 per share 12 months later, then its capital appreciation is $4.50. If GE paid a quarterly dividend of 25 cents, then it pro- vided shareholders with another dollar. That's a return of $5.50 in all. Divide $5.50 by $50 and you get 0.11, or 11 percent.

Now, assume that you begin with $10,000 today and invest it in a broadly diversified portfolio of stocks (like the S&P index itself) that returns an average of 11 percent a year. There is no *guarantee* that you will get an 11 percent return, of course, but history is a pretty good forecaster. At this rate, roughly every six and a half years, the value of your portfolio will double. A quick- and-dirty way to find how long it takes an investment to double is by using the "Rule of 72." Divide the yearly percentage rate of growth (in this case 11) into 72, and you get about 6.5. By comparison, at a rate of growth of 18 percent, doubling time is just four years; at 4 percent, it's 18 years.

But back to our $10,000. After six and a half years, it grows to about $20,000; after 13 years, to $40,000; after about 26 years, to $160,000; after 52 years, to well over $2 million.

Here is another way to think about the miracle of com- pounding over time. During the first six-and-a-half-year period you own your portfolio, it grows by $10,000; during the fourth six-and-a-half-year period, it grows by $80,000.

Holding onto an investment for 26 or 52 years is not so far- fetched as it sounds. If you begin at age 30, you can build a $10,000 stake into over $1 million before you are about 70— which will be a relatively young age (one hopes) by then. In Chapter 4, you will hear the story of a woman named Anne Scheiber, who managed to turn a $5,000 nest egg into $20 mil- lion merely by buying and holding good stocks.

Now, understand that, in 26 years, $160,000 won't have as much purchasing power as it does today. Inflation erodes the value of money. Guessing the rate of inflation over the next few decades isn't easy, but let's say it is 3 percent on average, a little higher than during the decade of the 1990s. At 3 percent, a dol- lar 26 years from now will have the purchasing power of a little less than 50 cents in today's currency. In other words, $160,000 will buy about what $80,000 does today. Still, that's not a bad gain on your investment: $10,000 rising to $80,000 in less than a generation.

The power of time is the reason that investors should start early. How early? Think birth. If parents are prescient enough, they can set up a sort of Social Security plan of their own for their child. (See Chapter 24 on investing for kids.) Simply put $5,000 into an investment that we'll assume will return an annual average of 10 percent (probably a mix of stocks and a few bonds). By the time the child is 65, the $5,000 will become $3 million. That should be enough to purchase an annuity—an investment contract with an insurance company that provides for an income—of $200,000—which, after accounting for likely inflation, should be about double what the average retiree gets today from Social Security.

But don't count on parents. Say that your goal is to retire at age 60 with $1 million. Start by age 29 and invest $5,000 per year (again at 10 percent) and you'll reach your goal. But if you wait until you are 39 to begin (investing the same $5,000 a year at 10 percent), you'll accumulate only $300,000.

Here is an even more dramatic example of the power of starting early: One investor decides to begin investing at age 25. She puts $2,000 a year into a portfolio of stocks and bonds that return an average of 10 percent a year (again, no great shakes). At age 35, after investing a total of $20,000, she stops and never adds another penny to her account. But the value of her fund continues to grow, and by the time she is 65, she has $546,197.

A second investor also wants to invest, but he waits until he is 35 before starting. He, too, invests $2,000 a year in a mutual fund returning 10 percent a year. But he invests for a full *30* years—a total of $60,000. How much does he have age 65? Just $328,988.

Time not only gives you the opportunity to exploit the miracle of compounding; time, as I'll show you, also moderates risk. But first

3. **With stocks, it's the *business* that counts.**
Study the balance sheet and the income statement, not the stock page.

A share of stock, after all, is a piece of a business, so it stands to reason that its value depends on how the business performs. When a corporation is launched, its founders issue shares to raise money in order to rent space, pay employees and generally get off the ground. The shareholders might be willing to wait for a few years, but ultimately they want to see a flow of cash coming out of the business and into their pockets.

When a company's revenues exceed its expenses, it generates profits. Some of those profits have to go back into the company to make capital investments in new property and machines, but the rest—the free cash flow—is available for the shareholders. The company can either pay them dividends (typically, every three months) or it can keep the free cash on the shareholders' behalf for later use (avoiding an extra level of taxes). But, in the end, the reason to invest in a company is the profits—or, more precisely, the free cash flow—it will throw off.

What determines the price of a stock in the long run is investors' estimates of what that cash flow will be in future. Projecting cash flow isn't easy, and events every day—a product shortage, new competition, a change in management—affect the guessing game. But, in the end, the way to tell whether you should buy a stock is through an examination of the business.

The past is not a perfect guide to the future, but it is the best we have, so, first, look at balance sheets, which show a company's assets (what it owns) and its liabilities (what it owes), and income statements, which show how much money the company is making or losing every quarter. (I will show you how to examine these financial statements, with ease, in Chapters 12 and 13.) Next, look at the business itself: what's the likely demand for its products, how good is the management, how tough is the competition. I like to own a business that has a moat around it, to protect it from competitors that will cut prices and reduce profits (for details, see Chapter 8).

A moat might be a patent—which is why I like pharmaceutical stocks so much. For a set number of years, no one can make Viagra but Pfizer. Or a moat might be a great brand name like Coca-Cola or Mercedes-Benz—or even cartoon characters like Walt Disney has in Mickey Mouse and Snow White. Or it may be a strong network of leases, a kind of geographic moat, like Starbucks, the coffeehouse chain, owns. Or it may simply be a reputation for service, like that of Home Depot. Competition may be wonderful for consumers and for the economy as a whole, but I prefer businesses with as little as possible.

I also look for companies that . . .

- **Have had a consistent track record of increasing their earnings at a rate of at least 7 percent a year for the past ten years**
- **Have a good chance of prospering 50 years from now (in other words, you shouldn't invest in hula hoop manufacturers)**
- **Don't have huge capital demands for the profits they make (in other words, they don't have to build expensive new plants every few years like semiconductor makers do)**

While numbers are important, you should not get carried away by quarterly earnings reports, the way that nearly all Wall Street analysts do. Clayton Christensen of the Harvard Business School notes that analysts are "theory-free investors. All they can do is react to the numbers. But the numbers they react to are measures of past performance. That's why [analysts] go in big herds. [They] have enshrined as a virtue the notion that you should be data-driven, [but] if you wait until the data are clear, the game is over." He's right—a grounding in *ideas* about companies is more important than an obsession with last quarter's profits.

4. **Own stocks not individually, but in portfolios.**

When you own just a few stocks, or even a lot of stocks in just one economic sector, you are inviting trouble. The fate of any business is utterly unpredictable, but history shows that the fate of the stock market as a whole is closely connected to the fate of the economy, which has been awfully consistent over the past 60 years. So, instead of owning a few individual stocks in a few sectors, you need to own *portfolios* of many stocks in many sectors—in an effort to reduce your risk through diversification (see Chapters 3 and 10).

For example, in the year 2000, Microsoft, which was then the largest company in the world in terms of market capitalization—that is, the value, according to the stock market on a given day, of all its shares of stock—fell 63 percent. The profitable online auction company, eBay, Inc., dropped from $127 to $27. In the fourth quarter alone, PBHG Technology and Communications, a $3 billion mutual fund, lost more than half its value.

Technology, however, is not the stock market, as I emphasize in Chapter 41. Practically every sector—from tobacco to oil service to health care—is more risky than the market as a whole (just as an individual stock is more risky than the sector of which it is a part). In 2000, the real estate sector returned a healthy 27 percent after falling 3 percent in 1999 and 16 percent in 1998. But in 1997, real estate returned 23 percent and in 1996, a hefty 32 percent. In fact, four-fifths of all sectors, or industries, rose in 2000, the year tech took its big swan dive.

Look at the stock market as a whole—even in 2000, a year in which the Federal Reserve aggressively raised interest rates, oil prices tripled and the U.S. took a month after the election to decide who was president. The S&P's high point during 2000 was 1527; its low was 1265. Now, that is not a very wide range. It is the equivalent of a stock that varied, during the course of an entire year, between a high of $15.27 and a low of $12.65. The Dow varied between a high of 11,311 and a low of 9796. Think of a stock bouncing merely between $28 and $24.50. But then consider individual stocks, even ones you might assume are pretty calm. Gillette, the razor maker, bounced between $42 and $27—twice as risky as the market. General Motors was even bumpier, varying between $94 and $48.

A certain amount of volatility in price is inherent in stocks. A portfolio that includes the entire market will produce what's called "systemic" or "nondiversifiable" risk. That's the risk that comes with the territory—with owning, say, the 500 stocks of the S&P index, a good proxy for the entire market. But a second kind of risk is called "idiosyncratic"—the bumpiness associated with individual stocks. This risk can be eliminated, as I show in Chapter 10.

How many stocks do you need to own to bring risk close to systemic levels? That's a matter of controversy among economists, but the answer is lower than you would expect. If you choose wisely, giving representation to sectors reflecting the entire economy, then a portfolio of around 30 stocks should do the trick. Clearly, it may be difficult to pick and manage such a portfolio yourself. You may need help, and later I will show how to find it. One approach is to manage a small portfolio of your own and to buy mutual funds as well (see Chapter 3).

Just don't be surprised by the wild riskiness of individual stocks you own. It's perfectly natural. Look at the 15 stocks that my co-author Kevin Hassett and I highlighted in our 1999 book on stock valuation, *Dow 36,000*: Sixteen months after publication, this little portfolio had returned more than 12 percent, a good showing during a period when the S&P lost about 1 percent. But individual stocks among the 15 were all over the lot—from a loss of 53 percent for Microsoft to a gain of 75 percent for DeVry, a fine company that runs a chain of technical schools. Five stocks lost at least 18 percent each and four stocks gained at least 41 percent each. Incredibly, only one-fifth of the stocks were essentially flat (that is, their returns lay between plus-or-minus 15 percent). That's volatility, and it's not unusual. Protect yourself with a diverse enough portfolio to dampen risk.

5. **When you hold a stock long enough, it becomes less risky than a bond.**

   What is risk anyway? If an investment increased your purchasing power by a specific amount per year—10 percent, say—then there would be no risk in it. Investing would be a lark. By definition, risk is the possibility of harm or loss, and when you invest—that is, delay gratification and give your money to someone else to use—there is *always* the chance that you will lose it, in whole or part. Even bonds issued by the United States Treasury carry risk—not so much that you won't get your principal back but that this money, eroded by inflation, won't be able to purchase much.

In financial jargon, risk is usually defined as volatility—the ups and downs of an investment's return. While the returns of bonds and cash don't bounce around a great deal, the returns of stocks do. This kind of riskiness may not sound so terrible. If you plan to hold onto your shares for, say, five years, what's the difference whether they rise every year at 10 percent or whether in some years they rise 60 percent and in others they fall 30 percent? For a superhuman investor, there is no difference at all, but for most investors, the difference is huge.

Volatility affects behavior, and prudent behavior is the key to investing success. It is hard to live up to Aristotle's ideal of moderation when your Cisco stock drops by half in a month. While a rational response to a decline in the value of your favorite stock may be to buy more, the *real* response of most investors is cold fear, leading to an impulse to sell—often at just the wrong time.

In theory, volatility can be the investor's best friend—since it offers good stocks at bargain prices. In practice, volatility is usually the investor's worst enemy—since it induces him to act irrationally. In real life, stock-market risk is a necessary evil. It is what makes investing difficult.

The good news, however, is that stocks are risky in a particular way. Taken individually, they are wildly volatile in the short term, and moderately volatile in the longer term. Taken

together—in an index like the S&P 500 o.
Industrial Average with its 30 stocks—they
in the short term but not more volatile than
longer term.

Here's one extreme example: On Monday, Oct.
Dow fell a sickening 554 points—at the time, the
day decline ever. But on Tuesday, the Dow rose an unpressive
337 points. The net effect was tiny—a decline of less than 3 percent, which is the equivalent of a stock falling from $30 to $29.
For the first 10 months of the year, the Dow had risen robustly,
and it was still well ahead even after the horror of that Monday.
If, as a contemporary Rip Van Winkle, you had fallen asleep on
Jan. 1, 1997, you could have awakened on Hallowe'en with a big
smile and said, "Fine. The market is up 16 percent." And, then,
of course, you would have gone back to sleep.

In microcosm, the experience of 1997 describes the stock
market very well: Crazy things happen in an hour or a day or a
week, a year or even a few years. But, if history is a guide, the
market's bumpiness is smoothed out over time. The longer you
hold stocks, the less risky they become.

This idea is so counter-intuitive that it needs more explanation. In 1995, Jeremy Siegel, a professor at the Wharton School
of the University of Pennsylvania, wrote a book called *Stocks for
the Long Run* that pulled together data on stocks and bonds, their
returns and their risk, going all the way back—believe it or
not—to 1802. He found some frightening facts. For instance, the
best year for the stock market produced a gain, after considering
inflation, of 67 percent. So an investment of $100 became $167.
But the worst year produced a loss of 39 percent. So $100
became $61. The range of results, from top to bottom, was more
than 100 percent of the original stake! But, at the same time,
Siegel's research convinced him that, over periods longer than a
few years, the riskiness declines significantly.

His conclusion was that "the safest long-term investment has
clearly been stocks and not bonds." He found, for example, that
there has *never* been a period of 17 years or longer in history in

a diversified portfolio of stocks (the S&P 500 or its predecessors) did not produce a positive return after inflation. Bonds were another story. Looking at every overlapping 20-year period since 1802 (that is, 1802–21, 1803–22, up to the present), Siegel discovered that the worst period for stocks produced a total return, after inflation, of more than 20 percent. The worst 20-year period for bonds, after inflation? *Minus* 60 percent!

The most common way to measure risk is through standard deviation—a figure that tells how much returns vary, from year to year, as compared to the average. For instance, if a portfolio of stocks produced returns of 11 percent every single year (or 3 percent, for that matter), then its standard deviation would be zero. The portfolio would not be risky at all. In fact, the S&P 500 has a standard deviation of about 20 percent over calendar-year periods. Remember that the S&P has returned an average of 11 percent annually. So, according to the rules of standard deviation, the index produces returns in two-thirds of all years that fall in a range 20 percentage points higher and 20 percentage points lower than the average—or from plus 31 percent to minus 9 percent. Now, *that's* volatile!

But Siegel found that, when investors held stock portfolios for 10 years without selling them, volatility plummeted to a standard deviation of just 5 percent, meaning that returns in two-thirds of the years fall into a range between plus-6 percent and plus-16 percent. And for investors who held stocks for 30 years, volatility dwindled to nothingness—a standard deviation of about 2 percent, which is lower than the risk of U.S. Treasury bonds (after accounting for inflation in both cases).

The history is clear: Hold stocks long enough, and they become no more risky than bonds. That may be the most important principle of the Secret Code.

6. **Don't trade stocks.**

Many investors are convinced they can own stocks for the short term. They reason that the bad times that knock stock

prices down are foreseeable, and, even if they miss the beginning of a downturn, they can sell shortly after it begins and
buy back shortly after the recovery starts.

This is dangerous thinking.

The practice of jumping in and out of stocks is called "trading." It does not work, period. In 1998, two economists, Brad M.
Barber and Terrance Odean of the University of California at
Davis, conducted an extensive study—the first in history—of
the actual stock records of 64,715 customers of an unnamed discount broker between 1991 and 1996. They found that, over
these five years, the average investor earned a gross return of
17.7 percent annually, beating the market as a whole, which
returned 17.1 percent. Unfortunately, however, after transaction
costs—mainly brokerage commissions—the net return (what the
investors actually earned) was 15.3 percent.

But, more important, the 12,000 investors that did the most
trading got the worst net returns (an average of only 10 percent)
while those who did the least trading got the best returns (17.5
percent). In other words, assuming that these returns continue
for another 15 years and that each group started with $1,000,
the active traders would end up with $6,700 while the passive
investors would end up with $25,200. "Our central message,"
concluded the two economists, "is that trading is hazardous to
your wealth."

But can't some investors time the market correctly? Maybe a
handful, but don't assume you are among them. Of market timing, John Bogle, the founder of the Vanguard Group, the well-
known mutual fund firm, has written: "After nearly fifty years in
the business, I do not know of anybody who has done it successfully and consistently. I do not even know anybody who
knows anybody who has done it successfully and consistently."

The best investors of the twentieth century made their fortunes by buying good companies and holding onto them for a
long time. For example, Graham's 1948 investment of $720,000
in GEICO, the insurance company that bypasses agents, was

worth $500 million a few decades later. Warren Buffett, Graham's protégé, has prospered by finding only a few companies (Coca-Cola, the Washington Post, See's Candies) and never selling them. "If the job has been correctly done when a common stock is purchased," wrote Philip A. Fisher, another highly successful investor, "the time to sell it is—almost never." (I'll explain the "almost" in Chapter 29.)

The reason trading does not work is embodied in Malkiel's "random walk." No one (without illegal inside information) knows what will happen to a stock price tomorrow. Predicting these moves is quite simply impossible. It's a fact you have to live with, despite cherished notions of your own genius. As a result, trading simply eats up profits through transaction costs—the commissions on buying and selling stocks, the sacrifice of the spread between a stock's "bid" and "asked" price and the "opportunity cost" (as economists call it) for being out of the market while you sit on cash and ponder when to get back in.

This last cost can be high. Imagine that you have $100,000 to invest but that, as a trader, you have an average of $20,000 of that amount out of the market, waiting for the right time to recommit it. History shows that cash earns about 4 percent annually while stocks return 11 percent. That means that the cost of market timing is $1,400 a year [$20,000 × (.11 − .04)]. In addition, market timers have a propensity to be wrong in dramatic ways. They get out of stocks at the bottom and fail to get back in until the stock has already turned around. "How is the investor to know when to buy back?" asks Fisher. "Theoretically, it should be after the decline. However, this presupposes that the investor will know when the decline will end. When a bear market has come, I have not seen one time in ten when the investor actually gets back into the same shares before they have gone up above his selling price."

No one at the New York Stock Exchange blows a whistle when a stock slump ends and shouts, "O.K., everyone back in the pool!" On the contrary. Turnarounds come swiftly and stealthily.

Just as the press was moaning about the horrors of investing in technology stocks, citing over and over the 39 percent decline in the tech-heavy Nasdaq Composite Index in 2000, these same stocks were recovering dramatically. In the first four weeks of 2001, Microsoft surged 41 percent and IBM 31 percent, Doubleclick and eBay doubled, the Nasdaq jumped 12 percent and the Street.com Internet index increased 30 percent. At this point, many momentum players (that is, investors whose trading follows trends) jumped back into the market. Too late—over the next four weeks, it lost all those gains.

One of my favorite analysts, the veteran H. Bradlee Perry of David L. Babson & Co. in Cambridge, Mass., put it best: "Over the long run (measured in decades), the market is usually very predictable. . . . But in the short term, prices are totally *un*predictable, because shifts in investor moods come quickly and they're very powerful, often carrying stock prices to extremes."

7. **The media have their own agenda, and it's not to make you rich.**
    If the way to make money in the stock market is to buy good companies and hold onto them for a long time, then paying attention to the minute-by-minute movements of the Nasdaq and the Dow is, at best, useless and, at worst, destructive. Entire cable networks are dedicated to bringing viewers the latest comments on particular stocks and sectors, predictions of what will happen in the next hour or week, daily charts of the movements of the S&P Utilities index and other short-term phenomena. Why? To grab your attention so that advertisers can sell you things.

It's hard to blame CNBC or CNNfn or Bloomberg for airing this kind of manic programming. They're in the business of selling eyeballs to advertisers. But what excuse do the viewers have?

Do you imagine that when you hear a positive bit of news about earnings on CNBC, you can rush to buy a stock and enjoy a little ride up before others catch on? That's dubious—and, if you are in for the long haul, it is just plain silly. What you want from the media are smart, analytical stories about *businesses*. For example, nearly 20 years ago, I learned about the revolution in steel mini-mills by reading an article in the *New York Times*. Yes, everyone else saw it, too, and it may have pushed up the price of Nucor in the short term, but, to a long-term investor, it was a revelation—a spur to further research and a warning that the big steel companies were falling on hard times.

An interview with a CEO on CNBC might tell you whether the fellow is glib, and you may even learn about a business. But, thanks to time constraints, opportunities for such insight on television are rare, and the risks of distraction overwhelm the benefits. The Secret Code teaches you to ignore the media frenzy (see Chapter 22).

As a columnist for the *Washington Post*, I once tried to convince the editor to drop the five pages of stock tables the business section consumed every day and instead use that precious space for articles about companies—local and national—in which investors might want to become partners and for articles about managers of portfolios of stocks (at the time, mainly mutual funds) in which readers might want to invest. I failed.

The way to succeed in the stock market is to concentrate on what matters and to block out the noise. There is, very simply, no reason to know what a stock is doing day to day or week to week. A good rule is to check stock prices no more than once a month—or once a year if you have the discipline.

8. **Pay no attention to the Fed.**

The Federal Reserve Board sets short-term interest rates, and those rates affect stock prices—for three reasons. First, most companies have borrowed money in the past and want to borrow more in the future, so when interest rates rise, a firm's costs rise, thus its profits fall. Second, consumers frequently borrow to make purchases; high rates discourage them, and hurt sales up and down the line for businesses. Third, high interest rates draw investors out of stocks and into bonds, which pay better.

Still, one of the principles of the Secret Code is to ignore the Fed. Why?

Between the end of World War II and 2000, there were nine recessions, but each was short and was followed by a quick recovery. The economy has grown at a rate of about three percent, on average, after inflation. So I make two assumptions: The first is that the Fed will do a decent job maintaining the value of the dollar (its central task), and, for that reason, it should play no role at all in your long-term investing decisions. During the 1990s, for example, the Fed raised rates, then lowered them, then raised them, then lowered them, then raised them again. The net effect was that the economy steamed ahead, averaging about 4 percent growth for most of the decade. Investors who were transfixed by the Fed either had sleepless nights or made regrettable, expensive trades—or both.

My second assumption is that the economy itself will continue to grow—with dips, of course—at the same rate it has for the past 60 years. Again, don't worry about it. In the short term no one can predict the course of the economy or the actions of the Fed, and there is no use fretting about something you can't know, or do anything about. In the long term, however, the economy has been pretty predictable.

So forget the Fed. Forget the economy. Forget the stock pages. Forget the kinds of things that financial journalists concentrate on. Instead, pay attention to the businesses you are buying and to your own behavior as a shareholder. That's what the superior investor does, and it is more than enough to worry about.

9. **For short-term investments, buy bonds and only bonds.**

The case for stocks over bonds is easy to make. History shows that stocks return twice as much. "When you buy a bond," writes Peter Lynch, the former manager of the most successful mutual fund in history, Fidelity Magellan, "you're only making a loan, but when you invest in a stock, you're buying a piece of a company. If the company prospers, you share in the prosperity. If it pays a dividend, you'll receive it, and if it raises the dividend, you'll reap the benefit. Hundreds of successful companies have a habit of raising their dividends year after year. . . . They never raise the interest rate on a bond."

Still, remember that with stocks, returns, year by year, are utterly uncertain. Day by day, it's even worse. Take a relatively tame stock like that of Merck & Co., the giant pharmaceutical house. In early January of 2000, Merck traded at $65 a share; a month later, it had jumped by one-fifth, to $78; a month after that, it had tumbled to $54, a loss of one-third. But by June, it was back up 40 percent; then down the next month by 15 percent. By November, Merck had soared to $90, a gain of nearly half in less than four months. And that's Merck!

With bonds, in the short term, the ride is much smoother. (See details on all types of bonds in Chapters 42 to 46.) A bond is an I.O.U. In other words, when you buy a bond, you are lending money to a government agency or a business. The deal is usually simple: For example, you give the U.S. Treasury $10,000, and it may promise to pay you the $10,000 back in five years, providing you with interest of 5 percent annually (or $500) along the way. If you decide to sell the bond before it reaches maturity in five years, you may get more or less than you paid, depending on market conditions. Generally, you sell a Treasury bond to another investor, and what she will pay is determined by whether interest rates have gone up or down in the meantime. If rates have risen, you will get less than what you paid; if they have fallen, you will get more.

But in the short term—five years or less—even the risk of interest rates rising pales compared to risks involved in stocks. The principle is this: Because they are so risky, stocks are a terrible investment for short periods. For short-term investing, stick to bonds. Naysayers like to criticize the stock market for being like a casino. Actually, for long-term investors, it is the *opposite* of a casino. At a casino, the house has an edge of about 5 percent in a game like roulette. On average, whenever you bet $100, the house makes $5. Stay at the tables long enough and you lose a lot of money. With the stock market, by contrast, *you* are the house, and your edge is 11 percent. It is, in fact, very difficult to lose money in the market over the long term even if you are trying. The Prudent Bear Fund, for example, a mutual fund that takes a pessimistic view of stocks and tries to profit by selling them short (a short-seller makes money when prices fall), lost 46 percent of its value in the five years ending in 2000.

In the short term, however, the stock market *is* a casino, and you should treat it that way. When I wrote a column for the *Washington Post*, I received a phone call one day from a man who had saved $20,000, enough to send his daughter to college. She would begin in two years. "Meantime," he asked me, "what stocks should I buy to see if I can make that $20,000 grow?"

I have a policy of not giving investment advice to readers about their special situations—especially over the phone. But I couldn't restrain myself. "What stocks to buy? None!" I blurted out. "The market is very, very risky over two-year periods. You could lose 40 percent of your money. That's what happened to people with diversified portfolios over 1973 and 1974. How would you explain to your daughter that you had enough to send her to college but that now you were $8,000 short?"

Instead, people in such circumstances should buy a bond, preferably from the U.S. Treasury, that matures right around the time they need the cash—for tuition, a down payment for a house or a trip around the world. That way, they know where they stand, and they are rewarded, with almost no risk, for delaying gratification. By buying a bond, the man who called me would have added another $2,000 or so to his tuition fund. By buying stocks, he might have doubled his money—but he might have lost half of it, too.

What about cash? In investing terms, cash is very short-term debt—certificates of deposit, a savings or checking account, Treasury bills, a money-market fund account. In each of these cases, you are actually lending money, usually to a bank or a government agency, but the loans you make mature very quickly.

This means that you are taking almost no risk but also getting almost no reward. Cash typically produces returns that are a tiny bit above inflation; currency stuffed under the mattress, on the other hand, loses ground to inflation. Cash is for extremely short-term needs (over the next week or month) and as a fund for emergencies. Otherwise, keep very little of it around.

10. **Do** sweat the small stuff: expenses, taxes and inflation.

That stuff isn't really small, but it's frequently ignored—which is why the Secret Code for expenses, taxes and inflation is detailed in Chapters 16 through 18. Since investing is not a game but a serious endeavor to provide income and comfort, it's not the score you rack up each year—like a mutual fund advertising its latest returns—that counts. What counts is your purchasing power—after expenses, inflation and taxes. If you don't pay attention, the bite can be enormous.

Take mutual fund expenses as one example. Assume you invest $10,000 in a fund that produces a return of a little under 12 percent annually for 30 years. With no expenses at all, your $10,000 would grow to $300,000. With expenses of 1 percent annually, the account would grow to $229,000; with expenses of 2 percent, to $174,000. That's right: $123,000 in expenses on a $10,000 investment! Expenses benefit from the miracle of compounding, just as earnings and dividends do, but in this case, the investor is the loser—the *big* loser.

With taxes, stocks enjoy a major advantage over bonds. When you make a stock investment of $1,000 and hold the shares for 20 years, you should have close to $10,000, but during that entire time, there's no need to pay a dime in taxes—unless, of course, the stock throws off dividends. The capital gains tax applies only to profits that investors *realize* when they sell their stocks at a profit. No sale, no tax. And, even with a sale, the top rate is just 20 percent. U.S. Treasury and corporate bonds, on the other hand, pay interest that's taxed at the ordinary-income rate, which can be well over 30 percent, and those taxes are payable every year. As a result, the effect of compounding is muted. Say you buy a $1,000 bond that pays 6 percent interest, and say your tax rate is 31 percent. The first year, interest is $60 but taxes are $18.60. As a result, if you reinvest the interest, you earn 6 percent only on $41.20, not on the full $60. The difference mounts up over time. There are ways to avoid paying taxes on your bond (and stock) investments each year, and this book will show you how. But ignorance of the law—and it's complex!—is no excuse for the superior investor. Paying taxes you don't need to pay is dumb.

Inflation kills. It's the reason that bonds lost 60 percent of their purchasing power between 1972 and 1981. At a rate of 4 percent a year, inflation reduces the value of an investment by half in 18 years and by three-quarters in 36 years. By then, $1 million will buy what $250,000 can buy today. Or, to put it another way, a $1 million nest egg, throwing off 6 percent income, will provide a retiree with the purchasing power of $15,000 a year in today's money. Ouch!

Is there a way to avoid the ravages of inflation? Yes, buy stocks. Many businesses are hurt by rising wages and other expenses—and the rising interest rates that come with inflation—but, at least, they can raise their *own* prices. Another solution is to own what may be the greatest contribution of the Clinton Administration to American life: Treasury Inflation-Protection Securities, or TIPS. These are bonds that pay a base "real" interest rate plus extra interest that adjusts to the rise in inflation each year. So if the real rate is 3 percent and inflation rises to 10 percent (it's been even higher), you get 13 percent that year while conventional bondholders may be collecting just 6 percent.

But there's a catch. TIPS are taxed in a disadvantageous way. They get you either coming or going—or they will if you don't follow the Secret Code. (For more on TIPS, see Chapter 46.)

Those are the ten principles for superior investing. Now, here are the details.

PART I ○

THE BASICS

YOUR GOALS DETERMINE YOUR INVESTMENTS

AFTER THE STOCK MARKET has run up nicely for a week or so, I often find friends—or children of friends—tell me they want to start investing. "How to do it?" they ask.

But "how" should come second. "Why" comes first.

Before you start to invest, know the reasons. To make money, certainly. But for *what*?

If you are 25 and saving for a retirement that's 40 years off, you should structure your investments in one way. If you are 70 and need regular income, you should structure them in another. If you are 30 and raising money to buy a house in a few years or a trip around the world by the time you're 35, your investment strategy should be completely different. Even the smallest investor, and $500 is a valid place to start, needs to know her goals.

The Secret Code works for all investors, from novice to experienced and in between. We all need to assess our goals every few years. I am not talking about filling out one of those interminable forms that financial advisors so dearly love, with questions asking you to rate your level of risk aversion and to list all your monthly expenses, from haircuts to gasoline.

Instead, just write your *objectives* out on a piece of paper—concrete goals in clear English with the sentence beginning "I" or, for couples, "we."

For example: "I want to have at least $2 million in financial assets [stocks, bonds and cash] by the time I am 60." "I want to own my own house with a $50,000 down payment when I am 35." "We want enough to send two children to graduate school before we're each 50."

What else? Just three things: 1) Make an estimate of your income over the rest of your working lifetime and take a guess on how much of it you can save. 2) Get a feel for how scared you are of owning stocks, whose prices can fluctuate wildly, day to day but, if you *are* scared, defer final judgment until after you are finished this book. And 3) Examine your tax situation. If you're in a medium or high tax bracket, do you have tax-deferred accounts like IRAs and 401(k) plans? Those plans, with few exceptions, are for retirement money only. Put as much as you can into them. If you don't have adequate tax-deferred accounts, then start your own, something I call a Low-Tax Retirement Account, which in many ways is superior to an IRA. The LTRA (not actually available from investment firms but easily constructed by any investor) is based on the best loophole in the tax code: You don't pay capital gains on something unless you sell it. Stuff your LTRA with non-dividend-paying stocks and hold onto the account as long as you can. Unlike an IRA, you can break into it whenever you want, for whatever you want, and pay no penalty—just whatever taxes are due, at the capital gains rate, rather than at the ordinary-income rate of most IRAs.

Writing down your goals and resources is the first step for any superior investor. Actually buying the assets—stocks, bonds and cash vehicles—is the second. And acting sensibly after you buy those assets (which generally means not selling when the going gets tough) is the third.

No one, of course, is able to follow a life plan precisely, but it's absolutely necessary before you buy a single share of stock or any other investment.

THE LONGER YOUR TIME HORIZON, THE MORE STOCKS YOU NEED TO OWN

IMAGINE THAT YOU ARE 40 and have spent every penny you have ever earned. Then, with no savings, you suddenly come into an inheritance of $100,000. What should you do with the money?

If you decide to invest it (at last!), there are only three good choices: stocks, bonds and cash.

Stocks: When you own shares of stock, you own a piece of a corporation; you literally *share* its fortunes. You have a claim on the company's profits. Some of those profits you may receive every three months in the form of dividends. The rest of the profits are reflected in a rising stock price. As the company's fortunes grow, so will its price, though that link isn't tight. Stock prices bounce up and down in the short term as investors become elated or depressed about the company's prospects, but, in the long term, one thing is certain: the stock of a company that does well will rise, and the stock of a company that does poorly will fall.

Bonds: Think of a bond as an I.O.U., a loan that an investor makes to a company or a government agency. Unlike many loans that banks make, bonds represent debt that can be traded among investors, just like stocks. Also, like most stocks, a bond pays an investor income usually twice a year. But, unlike stocks, those payments are set at the time the bonds are issued (which is why bonds are called "fixed-income" investments). Dividends can vary year by year according to profits of the company and the wishes of management, but the interest on bonds stays the same—except in the rare case that the bond's issuer can't make the payments. For example, if the U.S. Treasury issues a 10-year bond carrying a coupon (or interest rate) of 6 percent, then an investor who buys $10,000 worth of 10-year bonds gets $600 in interest a year. Also, if she buys the bond when it comes out and holds it until it matures, she will get her $10,000 back. But if she decides to sell before maturity, the price of the bond could be higher or lower. If market interest rates have risen in the meantime, she might get $12,000; if they have fallen, she might get $8,000.

Cash: In financial jargon, the term "cash" refers to short-term debt, including Treasury bills (which mature in no more than a year), bank accounts (when you have one, you are lending your own bank money, a loan you can call in at any time by writing a check), bank certificates of deposit (a longer-term commitment than a checking account), and money-market funds (which are pools of bonds that are just about to mature).

So how do you decide among these three kinds of investments?

There are two factors to consider: return and risk. First, return. Over the past 75 years, stocks have returned an average of about 11 percent a year, a total of dividends and price increases; long-term Treasury bonds have returned approximately 5 percent; and cash (represented by three-month Treasury bills) has returned around 4 percent. Inflation has averaged about 3 percent, cash has stayed a tiny bit ahead of rising prices; bonds have given investors returns of about 2 percent after inflation; and stocks about 8 percent after inflation.

So the choice seems obvious—put it all in stocks!

Not so fast. Risk plays a key role in investing. While the *average* return of a diversified portfolio of stocks—the 500 companies of the Standard & Poor's benchmark index, for example—has been 11 percent, those returns have varied considerably from year to year. In 1999, for instance, the S&P gained 20 percent, but in 2000 it lost 9 percent.

For returns to be meaningful, they have to be expressed in *real*—that is, after inflation, terms. What's important is purchasing power. If an investment returns 8 percent in a year, but inflation is 10 percent, then you have done worse than if the investment had returned just 3 percent in a year of 2-percent inflation.

In the stock market, risk is usually defined as volatility—that is, the extremes of a stock's (or a market's) ups and downs. A popular way to measure risk is through standard deviation, an indication of how much annual returns vary from average returns. For instance, if stocks simply returned 8 percent (after inflation) every year, there would be no risk at all for a standard deviation of zero. In fact, the annual standard deviation of the S&P 500 index, as I noted in the Introduction, is a whopping 20 percentage points. What does that mean for a typical stock?

Let's take as an example McDonald's Corp., the largest restaurant chain in the world. McDonald's is actually *less* risky than the average stock. Its "beta" (another way to measure volatility) is just 0.85, or 15 percent below that of the typical large U.S. company. But in 1998, the price of McDonald's shares varied from a low of $22 to a high of $40 and in 1999, from a low of $36 to a high of $50. So, depending when you bought shares in 1998 and sold them in 1999, you could have doubled your investment or lost 10 percent of it.

In the short term, bonds are much less risky than stocks—which makes sense because they pay the same amount in interest every year. But that does not mean bonds aren't risky. As Irving Fisher, the Yale economist, wrote in 1912, "The man or woman who invests in bonds is speculating in the general level of prices, or the purchasing power of money." Bond investors are betting that inflation will be tame; if it rises, they could lose big. Cash is the least risky investment of all since short-term rates tend to rise and fall along with inflation itself. Real returns for cash are very consistent but barely worth the attention of an investor. Cash is a resting place for money that will be used shortly.

So, the difference is clear: With stocks, you get high returns but also high risk. With cash, you get low returns and low risk. Long-term Treasury bonds fall in between.

But those differences are only in the short term. Over *longer* periods, the riskiness of stocks declines dramatically. Standard deviation falls to the single digits.

For planning your investments, then, the rule is this: If you can put your money away for a long time, put it into stocks, but for shorter-term investments (5 years or less) choose bonds or cash. When Jeremy Siegel examined every 10-year period from 1871 to 1996, he found that stocks beat bonds 82 percent of the time. He also found that, if you had invested in stocks just before the 1929 Crash and then held on for 30 years, a $1,000 investment in stocks would have become $5,650 after inflation; in bonds, $1,410; in cash, $790.

So back to the example at the start of this chapter. If, at age 40, you can afford to put the $100,000 away until retirement at, say, 65, then the entire amount should go into stocks. If history is a guide, the $100,000 will grow to about $1.5 million in stocks, compared with about $400,000 in bonds and, based on the record, the two investments will be equally risky, or volatile. It's not a tough choice.

CHAPTER THREE

DON'T OWN STOCKS AND BONDS; OWN A PORTFOLIO

ONE OF THE BIGGEST MISTAKES investors make is owning stocks and bonds. Instead, they should own *portfolios*. A portfolio, very simply, is a *group* of stocks or bonds or a mix of both that has a structure and a logic. It's a collection, not a random agglomeration.

For example, assume that, at age 30, you decide that over the next 20 years you want to put 80 percent of your investment cash into a group of stocks and 20 percent into a group of bonds, then gradually move more money into bonds as you get closer to retirement. That's a plan in keeping with the Secret Code since it emphasizes stocks for the long term and bonds for the short. The consequences of inappropriate allocation can be profound. Consider two 30-year-olds who, in 1990, had $40,000 to invest. The first put one-fourth of his money into stocks and three-fourths into bonds. The second, more sensibly, put three-fourths into stocks and one-fourth into bonds. The first had $140,000 after 10 years; the second, $260,000.

But how do you put an investment plan into practice? *Not* by buying a few stocks today and a few more in a month with no strategy in mind. Instead, you need a portfolio.

A solid portfolio requires diversification because the more stocks of different types you own, the less volatile your overall holdings will be—the value won't bounce around like crazy, scaring you into selling at the wrong time. So a portfolio might look like this:

- **50 PERCENT:** Large-company stocks like General Electric, IBM and Wal-Mart. These solid citizens provide stable capital appreciation (in other words, their prices tend to go up 10 to 12 percent annually, on average).

- **20 PERCENT:** Small-cap stocks. ("Cap," or capitalization, is the dollar value, based on today's stock-market price, of all the shares a company has issued; small-cap stocks are usually defined as having caps under $2 billion.) Typically, small-caps return more than large-caps, but they are more volatile (for more on small-caps, see Chapter 40).

- **10 PERCENT:** Stocks for income, such as real estate investment trusts (REITs), which, in turn, own portfolios of income-producing property, like apartment buildings and shopping centers. Income from stocks comes in the form of dividends, and the biggest dividend-payers, in addtion to REITS, tend to be utility, energy and tobacco stocks. They provide a steady stream of cash—though be aware that it's taxable at the ordinary-income rate, not the capital gains rate.

- **20 PERCENT:** Bonds, either those issued by the U.S. Treasury or by state and local authorities. The latter are municipal bonds, and the interest they pay is exempt from federal (and sometimes state and local) taxes (see Chapter 44).

What about foreign stocks? My strong belief is that the stocks of companies that are based outside the U.S. should *not* be in a separate asset category (see Chapter 34 for details on international stocks). For instance, some of your large-cap portfolio might consist of foreign stocks, but they should be chosen not by the country of origin but by industry and individual quality. Own the best companies you can find, wherever they are headquartered.

You should have a cash reserve as well, held in bank accounts, money-market funds, certificates of deposit or Treasury bills, but the cash can be considered separate from your investment portfolio (see Chapter 47). Just be aware that, in emergencies, cash comes in very handy. You should not have to sell your stocks and bonds to raise it.

Each portfolio should be broken down into sub-portfolios. For instance, there are many ways to hold the 50 percent of your portfolio that's in large-cap stocks. You can buy shares in individual companies, in which case you must be sure that you have balance across industries. Of 12 stocks, don't buy 10 oil companies, a retailer and a semiconductor firm. Sectors are highly volatile themselves, and oil stocks can be depressed for years before bouncing back; your two other stocks won't provide much balance. Diversification is a key requirement for a superior investor. You will hear more about it later, but, for now, just understand that you need it.

You can hold your sub-portfolio in any of six ways:

- **INDIVIDUAL STOCKS:** These are easy to understand, shares that represent ownership in companies themselves. You buy stocks through a broker, on-line, over the phone or in person, or, in more and more cases, straight from a company that offers a direct-purchase plan (just go to the website of almost any large firm, from Campbell's Soup to ExxonMobil). When you buy stocks, you usually pay a commission, which can range from a few dollars all the way to 2 percent of the purchase price. Higher commissions usually, but not always, indicate more service from the broker, including research, recommendations and hand-holding. (Lately, many brokers are being compensated with a fixed proportion, often 1 percent, of the total assets in an account, so they have less incentive to urge you to trade. That's a good system.) When you own individual stocks, you control your own destiny, buying and selling according to your own (or your broker's) wish.

- **MUTUAL FUNDS:** A mutual fund is itself a portfolio—on average, about 100 stocks (or bonds, or a mix) that are managed by a professional. Within a few restrictions set in the fund's charter (for example, there may be a limit of 20 percent foreign stocks or 10 percent bonds), the manager has free rein. Mutual funds usually fall into "style" categories; they concentrate in large-caps, small-caps, mid-caps, value (that is, stocks that are being shunned by investors), growth (high-fliers), industry sectors (health care, energy, etc.), and a lot more. As an investor, you own a piece of all the stocks in a fund, which usually provides you with more diversification than you could get on your own, as well as bookkeeping and (you hope) good management. For their work, mutual fund companies charge annual fees, typically between 1 percent and 2 percent of assets (though some charge less than one-fifth of a percentage point). So, if you own $10,000 in shares of a mutual fund, you will usually pay $100 to $200 in expenses annually. While that may not seem like much, it can add up over time (see Chapter 18). Some funds also charge up-front fees called "loads" which are essentially commissions to brokers and advisors who sell you funds (you can also buy funds directly over the phone, at fund company offices or on websites). Other funds charge loads when you sell. Mutual funds have drawbacks besides their costs. First, you don't know exactly what you own since most funds report their stock holdings only every six months and most managers are manic traders, turning over their entire portfolios at an average of once a year. Second, the fund manager's decisions can lead to big, unexpected tax bills for you (see Chapter 16). Third, after expenses, most funds over the past 20 years have not beaten the benchmark Standard & Poor's 500-Stock Index. In other words, many fund managers are not that good at their chosen profession.

But well-selected mutual funds are a godsend to small investors, who can leave the stock-picking to an expert. How do you find the best funds out of the 8,600 choices that prevailed in 2000? Check out record-keepers like Morningstar Mutual Funds (www.morningstar.com) or the Value Line Investment Survey (www.valueline.com) or a fine mutual fund newsletter, the No-Load Fund Investor (www.sheldonjacobs. com), edited by Sheldon Jacobs. My own favorite core mutual funds include Fidelity Growth Company, T. Rowe Price Dividend Growth (which looks for firms that increase their dividends year after year), Janus (which has a tightly focused portfolio and is thus more volatile than most funds), the redundantly named American Funds Growth Fund of America, TIAA-CREF Growth & Income (with very low expenses), Dreyfus Appreciation, Smith Barney Aggresssive Growth (with an average annual return of 30 percent, the only large-cap growth fund among the top 20 performers for the five years ending June 2001), Legg Mason Value, Merrill Lynch Fundamental Growth and AIM Constellation. But searching out great funds is something you can do on your own. Look for a long-term record (at least five years) of consistent growth under the same manager, low turnover, low expenses and an intelligently balanced portfolio. You will have to learn more of the Secret Code before you can make your choices, but the fundamentals of fund selection are simple.

- **FOLIOS AND SUCH.** A few years ago, a former commissioner of the Securities & Exchange Commission, Steve Wallman, invented a new kind of mutual fund called the FOLIO. (Full disclosure dept.: Steve is a friend of mine, and I once wrote a weekly column for the website.) Like a mutual fund, a FOLIO is a portfolio of stocks with a theme—large-cap growth, small-cap value, real estate, technology, and so on, plus some special portfolios that comprise the stocks in the Fortune list of Most Respected Companies or the stocks of the firms with the most women on their boards of directors. But, unlike a mutual fund, with these vehicles, the investor herself does the management, deciding, after the FOLIO is purchased, whether to buy some stocks or sell others. This extra control is just what many investors need, but others find scary. Companies like Folio(fn), the investment firm that Wallman heads, usually sell these portfolios either pre-packaged or custom-made to your specifications and normally including about 30 stocks for a flat annual fee, with no charge for stock trading. The fees, between $300 and $400 a year, make FOLIO-style investing attractive for slightly better-off investors. With a $60,000 investment, the company's take is only about one-half of one percent of your assets annually.

- **UNIT INVESTMENT TRUSTS.** These are like mutual funds, except that their contents are fixed for a specific duration, a year or more. UITs are issued by investment firms, which usually charge hefty commissions. Another variation that has become popular in recent years is the Defined Asset (or Equity Investor) fund, also packaged by a large firm and actively traded in the market. Most of these trusts have a theme: energy, broadband, "Baby Boom Economy," utilities. UITs are especially popular, as they should be, with muni-bond investors since they provide a combination of diversification and control that is hard to find elsewhere.

- **CLOSED-END FUNDS.** A conventional mutual fund is open-ended—that is, as more investors add cash, the fund simply gets larger, which means that the manager has to find places to put the new cash. (Also, as investors *subtract* cash or redeem their shares, the manager needs to sell stocks to raise the money, often an unpleasant and expensive procedure, especially if the fund is invested in illiquid, lightly traded stocks.) The price of a mutual fund's shares is determined by adding up the value of all its stocks (or bonds) at the end of each day and dividing it by the number of shares. The price is also called "net asset value," or NAV, and the mutual fund company agrees to pay the NAV to you in cash whenever you redeem your shares. Closed-end funds comprise similar, managed, diversified portfolios, but their shares are floated in an Initial Public Offering (IPO) like the shares of an individual stock. A closed-end fund might begin by raising $10 million from the public by selling 1 million shares at $10 each. The fund then takes the $10 million and uses it to buy stocks. New investors have to buy their shares from current investors (usually on the New York Stock Exchange), and the price is set by supply and demand and can sometimes differ from NAV. One of my favorite closed-ends is Tri-Continental, started in the 1920s and trading on the NYSE under the symbol TY. It owns a well-balanced portfolio highlighted by such stalwarts as Microsoft and General Electric and returned an annual average of 12.5 percent for the 10 years ending in June 2001, a little less than the S&P benchmark but at lower risk. Yet Tri-Continental's stock consistently trades at a discount of about 10 percent to its NAV. In other words, a share of TY trades at a price that's less than the market value of the stocks it represents. Will the gap ever close? Probably not, but it is unlikely to widen much, either, and it's a well-run portfolio. Closed-end funds are particularly good investments if you want to buy the illiquid stocks of a single country or a regional emerging market: Argentina Fund, Asia Tigers Fund and the wild Turkish Investment Fund, which is the single most volatile fund I have ever found: From January 1998 to June 2001, it returned a total of 14 percent, but that's after quadrupling in 1999 and losing nearly half its value in the other years. Turkey aside, closed-ends can't eliminate risk, but they are much better at dampening it than traditional mutual funds.

- **EXCHANGE-TRADED FUNDS.** These are relatively new phenomena. ETFs are similar to closed-end funds and trade the same way on the exchanges, but they usually include the stocks that make up an index, like the S&P 500 (those ETFs are called Spiders, derived from SPDR, Standard & Poor's Depositary Receipts) or the tech-heavy Nasdaq 100 (symbol: QQQ) or the 30-stock Dow Jones Industrial Average (symbol: DIA, called "Diamonds"). Other ETFs focus on sectors, such as the iShares series from Barclay's: chemicals, real estate, tech, etc. Since ETFs are run by computers and not actual human beings, they charge low expenses—no more than one-fifth of a percentage point for the most popular. Index mutual funds such as Vanguard Index 500 offer the same package of stocks as ETFs with similarly low expenses, and it rarely matters which one you buy. ETF prices move in lockstep with the price of indexes. For example, Spiders trade at one-tenth the value of the S&P 500: $110 when the S&P is 1100. Diamonds trade at $1/100$ the value of the Dow, and so on. Choosing between index funds (or ETFs) and actively managed portfolios isn't easy. The odds favor indexes, but I put my own money in a mix of index ETFs, and managed mutual funds like Fidelity Contrafund and Mutual Shares.

Small-cap and income-producing stocks can be found in portfolios of these same six flavors. Individual small-caps are difficult to pick on your own, so I tend to prefer mutual funds like Wasatch Core Growth or Merrill Lynch Small-Cap Value. For income, individual stocks are easier to choose, but also look for mutual funds with the phrase "equity-income" in their names, an indication they specialize in high-yielding stocks. A standout in recent years has been Fidelity Equity-Income II. Top holdings for the fund recently included American Express and Fannie Mae, which provides money for mortgages. (By the way, if you had bought $1,000 worth of Fannie in 1983, your dividends in the year 2000 alone would have totalled more than $800.) Also, portfolio investing is the best way to own highly risky sectors, such as technology. The tech portion of my own holdings is mainly represented by the Nasdaq 100 ETF, but such funds as Seligman Communications and Information and Janus Mercury have proven their mettle in a tough market. Finally, don't overlook funds that lean toward value or underappreciated stocks. My favorites here include Tweedy Browne American (and Global) Value, Dodge & Cox Stock and Franklin Templeton Mutual Shares.

Bonds are also sold as mutual funds, closed-ends and UITs, but the Secret Code dictates that you hold all bonds to maturity (see Chapter 43), so individual bonds are a better choice.

Finally, stay away from the kind of mutual fund that offers a mix of stocks, bonds and cash. Nearly all stock funds allow managers to own a scattering of bonds, and most keep a few percentage points' worth of cash on hand for redemptions. But "balanced" or "asset allocation" funds, at the manager's discretion, will move their assets around among stocks and bonds, varying the ratio, say, from 70 percent stocks-30 percent bonds to 50-50. Superior investors do not give up control over asset allocation to a fund manager. *You* do the allocating; let the fund manager do the stock- and bond-picking.

PART 2 ∘
PRINCIPLES OF
THE CODE

BUY AND HOLD

THROUGHOUT THIS BOOK, you will hear three words: "buy and hold." They comprise the best investing advice to give but the hardest to put into practice. Maybe this story will help.

In 1944, a young lawyer named Anne Scheiber retired from her dreary job at the Internal Revenue Service. Despite her graduate degree, she was repeatedly denied promotions, and she never made more than $3,150 a year (the equivalent of about $35,000 in 2002). Still, she managed to scrape together $5,000 in savings, and she put it all into stocks.

Over the next six years, stock prices doubled, and, in 1950, with her profits, she bought 1,000 shares of Schering-Plough Corp., the drug company (at the time, it was called Schering Corp.), for about $10,000. It became her largest holding. When she died in 1995, those 1,000 shares became, through splits, 128,000 shares, worth $7.5 million. (Schering would quadruple again in the six years after Scheiber's death.)

Using dividends and profits, she bought other stocks as well. Among her long-term holdings, Coca-Cola Co. increased in value from $28,000 to $720,000 during the last 15 years of her life, and that doesn't even count dividends. As a Peter Lynch–

style investor (see Chapter 33), she bought Loews because she liked the movie theaters, even though the company later became a tobacco-and-insurance company. Her Loews stock was eventually worth $2.2 million at her death. Her Pepsico stock was worth $1.6 million; Bristol-Myers Squibb, $900,000; Allied-Signal (now part of Honeywell), $1 million. In all, Anne Scheiber parlayed her $5,000 savings into an investment account valued at $22 million.

Then, she gave it all away to the startled folks who ran Yeshiva University in New York. She never attended Yeshiva, but every weekday morning, in her frugal way, she read the *Wall Street Journal* in its library. She was grateful.

How did she do it? Nothing special. "She just held onto what she bought and never sold anything," her broker, William Fay of Merrill Lynch, said after she died. "She believed in these companies. She just stayed with them. She didn't care if the market was up or down." All of her stocks went through rough patches—all of them. There was a time, "during the '70s when Schering dropped off and lost half its value," Fay said. But Scheiber didn't sell during the inflation and recession of the 1970s. She held through it all: the Kennedy assassination, the Korean War, the Cold War, the oil embargo. . . . She held.

Scheiber's experience reinforces five basic lessons of the Secret Code:

- **START EARLY.** Scheiber herself was 51 when she invested her $5,000, but she was 101 when she died. Becoming a centenarian may be part of your life's plan, but there's no guarantee. More sensible would be to start investing at 25, planning to use the proceeds when you're in your 60s, 70s and 80s. The point is that the miracle of compounding needs time to work, and what you can reasonably expect is that $5,000 will grow to about $600,000 in 50 years. Not bad.

- **BUY STOCKS.** As an IRS auditor dealing with estates, Scheiber noticed that the very rich tended to own lots of common stock. Today, tens of millions of Americans have caught on, and more than half of U.S. families have equity accounts. If Scheiber had invested only in bonds from 1944 to 1995, her $5,000 would have grown only to about $100,000. She did not, however, invest *exclusively* in stocks. Like most older people, she began moving some of her assets into fixed-income investments. Fay urged her to buy tax-exempt municipals in the late 1970s, a sensible move for a typical woman in her 80s (who might worry about having enough to live on) though unnecessary for someone with Scheiber's wealth. At the time of her death, Scheiber's bond holdings amounted to $8.1 million; together, her stocks and bonds generated more than $800,000 in dividends and interest annually, most of it tax-free. But moving into bonds undoubtedly reduced the value of her total portfolio.

• **MINIMIZE TAXES.** Scheiber got her revenge on her former employer. Not only did she deny the IRS estate taxes at her death by giving all her securities to Yeshiva, but also she denied the IRS capital gains taxes during her life. One of the pleasant quirks of the tax code is that profits become taxable only if you sell stocks. If you keep them and pass them along to your heirs, you avoid the tax.

• **DIVERSIFY.** Scheiber did most of her own research, and the stocks she picked were hardly exceptional discoveries: drug companies, soft drinks, utilities. She bought solid firms with good balance sheets and strong reputations, rather than trying to find the next Microsoft in its cradle. "She focused on franchise names," said Fay. Among them: Exxon, Chrysler, Warner-Lambert, Pfizer. "She was drawn to these stocks by their products," said Fay. As an elderly person, for instance, she understood pharmaceuticals. But the portfolio was also diversified, allowing her to dampen the inherent riskiness of equities (see Chapter 10).

- **BUY AND HOLD.** Scheiber's greatest talent, however, was a knack for hanging onto what she owned, no matter what. Yes, occasionally there are times to sell (see Chapter 29), but fortunes are made through holding, not through trading. She also followed the admonition of old wealth not to touch capital. She never dipped into her Merrill Lynch account, instead using the dividends and interest to buy more stocks and bonds. She lived in a tiny $400-a-month rent-controlled apartment on West 56th Street in Manhattan, getting by strictly on her small IRS pension and Social Security. (By the way, spending some money on herself would not have been so terrible. So what if she died with only $20 million instead of $22 million?)

At every moment in stock-market history, smart people can make a good case for selling stocks. Newsletter editor James Grant, for example, warned throughout the 1990s that stocks were overvalued. I like Grant, and there were times when his wit disarmed me, and I began to agree to him. He told me in late 1996, for example, with the Dow at 6000: "The last 4,000 or 5,000 Dow points have taken us rather by surprise. We have been implacably disbelieving and unprofitably bearish." But the Dow rose to 7900 by the end of the next year.

Be wary of people who want you to sell, and take solace this way: It would be nice if someone could actually predict consistently when markets would rise and fall, but no one can. So why try? The delightful thing about the default position—holding on—is that it produces riches over time. That's why, every day in every market, you should remember Anne Scheiber.

CHAPTER FIVE

STOCKS ARE CHEAP

FOR AN INCREDIBLE STRETCH of 18 calendar years, from 1982 to 1999, the S&P 500 index fell only once, and that was a mere 3 percent decline in 1990. Sure, there were rough patches, such as the one-day 500-point drops in 1987 and 1997, but, in general, it wasn't hard to be a buy-and-hold investor during the 1980s and 1990s. If you had put a total of $10,000 into the 500 S&P stocks at the start of 1982 and kept it there, you would have accumulated $193,600 by the end of 1999. After inflation, your $10,000 grew to $120,000. It was a glorious two decades, a Golden Age.

But was it a *fluke?* From 1926 to 1999, a diversified basket of S&P stocks declined in 20 calendar years, but only *one* of those years occurred between 1982 and 1999. If the Golden Age was an anomaly, how can investors protect themselves in more normal times? Is a simple buy-and-hold strategy, of the sort that made Anne Scheiber rich, enough?

First, let's review the bidding: For five unprecedented years in a row, the S&P produced returns of 20 percent or more. Then, in January 2000, the index dropped 5 percent. A remarkably accurate signal called the "January Effect" holds that, as January goes, so goes the year. And, in fact, during the 1990s, the market had fallen only twice in January, in 1990 (a losing year) and in 1992 (a lackluster one). In 2000, true to form, stocks kept falling: in February, April, May, July, September, October and November. The S&P finished the year down 9.1 percent, after accounting for dividends of 1.1 percent. It was the worst performance since the horrible recession of 1973–74. It didn't end there: Shares continued to drop during 2001, and technology stocks were devastated. The Nasdaq Composite Index peaked over 5000 in March 2000 but fell below 1500 after the September 2001 terror attacks. The beginning of the new millennium provided a lesson in humility.

But which was the lesson: that stocks don't go straight up forever, or that the 1980s and 1990s were some sort of weird exception to the rules of the market? The bears, emerging from hibernation, believed that the year 2000 was the start of a process that would bring stocks back to the norm. In the spring of 2000, just as the Nasdaq was crashing, Robert Shiller, a mild-mannered Yale economist, published a book called *Irrational Exuberance*. Its title was taken from a phrase used by the chairman of the Federal Reserve Board, Alan Greenspan, in a speech on Dec. 5, 1996, at the annual banquet of the American Enterprise Institute, the Washington, D.C., think tank where I work. Greenspan warned that stockholder enthusiasm might be getting out of hand. Greenspan was wrong, and he later changed his pessimistic view of markets. When he gave his speech, the Dow Jones Industrial Average stood at 6437, having risen from 3686 just two years earlier. Within three years of Greenspan's uttering the phrase "irrational exuberance," the Dow had soared another 5,000 points.

Shiller had been warning about what he considered the market's high levels for years (in fact, he and John Campbell, a Harvard economist, had briefed Greenspan before the 1996 speech, telling him that shares were on the verge of dropping by half or more), but, for his book, the timing was exquisite. His basic argument was the mantra of the Wall Street-and-academic establishment, which had been drowned out in the boom years:

Stocks can't exceed their historic valuations for very long without taking a fall. "Valuation" is an indication of the market's enthusiasm about a company, since stock prices taken alone are meaningless. The Secret Code on valuation is explained in detail in Chapter 11, but you have probably heard of the most common valuation indicator: the price-to-earnings, or P/E, ratio, which tells how many dollars it takes to buy a dollar of a stock's profits. My view, as you will see, is that P/Es are not particularly significant, but there is no denying their popularity, indeed, their tyranny.

The establishment notion is that when they go up too high, P/Es must come down. This process is called "reversion to the mean"—and, obviously, there is some truth to it. That's why it's so pernicious. What goes up always does go down, but no one can predict when, by how much or how long it will stay down before going up again. For example, P/Es exceeded the academic "speed limit" for nearly the entire decade of the 1990s, and an investor who bailed out when P/Es hit a ceiling of 14 or 15 would have missed quadrupling his money.

One reason it is hard to believe in a natural limit on stock prices is that many companies exceed that limit regularly. Since 1985, the average annual P/E of Wal-Mart Stores has never been below 18, and most of the time it was over 30. During the 1990s, while it was supposed to be dangerously overvalued by P/E standards, the benchmark Standard & Poor's 500-Stock Index produced an average annual return of 18.2 percent—its greatest decade in history.

Still, there is no denying that during the 1990s, some stocks became overvalued, especially technology stocks. Many investors were convinced that the Internet would produce vast new wealth and that shareholders who got into tech stocks early—even before companies showed profits—would prosper. For a company with no earnings, *any* price makes the P/E ratio infinite, and valuations in many cases became absurd. Based on its stock price in early 2000, the value of Yahoo! Inc., a popular Internet site that was actually making a profit, was more than $100 billion. In other words, investors were saying that it was worth more than the New York Times Co., Dow Jones (publisher of the *Wall Street Journal*), the Washington Post Co. and Gannett (publisher of *USA Today*) *combined*. Excite@Home, a company that provided Internet access to consumers and businesses, never made a profit from its inception, yet in 1999, it was trading as high as $99 a share, for a market capitalization of $40 billion, three times as great as FedEx Corp., which, at the time, had $17 billion in revenues and more than $600 million in after-tax profits. Excite@Home declared bankruptcy in 2001. The "greater-fool" theory had gripped many investors—the notion that I may be a fool to pay $30 a share for a company like TheStreet.com, but I can always find a greater fool to buy my shares for $40. In fact, shortly after its debut, this particular company, which never made a profit, peaked at $70 a share but, by September 2001, was trading at 96 cents. Yahoo went from a high of $250 to a low of $7.75.

Yes, there were excesses, and it was hard for investors to maintain their equilibrium, in the face of both the high prices and the low. Superior investors nourish a simple idea: buy a stream of profits. The corollary is to stay away from companies that don't have a proven track record of earnings. I will make this concession: If a company has not shown profitability yet but you truly believe in its products and its management, then be sure that your investment in its stock is only a small part of a broader portfolio. Remember that during the early 1990s, America Online made practically no money at all. In 1996, it traded at a P/E of over 200, in 1997 it lost a hefty $72 million, and in 1999 its P/E was over 400. Yet AOL, which merged with Time Warner in early 2001, has proven a fabulous investment. Investing $10,000 in 1993, you would have had $5 million by 2001.

So the absurd heights reached by stocks like E*Trade Group, CMGI and CNET Networks comprise a good warning but not a rule to live by. They do not prove, for example, that a P/E level of about 15 constitutes, as the academics believed, an impenetrable ceiling. In all the turmoil of this period, a heretical idea began to emerge, one that had *nothing at all* to do with Internet stocks: What if investors began, in the early 1980s, to wake up to the true value of average, Dow-style stocks and began bidding up their prices to a higher, but at the same time more *sensible*, level?

Kevin Hassett, an economist at the American Enterprise Institute, and I looked at this question closely and came to some surprising conclusions, first in an article in the *Wall Street Journal* in 1998 and then in a book the next year. The book was called *Dow 36,000*, and the title reflected what we called the "proper level" of the stock market, as reflected by the Dow Jones Industrial Average, a well-known stand-in for the market as a whole.

Our conclusion reflected the results of an inquiry into the risk and returns of stocks and bonds. Our logic went like this:

1. Over the long term, a diversified portfolio of stocks is no more risky—when we look at after-inflation returns— than an investment in bonds issued by the United States Treasury. Recall that Jeremy Siegel had found that inflation was so devastating to Treasury bonds that, when they were held for long periods, they were just as risky as stocks—in fact, more risky. The worst single year for stocks since 1802 produced a loss of 38.6 percent, after inflation, but the worst 10-year period since 1802 produced an average annual loss of only 4.1 percent, and the worst 20-year period produced an average annual *gain* of 1.0 percent. But for bonds, the worst 20-year period produced an average annual *loss* of 3.1 percent. Over one-year periods, stocks beat bonds roughly 60 percent of the time, but over 30-year periods, stocks beat bonds 99 percent of the time. That's an amazing consistency.

2. Then we took the next logical step, the one that Professor Siegel had avoided: Although stocks were no more risky than bonds, they been priced as though they *were* more risky. Investors were so afraid of stocks that they kept

their prices low—which is another way of saying that their returns had been high. This is not an easy concept, but think of it this way: Say a company pays out $1 a share in dividends. That's the return. If the stock price is $100, then the return is relatively low, just 1 percent ($1/$100= 0.01). But if the price is lower, say, $20, then the return is high—5 percent ($20/$100 = 0.05). Stocks returned too much because they were too cheap.

3. Stocks have been priced so low that they have historically provided a *risk premium* of about seven percentage points over the benchmark Treasury-bond return. A risk premium is an extra return to compensate for extra risk. The higher risk, the higher the return. For example, a high-yield, or junk, bond, issued by a shaky company, will typically pay a risk premium of several percentage points above the Treasury rate, giving investors a bonus so they will buy a riskier investment they would otherwise shun.

4. But the risk premium for stocks is based on an erroneous assumption—that stocks are *way* riskier than bonds. In fact, for long-term shareholders, they are not. Because of this premium, investors have been getting a delightful unearned dividend for owning stocks instead of bonds.

5. There is plenty of evidence that, beginning in the early 1980s, investors started to catch on to this great deal. They began to bid up the prices of stocks and, thus, bid down the equity risk premium. The Dow Jones Industrial Average, an exceptionally good proxy for the market as a whole, went from 777 at its depths in August 1982 to 2753 by the end of 1989 to 5117 by 1995 to over 10,000 by 1999. Dr. Hassett and I determined that this process was perfectly rational and would continue, with breaks, of course, for bear markets caused by outside events like oil shocks and wars. ("Stocks will not go straight up," we

wrote. "They never do.") For how long would this secu-
lar (or long-term) rise last? Roughly until the Dow got to
about 36,000, where, by our research, we concluded it
would be fully valued and the irrational risk premium
would no longer exist ("It is impossible to predict how
long it will take. . . . It could take ten years or ten weeks.")
At that point, stocks would, on average, return about 5
percent or 6 percent annually, which is the historic
growth rate of earnings and cash flow.

There, in brief, is the Dow 36,000 theory. Its main message is
that stocks are an especially good buy at this point in history.
Not long from now, investors will have bid up the prices of
stocks to a fully-valued level and the revaluation period will be
over. Stocks will still be a decent buy, but, for long-term
investors, they will be only slightly more attractive (mainly for
tax reasons) than bonds.

But while Professor Shiller's timing was magnificent, ours was
not. Our book appeared just as the market was completing its
10th record-breaking year in a row. In 2000, tech stocks crashed
and the S&P suffered its worst year in a quarter-century. In early
2001, we reviewed our theory to see if we should revise or
recount, and instead we came away more convinced than ever
that we were right, despite terrorism and economic slowdown.
Why? The theory is based on two assumptions.

The first is that investors will continue to act rationally. Yes,
investors are not computers. They are humans, and humans are
emotional. In fact, the best description of their behavior is the
metaphor of Mr. Market, which the late Benjamin Graham, the
great investor and Columbia University professor, invented in
the middle of the last century. "Without fail," as Warren Buffett,
Graham's student, described him, "Mr. Market appears daily
and names a price at which he will either buy your interest or sell
you his." But the main characteristic of Mr. Market is that he
"has incurable emotional problems. At times he feels euphoric
and can see only the favorable factors affecting the business. . . .

At other times he is depressed and can see nothing but trouble ahead for both the business and world." When he's manic, Mr. Market demands high prices; when he's depressed, he will sell (or buy) cheaply.

Investors should take advantage of Mr. Market's moods, but they should not be influenced by them. In the long term, stock prices reflect the underlying cash flows generated by a business—the riskiness of those flows and the returns those flows produce. For the Dow 36,000 theory to be valid, investors must continue to understand the truth of the long-term nature of stocks and not revert to their Mr. Market–like ways. So far, so good. The market decline of 2000 and 2001, did not chase small investors from stocks. In fact, between January 2000 and July 2001, stock mutual funds experienced a net *inflow* of more than $300 billion in new cash. Yes, some investors took money out of mutual funds, but new money overwhelmed those redemptions. In the face of Mr. Market's depression, investors *bought* mutual funds just as they should.

The second assumption is that the economy in the future will be pretty much like it has been in the past. Chapter 9 discusses in depth the importance of the economy in investing, but, for now, understand that rational investors don't need a New Economy paradigm to justify putting their long-term money into stocks. A growth rate of 2.5 percent in real, after-inflation, terms will do just fine. That was the consensus assumption for the next decade's growth when we started writing *Dow 36,000*. But now, there is good reason to believe that the economy will grow *faster* in the years ahead. The Congressional Budget Office, which tends to be conservative, in August 2001 projected 3.2 percent growth from 2003 to 2011. Economic growth is tied directly to earnings growth, which is tied directly to stock-price growth.

But what about the economic slowdown that began late in 2000 and then intensified? The economy had been growing at a remarkable 4 percent for the previous eight years. The rate was over 5 percent by mid-2000 but declined to just above zero by mid-2001. Why? Four reasons: 1) A severe oil shock, which tripled the price of a barrel of crude. Eight of the nine recessions (that is, declines in national output lasting six months or more) since World War II were preceded by an oil shock. 2) A Federal Reserve mistake, which kept interest rates too high throughout 2000. The Fed began to lower rates in January 2001, but the damage was done. 3) The drag from high tax rates, which had drifted upwards during the 1990s until they hit record levels achieved only during World War II. 4) Increased intervention in the economy by federal regulators and attorneys, most significantly the decision to try to break up the single most important high-tech company, Microsoft. In light of all these developments, plus the collapse of ridiculously high-priced high-tech stocks and the horror of September 11, 2001, it was a wonder that the Dow lost as little as it did. And in all four areas, the marketplace or the federal government was moving to mitigate the problems as oil price, interest rates, tax rates and regulatory intervention began to fall. Every slowdown in history has been accompanied by falling stock prices, and every slowdown has ended with stock prices eventually rising to a new, higher level.

The lessons of the Secret Code are clear: Stocks are cheap; buy the best you can find and hold them, in a cool and unemotional way, for the long term; ignore the chaos and ignore the economic ups and downs; in the end, as a long-term holder, you will come out far, far ahead.

Also understand that you don't need to buy the Dow 36,000 theory to buy stocks. Think only of the rudiments of investment history: The market has returned an annual average of 11 percent a year since 1926. Say that figure declines sharply for some unknown reason to 8 percent. In less than 30 years, a $10,000 investment in stocks should rise to about $100,000 while a $10,000 investment in bonds will become less than $50,000. The case for stocks remains overwhelming.

BE A PARTAKER, NOT AN OUTSMARTER

THERE ARE TWO KINDS OF INVESTORS: Outsmarters and Partakers.

Outsmarters believe they're so clever they can beat the system, through inside advice and superior brainpower. Partakers understand that the best way to make money is to share in the profits of successful businesses, by buying stock in Citigroup, AOL Time Warner or Vivendi, for example.

Many investors, especially baby boomers, who are convinced they were born more brilliant than everyone else, begin their investing careers as Outsmarters. They invariably get outsmarted themselves.

That's exactly what happened to a young Arkansas couple named Bill and Hillary Clinton in 1978. They went into a typical Outsmarter deal—borrowing money to buy land in the Ozarks through Whitewater Development, a company they set up with an insider named James McDougal, along with his wife Susan. Real estate is especially tempting to Outsmarters since it's a game in which the other players often appear to be rubes. In this case, however, the Clintons and McDougals bought land for $880 an acre from a group that had purchased the property just 19 days earlier for $440 an acre.

The intention of the Whitewater investors was to find people to buy the lots at more than $880 an acre and make a big profit. But in the end, they found that such buyers did not exist ($440 an acre turned out to be the right number). The Clintons lost $68,300, according to an accountant's report they commissioned.

All right, I won't dwell on the Clintons. There are enough Outsmarters to pick on. There are, for example, day traders, who think they can profit from tiny ups and downs of stocks over minutes or hours. I do not doubt that some people can make a profit this way—after all, some people are born with the ability to throw a baseball 100 miles an hour or to do complicated long division in their heads. But beyond a tiny cadre of the super-talented and super-dedicated, day traders get eaten up by the transaction costs—the commissions, the spreads between bid and asked prices and the interest incurred in buying stocks on margin.

Other Outsmarters are bottom fishers. They figure they can identify stocks that have plunged but will soon emerge from the depths. Occasionally, a smart investor will win by betting on these kinds of stocks, but most of the time . . . . no. When a stock is exceptionally cheap, there is almost always a reason. The price of a stock, after all, is determined by the considered judgments of thousands, even millions, of investors. It could be "wrong," but chances are that it does reflect a rational assessment of all available knowledge about the company. At any rate, it's a good idea to assess any price from a posture of humility, not hubris.

Remember that a stock that's fallen can keep falling. Did Internet Capital Group look like a good buy after it had declined from $196 to $45 in the first four months of 2000? Investors who thought it did, got burned. Over the next year, it dropped to 34 cents. And don't forget that the only limit to how low a stock can go is zero. Outsmarters sometimes think that a two-dollar stock has some kind of floor beneath it. Nonsense! Shares of drkoop.com, Inc., were $1 a share in May 2000, but they were

19 cents a share a year later, a loss of 81 percent for any Outsmarters who thought a buck was a bargain.

Partaking, on the other hand, is the ticket to success in the stock market. Investing in an index fund like the Vanguard Index 500, which tracks the S&P 500, or in an exchange-traded fund like Spiders, an S&P proxy that trades on the American Stock Exchange, is a way to share in the long-term growth of the U.S. economy—an awfully good bet.

My own preference is partaking in the growth of great companies. Occasionally, it strikes me how incredibly generous the stock market is. At little cost, I can become a partner in a business like General Electric or Microsoft, tagging along on a very profitable ride. Who would ever want to take the risks of being an Outsmarter in an economy like this one?

READ THE GOSPEL

WHEN THE GOING GETS TOUGH, as it certainly has in recent years, bury yourself in Scripture, in the lives of the saints and their writings. Few of them have been martyred, but all of them went through terrible times and prospered.

Who are they? Benjamin Graham, John Templeton, Philip Carret, Philip Fisher and maybe a dozen more.

The late Ben Graham, perhaps the greatest of them all, was an erudite classicist who loved Proust, Virgil and the German poets and translated books from the Portuguese. In 1926, he started managing the Graham Joint Account, a fund for private investors. Its value fell 70 percent in 1929 and 1930, but he persevered. One of his huge successes was GEICO, the insurance company that bypasses agents. His $720,000 investment in 1948 was eventually worth $500 million. (Today, Berkshire Hathaway, Inc., run by Graham's most famous student, Warren Buffett, owns all of GEICO.)

Graham made at least five important contributions to investing. First, he came up with the concept that investors, when they buy stocks, should think of themselves as becoming partners in a business. It's a frame of mind that helps keep you from selling a stock simply because it's gone down and that deters you from obsessing about its daily price.

Second, as John Train, the financial advisor and prolific author, writes, "Graham's greatness as an investor may well have consisted in knowing how to say no." Buffett puts it this way: Investing is like a special kind of baseball game where you can simply stand at home plate and wait for your pitch. In this game, they can't call you out on strikes, so swing at only what you love.

Third, Graham stressed the idea of a "margin of safety," trying to buy companies for substantially less than they are worth.

Fourth, he invented the notion of "Mr. Market," to whom we introduced you earlier. Mr. Market is the manic-depressive partner of all investors. Every day, he offers pieces of businesses for sale at prices that reflect his mood. As investors, our job is to exploit his mood swings, buying when he is deeply pessimistic.

Fifth, Graham taught (in Buffett's words) that you should "look at [market] fluctuations as your friend rather than your enemy—profit from folly rather than participate in it."

Graham is a classic value investor. In an age that focuses on big, quick scores, he seems a boring plodder. What about great investors like George Soros, the frenetic Hungarian-American billionaire whose Quantum Fund, from 1969 to 1997, produced returns of 300,000 percent? The truth is, Soros has little to teach the small investor. His technique is to jump in and out of currency, bond and stock markets, placing huge bets with borrowed money and often reversing his positions (from buying long to selling short) in just a few days. The Secret Code has advice for anyone seeking to follow the Soros technique: Don't try this at home.

No, it is the ancient saints, the ones who endured the worst trials, that deserve our attention. Take Phil Fisher, who started his career as a money manager in 1931, immediately after President Herbert Hoover had told America that prosperity was just around the corner (one of the worst prognostications of all time), and who was still teaching classes at Stanford 70 years later.

Fisher's greatest insight was the chapter on when to sell stocks that appeared in his 1958 book, *Common Stocks and Uncommon Profits*. He wrote, "If the job has been correctly done when a common stock is purchased, the time to sell it is almost never." The only major exception comes when something important changes for the company you own: new management arrives and falters, a key product fails, fierce and unexpected competition enters the market. (For more on Fisher's philosophy of selling, see Chapter 29.)

Fisher was also an early advocate of buy-and-hold investing. In the first chapter of his most famous book, he wrote, "Even in these earlier times [1913], finding the really outstanding companies and staying with them through all the fluctuations of a gyrating market proved far more profitable to far more people than did the more colorful practice of trying to buy them cheap and sell them dear." He also noted that too many investors passed up great opportunities to buy stocks simply because they believed that the P/E ratios at the time were too high. Consider one of my favorite companies, Starbucks Corp., the coffeehouse chain. For the year 1996, its P/E ratio averaged over 50, yet an investor who bought the stock then would have quintupled his money in five years. Ever since it became a public company, Starbucks has, year after year, sported average P/E ratios of 40 or 50, but the firm has increased its earnings at a rate of over 20 percent annually, so the price has risen sharply.

Two other points that Fisher makes are part of the Secret Code. First, he asks, "Does the company have a management of unquestionable integrity?" If it does not, then you should stay away from the stock. Even unproven accusations of fudging earnings can be enough for me to drop a firm from consideration. Remember what Graham and Buffett said about waiting for the best pitch. Second, Fisher warns against being *too* diversified. While spreading the risk is fine, it is foolish to own so many stocks that you don't have decent knowledge of each. Fisher even writes that owning five large-company stocks, each exposed to broad worldwide markets, can offer sufficient diversification in a portfolio. He gives as examples IBM, DuPont and Dow Chemical. As an update, I would add General Electric, Hewlett-Packard and Sony, but I still consider five stocks of any sort too few to own.

Philip Carret, who died in 2000 after a spectacular career that covered eight decades (he was still working three days a week at the age of 100), started the Pioneer Fund in May 1928. Not very good timing, but he stuck with it. Over the 55 years that he ran the fund, an investment of $10,000 became $8 million, even if an investor withdrew all the dividends produced along the way.

One of Carret's great contributions was recognizing the value of small companies. "I'm more conservative than most people," he told John Train. "Most people think that 'conservative' means General Motors, IBM, et cetera. But I've always been in offbeat stuff. They're less . . . affected by crowd psychology. . . . I avoid fads like the plague." In 1930, Carret laid down his "12 Commandments" for investors in his classic, *The Art of Speculation*. Here they are, as cataloged by Outstanding Investor Digest, a superb newsletter that was one of Carret's constant boosters, and paraphrased by me:

1. Never hold fewer than 10 different stocks covering five different fields of business.

2. At least once every six months, reappraise every stock that you own.

3. Keep at least half your total portfolio in dividend-paying stocks.

4. Consider dividend yield the least important factor in analyzing any stock.

5. Be quick to take losses and reluctant to take profits.

6. Never put more than 25 percent of your portfolio into securities about which detailed information is not readily and regularly available.

7. Avoid inside information as you would the plague.

8. Seek facts diligently, advice never.

9. Ignore mechanical formulas.

10. When stocks are high, interest rates rising and business prosperous, at least half a given portfolio should be placed in short-term bonds.

11. Borrow money sparingly and only when stocks are low, interest rates low and falling, and business depressed.

12. Set aside a moderate proportion of available funds for the purchase of long-term options on stocks in promising companies whenever available.

Some of Carret's commandments don't meet the criteria of the Secret Code, which eschews options (12) entirely and does not encourage switching out of stocks into bonds (10) except as an investor grows older. But overall, the rules are sound, especially Carret's views on inside information (7), reappraisal (2), fact-seeking (8) and diversification (1).

Sir John Templeton's specialty was finding international values at a time when few Americans looked for stocks beyond their borders. He was born in Winchester, Tennessee, in 1912, won a scholarship to Yale and went to Oxford as a Rhodes Scholar. He started his own investment firm in 1937, in the depths of the Depression, and managed to launch his flagship, the Templeton

Growth Fund, in 1954. It is still going strong as part of the Franklin Templeton family. In 1962, Templeton (later knighted as a British subject) started buying Japanese stocks, which the rest of the world shunned, at prices of just two or three times their annual earnings. By 1970, some 60 percent of his holdings were in Japan, but he began to sell as the growth rates slowed and prices rose. One of Sir John's best pieces of advice is to be "suspicious of extremely rapid growth. Ordinarily, it is unsustainable." In 1973, he used his immense wealth to start a prize for achievement in religion (the first recipient was Mother Teresa of Calcutta), and in 1992 he sold his firm but was still maintaining an intense interest in investing a decade later.

Templeton made his mark as a global value investor, but he built his success on sound, Secret Code principles. He urged investors to search for great companies at good prices and to ignore "market trends [and] the economic outlook. Ultimately, it is the individual stocks that determine the market, not vice versa. Individual stocks can rise in a bear market and fall in a bull market."

My own lasting impression of Templeton came from my first meeting with him in 1980, in a closet-sized room at the Union League club in Philadelphia where he was staying overnight while visiting his son. It was his modesty, serenity and confidence that struck me most. In the years since, I have learned that those are precisely the qualities that lead to stock-market success. Brash, frantic, skittish investors don't survive very long.

The Gospel According to Templeton, Graham, Fisher and Carret gives investors comfort and wisdom in tough times. And it can be boiled down to three simple rules: 1) buy good, growing businesses that you know about, 2) buy stocks that are out of favor, and 3) be patient.

BUY COMPANIES WITH A MOAT TO PROTECT THEM

EVERY BUSINESS is in a state of war with its competitors. The secret to winning that war is a good defense, and the best defense is a *moat*.

For some industries, however, there is little protection. Even before the terrorist attacks of 2001, the airlines were fighting their own war of attrition, so destructive that it had killed off many of the combatants: Eastern, Pan American, National, Air Florida are just a few examples. One of the surviving contenders, Northwest Airlines, is typical. It's poured so many resources into the battle that, even as a modest victor (it's the fifth-largest airline), it has little left—for shareholders, that is. Fare wars have driven down profit margins so that Northwest manages to keep only $2 for every $100 spent by travellers, and the need for new or renovated planes has cut into even those profits. For the five years ending in September 2001, Northwest's stock dropped 43 percent. Between 2001 and 2006, Value Line's Warren Thorpe predicts, the company's earnings will rise by 11.5 percent annually, not bad at all. But, because of demands for capital investment, cash flow (money available for investors) will rise at a yearly rate of just 4 percent, about the return on a Treasury bill.

Or consider venerable retailer JC Penney Co., with 1,160 department stores, 2,640 drug stores (mainly under the Eckerd name) and an extensive catalog and Internet business. Penney's revenues, at $32 billion in 2000, look impressive, but the company earned just 20 cents on every $100 in sales, and it was carrying $6 billion in debt. Long-term interest alone was costing $425 million a year—a lot of money for a company with earnings of $800 million in a *good* year, like 1997. Penney's problem is not hard to understand: It is engaged in vicious hand-to-hand combat, with such opponents on the battlefield as Wal-Mart, CVS, Walgreen, Sears and Target. No wonder Penney's lost nearly half its stock value between 1996 and 2001.

Here are two sectors, airlines and retailing, where the battle merely for corporate survival is so furious that investors are best advised to stay away. Warren Buffett likes to say he's a member of AA ("Airlines Anonymous"), trying to kick the habit of succumbing to buying shares in airlines (in his case, US Airways) that may look attractive but that rarely make much money. The same with retailing. Many times, a well-run chain will start winning the war for a while but then is forced to retreat. (There are exceptions, however, and I'll get to them in a second.)

Warfare is the prevailing environment in all sectors of the economy. It is wonderful for consumers since it means lower prices and better quality, but it can be hell for the competitors. No company can remain highly profitable for very long because profits attract other companies. I learned this in a small way in my own business. From 1986 to 1992, I was editor and part-owner of *Roll Call*, a twice-weekly newspaper that covered Capitol Hill. It had a great niche: an audience of staffers, House members and Senators that issue-advertisers pushing for legislation wanted to reach. And we had no direct competition. To reach the same audience, you had to buy space in the *Washington Post* for much more money and pay for excess readers (that is, non-legislative workers) you didn't need. After awhile, we were earning profit margins (earnings divided by sales) of 30 percent and more. But it was inevitable that a competitor would go up against us, and eventually one did. (Luckily, my partner Arthur Levitt, who later became chairman of the SEC, and I sold out the year before.)

Still, even in the most hard-fought parts of the battlefield, some companies are consistent winners. The reason, almost always, is that they have protection, a "moat" around their defensive position, their castle of assets. A moat keeps the enemy at bay. It can be a great brand name or a special way of doing business or a series of patents. Gillette has had a reputation for making high-quality blades for more than a century. Its brand name is so strong that it has captured 70 percent of the world market. While Gillette will occasionally suffer lackluster years (as it did in 1999 and 2000), it is highly unlikely that any company will storm its redoubt successfully.

Coca-Cola has a secret formula for a soft drink that its competitors have been unable to duplicate. That formula held off the enemy for decades, but, ultimately, it was Coke's brand name (the most-recognized word in the world after "O.K."), built over a century of advertising and word-of-mouth, and its worldwide distribution system (North America accounts for only 38 percent of total sales) that broadened the moat. While Coke's business, like Gillette's, has gone through rough stretches (between mid 1996 and mid 2001, the stock rose only 18 percent in all, partly because of the slowdown in Asia, Coke's growth market), its moat makes it a long-term winner. For the 30 years ending in June 2001, for example, the stock price rose 20-fold and that doesn't even count Coke's constantly increasing dividend went from 12 cents a share in 1985 to 72 cents in 2001. It is Coke's moat that has allowed it such a clean balance sheet: less than $1 billion in debt for a company with $2 billion in cash and nearly $10 billion (conservatively) in net worth for its shareholders. Even in a lackluster year like 1999, Coke earned 34 percent on its equity. Thanks to its moat, it is a great business.

Could a start-up company compete against Gillette or Coke or against Tootsie Roll with such brands as Charms and Junior Mints, or against the glorious William Wrigley Jr. Co., world's largest chewing-gum maker (Doublemint, Big Red, Hubba Bubba), a company with no debt and a dividend that rose from 11 cents in 1985 to 76 cents in 2001? It's doubtful. The barriers to entry do not involve huge investments in plants and machines but rather the generations it takes to build a strong brand name.

Think of it this way: All companies strive for monopoly (*legal* monopoly), but they never succeed because other firms insist on grabbing some of the wealth. Thus, war. Metropolitan daily newspapers were considered "franchises," or monopolies, up until lately. Then, competition from TV, radio, the Internet and weeklies began to eat into profits. Companies that specialize in dailies, like Gannett, Hollinger, Pulitzer and McClatchy, have found business good, but not great, in recent years. Moats, in other words, dry up.

The best moats are those protected by law. One example is patents, which shield inventions like pharmaceuticals from competition for a set period. Merck & Co. has been doubling its earnings every five years, in large part because it owns patents on such drugs as anti-arthritic Vioxx and cholesterol-lowering agent Zocor (see Chapter 36). Another moat of this sort is the government-regulated franchise, which local monopoly telephone companies enjoy. Fannie Mae and Freddie Mac, which provide financing for mortgages, have a broad moat—courtesy of an implicit government guarantee on their bonds. These firms are well-defended money factories. Fannie, for example, has increased its earnings every year since the early 1980s, and only once has the rise been less than 10 percent—highlighted in *Dow 36,000*. The stock rose 168 percent for the five years ending September 2001. Even in a recession, Fannie thrives: earnings doubled between 1990 and 1992.

Other companies dig their own moats and gain a reputation for a stout defense through excellent management (like General Electric), superb service (Dell) or cost-cutting (Wal-Mart). And you can find well-protected companies even in war-torn industries. Southwest Airlines is exceptionally well-guarded by a moat comprising its unique short-haul, low-fare, no-nonsense service and a highly motivated workforce. As a result, between 1991 and 2001, the company's revenues jumped from $1 billion to $6 billion and cash flow grew at an annual rate of 18 percent.

How do you find companies with broad moats? A long history of strongly rising earnings is a dead giveaway. A firm that is dangerously exposed to competition quite simply will not increase its profits at a fast clip for very long. But a firm like Automatic Data Processing, which has increased its earnings at a double-digit rate for 40 years *must* have a moat, otherwise it could not have been so profitable. ADP has blown away the competition in its major niche—payroll and tax processing for medium-sized firms—mainly through excellent service and efficiency. Microsoft is another example of a well-defended company. Despite the slings and arrows of outrageous legal action, the software company has continued to thrive thanks to its widespread operating system, powerful brand and rich human capital.

But even the broadest moats can be breached. Competition has begun to eat away at the profits of that brand behemoth, Procter & Gamble (Crest, Tide, etc.). Nothing is certain in investing, but when you find a company with a moat, make the most of it.

PART 3 ∘
PUTTING THE CODE
INTO ACTION

IT'S *NOT* THE ECONOMY, STUPID

NOTHING TRANSFIXES financial journalists like a meeting of the Open Market Committee of the Federal Reserve Board, America's central bank. Since 1913, it has been the Fed's job to maintain a secure monetary and financial system. It does this primarily by preventing the value of the dollar from being eroded too quickly by inflation. Higher interest rates tend to dampen inflation by slowing down the economy; lower rates do the opposite. While the Fed might pretend that it cares more about a stable dollar than about a booming economy, the truth is that it cares about both. So its job is a balancing act.

The Fed works in mysterious ways. When the Open Market Committee—the seven Fed governors plus the president of the New York Federal Reserve Bank plus, in rotation, four other Fed regional presidents—decides to lower short-term rates, the Fed starts buying Treasury securities, mainly from commercial banks around the country. It gives the banks cash (actually creating it out of thin air), making the banks more liquid. That process adds more money to the system, thus lowering interest rates. Money, like anything else, has a price that's determined by supply and demand. Increase the supply by adding liquidity, and you lower the price (that is, the interest rate). Conversely, when the Fed wants to raise rates, the Fed *sells* Treasury securities out of its inventory, thus pulling money out of circulation from the buyers, lowering the supply and boosting the price.

These open-market activities specifically target what is called the federal funds (or "fed funds") rate, which is what banks charge each other for overnight loans. The fed funds rate was under 1 percent in the mid-1950s and over 14 percent in 1982. More recently, it has fluctuated between 2 percent and 6 percent. For example, when the Fed became worried about inflation getting out of hand with the economy booming in the late 1990s, the Open Market Committee began raising rates from 4.75 percent to 6.5 percent in increments over the course of a year, starting in June 1999.

The Open Market Committee has eight regular meetings annually but can meet in emergencies at any time. On Jan. 3, 2001, the group, now worried about a slowing economy and possible deflation, or falling prices, with a dollar grown too strong, cut rates between meetings by half a percentage point (or 50 basis points). Other cuts followed, and by October 2001, the Fed had reduced short-rates to just 2.5 percent. Typically, when the Fed begins adjusting rates, it takes them down (or up) in a series of steps by a total of around 300 basis points. The Fed has the power to set a second rate directly—the discount rate, which is what it charges member banks to borrow. That rate has been less important in recent years, and reductions tend to be more symbolic.

Fed moves can sometimes have a dramatic effect on stock prices in the very short term, as they did after the surprise Jan. 3, 2001, cut, when the Nasdaq index soared 14 percent in one day. But much of the time, it is difficult to correlate specific Fed actions with price movements. The day of the Jan. 31 cut, the Dow was up only a few points and the Nasdaq actually fell. A sharp market decline also occurred in March 2001, also after rate *reductions*.

Still, over the long term (a year or so), Fed rate reductions are closely linked to rising stock prices. That stands to reason. While investors can sometimes act like spoiled brats, selling stocks when the Fed declines to satisfy their every whim, the market, in the end, reflects the performance of the businesses whose stocks are traded there. And those businesses improve when the Fed cuts rates, though the improvement can take a while, often nine months or more.

In my view, the Fed's failure to reduce rates in the fall of 2000, despite little threat of inflation, helped send the economy into the slump that began as that year came to an end. The Fed should have been aware that a tripling of oil prices at around the same time would slow the economy and that an oil hike plus a rate hike equals a poisonous mixture. The Fed does make mistakes, no doubt about it. But if you're a long-term investor, Fed mistakes are generally not worth your time. First, they tend to be corrected, and, second, they can't be predicted anyway. With the exception of the Great Depression, slowdowns in the U.S. economy have been brief (less than a year, typically), and the economy and the market have quickly recovered to a higher level.

Still, investors are deeply concerned about the Fed. Why? First, high interest rates mean diminished profits for corporations both because their own borrowing costs rise and because customers who buy big-ticket items on credit (only one in ten automobiles, for example, is bought with cash) have to shell out more each month on their installment loans. Second, when rates rise, bonds become more attractive in comparison with stocks, so demand for stocks falls and along with it prices. On the other hand, reduced rates mean reduced costs for companies and less enthusiasm by investors for bonds.

But, even though interest rates affect stock prices, my advice is to ignore the Fed entirely. And, while you're at it, you should ignore the *economy*, too. If you're in the stock market, you should be in for the long term, that is, a minimum of five years and, better, 10 or more, and over the long term, the Fed and the econ-omy behave with remarkable consistency. The Fed tends to do the right thing, and the economy rises, on average, at about 6 percent a year, including inflation.

In the short term, neither the Fed nor the economy is pre-dictable. So the Secret Code urges you not to worry about them. In an excellent letter to clients a while back, the veteran analyst H. Bradlee Perry of David L. Babson & Co. of Cambridge, Massachusetts, made just this point. Investors need to distinguish between what they can know and what they can't know: "Many investors . . . worry a lot about 'confusing outlooks' and, there-fore, expend far too much energy in fruitless attempts to forecast the *unforecastable*. Once we can admit what we *don't* know and understand that uncertainty is part of investing, we can focus our attention on what we *do* know."

What we do know are basic truths about stock investing. That, since 1926, the average annual return of the Standard & Poor's 500-Stock Index, the benchmark for equity managers, and its predecessors has been 11 percent, including dividends; that stock prices, again over the long term, are closely linked to cor-porate profits, which in turn are closely linked to the economy; that, by holding diversified portfolios of stocks for the long term, investors diminish their risk; and that the best stocks are those with a strong track record of rising earnings and a brand name or patent wall that is difficult for competitors to assail.

There's enough for Superior Investors to worry about. Worry that you don't own enough good companies. Worry that your portfolio doesn't have balance from income-producing stocks, value stocks or small-cap stocks. Worry that management changes may be sending one of your companies on the wrong path. In short, worry about your *portfolio* and the *businesses* that comprise it. Don't worry about the Fed. Don't worry about the economy.

DIVERSIFY, DIVERSIFY, DIVERSIFY

RISK—THAT IS, the volatility, or the ups and downs, of stock prices—is what makes investing difficult. Before dividends, stocks rise an average of about 9 or 10 percent annually, and if that increase were consistent, year after year, then stocks would carry no risk at all. Unfortunately, life isn't like that. In one week in March 2000, even a stock as seemingly stable as Procter & Gamble (the giant maker of consumer products and a profitable old warhorse that hasn't missed a dividend since 1890) fell from $88 to $53. Is there a way to smooth out this kind of frightening volatility?

One way is through diversification. That is, holding *a variety* of stocks, since economic events and investor passions don't affect all companies in the same way at the same time. When some stocks are hot, others are cold, and, when you own both kinds, the ride is often much smoother. In the late 1990s, many investors, distracted by the power of technology, neglected diversification. In the four years ending Dec. 31, 1999, the mutual fund Janus Twenty, highly concentrated in tech shares, quadrupled in value. Even more broadly defined growth stocks, shares with sharply rising profits and high price-to-earnings ratios, rose

22 percent in 1998 and 55 percent in 1999. Why diversify into traditional industries or value stocks, investors reasoned, if tech growth stocks were so strong?

Actually, high returns in a portfolio are more a danger sign than low returns. They typically indicate that your holdings are overweighted in a single sector. The market as a whole simply does not zip along at 50 percent growth a year. Sure enough, Janus Twenty fell 32 percent in 2000 while the Nasdaq Composite Index, heavily weighted toward technology shares, dropped 39 percent, and growth-stock mutual funds declined 11 percent.

The lesson of 2000 was not to bail out of funds like Janus Twenty but to make sure that the go-go part of your portfolio is balanced with tamer shares. In 2000, for example, mutual funds that specialized in U.S. value stocks, slower-growing companies that were out of favor with investors, *rose* an average of 10 percent. Merck, the reliable pharmaceutical house, jumped 40 percent. The Dow Jones Industrial Average itself lost less than 5 percent after dividends, one-eighth the decline of the Nasdaq. Diversification dampens risk, no doubt about it. But how much diversification is enough?

Before we tackle that question, let's understand what risk *is*. In financial markets, risk is almost always defined as volatility: the extremes of the ups and downs of stock returns (price increases plus dividends). What about the risk of bankruptcy? Volatility covers that eventuality, too, since a bankrupt company's stock usually drops sharply, to zero or close to it. A common way to measure the riskiness of the market as a whole is standard deviation, an indicator of how much the returns of the market tend, from year to year, to vary from the *average* return of the market. For instance, if, over five years, the market produced positive returns of 15 percent, 10 percent, 12 percent, 11 percent and 8 percent, it would not be very risky. It would have a standard deviation of only a few percentage points. But if it returned −26 percent, +37 percent, +24 percent, −7 percent and +7 percent (as it did between 1974 and 1978), then its standard deviation would be high.

The actual standard deviation of the market over the past three-quarters of a century has been about 20 percent. Because the average annual return over this period was 11 percent, this means that in two-thirds of the years going forward, investors can expect annual returns that will vary in a band that ranges from 20 percent more than average (or 31 percent) to 20 percent less (minus-9 percent, which, by the way, was the return in 2000, the worst year since 1974).

But, while these returns look very volatile, they measure only the broad market, the Standard & Poor's index of, roughly, the 500 largest U.S. stocks. Individual shares can have a volatility that is considerably higher than the average, or considerably lower. Their own riskiness is usually measured by *beta*, which compares their volatility to that of the market. A beta of 1.00 means that a stock, historically, has carried about the same volatility as the market. A beta of 1.60 (carried by Vitesse Semiconductor Corp., for example) means that the stock has been 60 percent more volatile; a beta of 0.65 (Kelly Services, Inc.) means that it has been 35 percent less volatile.

Over the short term, investing in individual stocks or even the stock market as a whole can be extremely risky. Prices rise and fall with gut-churning speed. We know, however, that over the long term, stocks dramatically outperform other investment options, like bonds. So the key is to hang in there and benefit from this powerful long-term trend. And that means that you have to be clear on what history is saying: not that each individual stock is guaranteed to be a winner but that the U.S. stock market as a whole has been a winning environment for long-term investors.

So your goal should be to match the risks and the returns of the *market*, not to create your own unique set of risks and returns. One easy way to mimic the market is to put your money in an index mutual fund. One, for example, that owns all the stocks of the S&P 500 or that, by using computer modeling, copies the performance of the Wilshire 5000, an index that includes all 7,000-plus stocks on the three major U.S. exchanges. Superior investors can use either approach with confidence.

Many investors, however, enjoy picking their own stocks or trying to find great mutual funds or prepackaged portfolios that can beat the market. That's fine. If selecting your own fund encourages you to get more involved in the market and to save and invest more of your income, then, definitely, pick your own. If the intellectual challenge and the intrigue of evaluating CEOs, products and consumer demand help you to invest early and often, then selecting stocks is the right approach.

With any portfolio, you have to accept the riskiness of the market as a whole. What you don't have to accept is anything on top of that, or what economists call *idiosyncratic* risk. Think of it this way: If your portfolio includes just one stock, you are accepting an enormous amount of idiosyncratic risk. Individual stocks can be very volatile. Consider Libbey, Inc., a tame stock. Shares of the maker of glass jars traded at $26 in March 2000. But two months later, Libbey's price was up by 25 percent; then in October it fell to $26 again. By January, Libbey was up one-third; then fell one-fourth two months later. In June, the stock hit a spectacular $41, tumbled to $33 in August, and recovered to $38 in September. And this is Libbey, which is 45 percent less volatile than the market as a whole. It is only a portfolio comprising many individual stocks that reduces risk since, on average, some go down but others go up.

The more stocks you buy, spread across various industries, the closer you get to matching the volatility of the market as a whole. The big question is how much diversification do you really need, how many different stocks should one investor own to eliminate, or nearly eliminate, idiosyncratic risk?

This is a tougher question than it sounds. Investment professionals have traditionally said that you can achieve adequate diversification with as few as 10 or 20 stocks. In 1977, a highly influential study by Bloomfield, Leftwich and Long found that owning 20 randomly selected stocks provided almost as much benefit from diversification as the benefit provided by the market as a whole. Indeed, they found a big drop-off in idiosyncratic risk with a portfolio as small as eight or 10 stocks. The three economists had studied the volatility of individual stocks compared with the market in the years 1965–1970, and their conclusions became the settled conventional wisdom, until the year 2000.

That's when a group of esteemed economists released an updated study. John Y. Campbell of Harvard, Martin Lettau of the Federal Reserve Bank of New York, Burton Malkiel of Princeton, and Yexiao Xu of the University of Texas at Dallas looked at the volatility of stocks, industries and the market as a whole during the period 1962–1997. They found that to achieve roughly the same volatility as the market, investors needed to own as many as 50 individual stocks. That's because, while the risk in the market and within industries hasn't changed much in recent years, the risk of *specific* stocks has been steadily increasing. The average stock is much more volatile than it used to be.

Why? The authors suggest a few reasons. For one thing, there's been a trend of breaking up companies into smaller, more focused firms—partly in an effort to attract investors, who find it easier to understand stocks in a single industry. Old-fashioned conglomerates had many businesses under one roof, so they offered a lot of diversification within one company. GE, one of the remaining successful conglomerates, today is involved in so many industries that it's a kind of mutual fund on its own. If aircraft engines aren't selling well in a given quarter, GE can compensate with better results in its plastics business. GE's volatility is about the same as the market's. But most companies today are concentrated in specific economic niches, which means a big short-term upside if a firm does well, and a big downside if it does not.

Another factor may be that many companies now go public at very early stages—often before they're consistently profitable. In the past, a firm had to achieve a strong earnings record before it launched an Initial Public Offering, or IPO. As a result, many of the companies listed on the Nasdaq, especially, are far riskier than their counterparts of 30 or 40 years ago. And perhaps most important, the authors note that with so many CEOs compensated with stock options, there's a greater incentive for management to make risky moves that may juice the stock price. Managers face the possibility of huge gains when their stock rises, but, since they hold options, the worst they can do is break even if it falls (in fact, they may even have their options "repriced" at a lower level, so they make money either way). In the long term, stock-option incentives for managers probably benefit shareholders, but they appear to increase volatility.

Is the increased volatility of individual stocks merely a passing fad? There is no way to know, but it is wise to take out some insurance. Campbell and his co-authors found a large difference between the riskiness of a 20-stock portfolio and a 50-stock portfolio. After examining the results, my own conclusion is that 30 stocks, chosen to reflect the variety of the broad market, should modulate volatility enough to give you a sensible portfolio. But be sure to balance your holdings: own tech stocks and real estate investment trusts; own oil service stocks and airlines; own manufacturers and consumer-goods sellers; own small companies as well as large; consider value as well as growth. And don't forget that the volatility of *any* portfolio falls sharply over time.

Choosing and tracking 30 stocks (or even 20) can be a tall order. Peter Lynch, former manager of the Fidelity Magellan fund, coined the term "diworseification" to denote a portfolio that's so loaded with stocks that an investor can't follow them all. (Lynch himself ran a mutual fund with more than 200 different stocks, but he had help.) John Maynard Keynes, the most influential economist of the twentieth century—and a successful investor, to boot—once wrote that "it is a mistake to think that one limits one's risk by spreading too much between enterprises

about which one knows little and has no reason for special confidence."

That's a good term, "special confidence." As an investor, you
need truly to love the companies you own (though don't become
so enamored that you can't jilt one or two when they don't
return the favor). Superior investors understand that you should
own as many stocks as you feel comfortable with—20 is a little
better than 10 and 40 is the max. Make sure they are in different businesses. And keep them for a long, long time.

P/E RATIOS

ON JUNE 30, 2001, a single share of stock in the Washington Post Co., publisher of the largest newspaper in the nation's capital and of the 3.1-million circulation magazine *Newsweek*, and owner of six TV stations, numerous small cable systems, and the Stanley H. Kaplan Educational Centers for prepping students to take college entrance exams, cost $574. On the same date, Oracle Corporation, the world's largest maker of database-management software, cost $19. Which stock was more expensive?

Oracle, by a mile. The newspaper company's stock traded at a price-to-earnings ratio of 18 while the software firm's stock traded at a P/E of 42. The P/E ratio indicates how many dollars investors are willing to pay to acquire a dollar of a company's annual earnings. Investors, at least in mid-2001, were paying twice as much for Oracle as for the Washington Post Co.

All by itself, the *price* of a stock means nothing. When entrepreneurs get together to start a corporation, they sell shares to raise money. How many shares? That's arbitrary. To raise $1 million, they may issue 10 million shares at 10 cents each or 100 shares at $10,000 each. Eventually, the company may go public—that is, either issue new shares or sell the existing shares (or a combination) to a broader audience. If the shares are then listed on the New York, American or Nasdaq exchanges, they need to carry a convenient price, usually somewhere between $10 and $60. But some stocks are as cheap as a buck a share, and, at the other end of the scale, a single "A" share of Warren Buffett's company, Berkshire Hathaway, Inc., has traded as high as $80,000, and the Washington Post, in March of 2001, hit a high of $651.

Normally, however, companies don't want their stock prices to get much above $100 since a high price discourages small investors from buying convenient 100-share lots, or even, in some cases, from buying a single share. To keep share prices sensible, companies split their stock, which simply means issuing more shares to current holders. If you own 100 shares trading at $100, and the stock splits two-for-one, then the next day you will own 200 shares trading at around $50. Often, a split creates excitement, and the stock rises briefly, but, in general, a stock split is a non-event. It doesn't matter whether your ten dollars comes in the form of two five-dollar bills or one ten-dollar bill.

Buffett, who often goes his own way, has never split the primary shares of Berkshire because he wants "quality" shareholders. That is, shareholders who are in for the long haul and who don't focus on price changes in the stock. (Buffett sits on the board of the Washington Post Co. and always had an influence on the late Katharine Graham and her son Donald, the company's CEO) "Would a potential one-share purchaser be better off if we split 100 for 1, so he could buy 100 shares?" Buffett once asked, rhetorically. "Those who think so and who would buy the stock because of the split or in anticipation of one would definitely downgrade the overall quality of our present shareholder group." By 1995, however, the price of an "A" share had soared beyond the reach of many investors, so Berkshire did issue a new "B" class of stock, with each share worth about one-thirtieth of an "A" share. At the time, "B" shares were still expensive, at more than $1,000 each (in October 2001, they were trading at $2,400).

But the point is that the absolute price of a share of stock is meaningless. What counts is its relationship to something else— its own price a year ago, for example, or the profits of the company that issued it. The most popular measure of such a relationship is the P/E ratio. Some are convinced the P/E is the true measure of a stock's value in the market. (You find it by dividing the price of the stock by the earnings per share of the company.) I do not. I am not a fanatic about P/Es. In fact, superior investors can get through their lives perfectly well without paying attention to them, for reasons I will explain.

Earnings per share, of course, is a figure, expressed in dollars and cents, that's derived by dividing the firm's earnings (or its official after-tax profits in a year) by the total number of shares outstanding. Earnings per share, or EPS, is a figure that you can find on any financial website or in a company's own press releases. The SEC requires listed firms to report their earnings every quarter, and stock analysts spend much of their time trying to predict what the EPS will be.

Some confusion arises over P/E ratios because different people have different definitions of a year's EPS. Do you use the most recent 12 months, the most recent full calendar year, the calendar year you are in (thus, projections are necessary), or some combination?

My favorite research service, the Value Line Investment Survey, takes the EPS for the last two full quarters and adds that to projections for the next two quarters. That's fine, but it's important, for comparisons, to know what you're working with. A P/E ratio that uses next year's predicted profits will usually be lower (and thus make the stock look more enticing) than a P/E based on last year's actual profits.

Despite its deficiencies, the P/E ratio remains the favorite valuation measure of analysts and investors. It does tell—as price alone does not—which stocks are popular, that is, which stocks investors truly want to own at a given moment. For example, between 1996 and 1999, the average annual P/E ratio for the market (based on the previous 12 months' profits) was about 20, but the P/E for airline stocks was 10. That is, it took only $10 to buy a dollar's worth of an airline's annual profits, but it took $20 to buy a dollar's worth of the average company's annual profits. By contrast, restaurant stocks over the same period carried a P/E ratio of 21; drug company stocks, 29. In 1999, Dell Computer had a P/E of 62 while many other high-tech stocks had P/Es over 100, and the average thrift (or savings and loan) had a P/E of 14.

Why the discrepancies? First, investors will pay more for a stock that has *consistent* earnings growth. Risk scares people, and they are willing to spend money to avoid it. Airlines, automakers and other companies in cyclical industries do not offer consistent profits, the way that pharmaceutical firms do. People get sick and need drugs whatever is happening in the economy, but they can cut back on flying and delay their car purchases in a downturn.

Even a well-run company like Delta Air Lines experiences wild highs and lows in profits. Delta had earnings of $4.69 per share in 1989, then $2.64 in 1990, then a four-year string of losses before becoming profitable again in 1995. In 1989, you could have bought Delta for as little as $24, at a rock-bottom P/E of 5, but that would not necessarily have been a great deal, considering what happened in the next five years: the stock barely budged in price. In 2000, Delta earned a record $7.40 for an average P/E that year of just 7. But in 2001, the company was expected to lose money again.

By contrast, despite a faltering economy, investors in mid-2001 were willing to pay a price representing a P/E of 18 for shares of Gannett Co., the giant newspaper chain, which had increased its profits at a steady clip in every year of the preceding decade, averaging 10 percent annual growth (at the same time, the Washington Post Co. and the New York Times Co. each had P/Es of 18 as well). Gannett does pretty well in any economy. General Electric, which may be the best-managed company in the world (see Chapter 37), was trading in mid-2001 at a P/E of 36.

Second, investors will pay more for profit growth. Consider a company like Merck, the giant pharmaceutical house, which typically carries a P/E ratio that is 50 percent higher than the stock market as a whole. During the decade of the 1990s, Merck lifted its earnings per share from 83 cents to $2.45. At the end of 1989, an investor had to pay $20 for every dollar of Merck's earnings, but by the end of 1999, those earnings had tripled, so, on the basis of his original investment, the investor was getting a dollar's worth of earnings for about $6. Not a bad deal at all.

Some analysts have worked out another ratio that takes growth into account. Find the expected growth rate for a company's earnings (again, available on websites like Bloomberg.com and SmartMoney.com) and divide it by the P/E ratio. If the result, called a "PEG" ratio, is greater than 1, then the stock is a good deal. An example is Apache Corp., the Houston-based oil and gas producer. In mid-2001, Apache had a P/E ratio of just 7, but, according to estimates by Value Line, it was projected to increase its earnings at an annual average rate of 10 percent for the next five years (after a 16 percent rate for the preceding 10 years). Divide 7 by 10, and you get 0.7—for a PEG ratio that's considerably less than one. This ratio of a ratio is better than a P/E alone, but it's still a very simplistic way to describe the real world of business, and don't forget, it's based on estimates of *future* earnings, which are sometimes far off the mark.

While we're at it, however, let's look at a ratio that provides an easier way to compare stocks with bonds. You find it by inverting the P/E, or turning it upside down, into an *E/P* ratio, which expresses earnings as a percentage of price. In 1989, an investor might have bought one share of Merck for $17 while the company was earning 83 cents. That's a P/E of about 20 (17/0.83 = 20.48) or an E/P of about 5 percent (0.83/17 = 0.0488). In other words, the investor's stake in Merck is producing a return, in terms of her share of after-tax profits, of 5 percent. Compare that to a long-term Treasury bond, which in December 1989 was returning 6.4 percent. The T-bond was yielding 1.4 percentage points more than Merck.

Now, fast-forward 10 years. Merck's earnings are $2.45, so the E/P, based on the original price paid by the investor, is 14.4 percent—a handsome return, and rising. If Value Line's earnings projections for Merck are correct, earnings should reach $4.80 by 2005 for a return in that year of 28 percent on the original investment. Meanwhile, the 30-year T-bond is still yielding 6.4 percent.

Merck is a fast-growing company, but the average firm, since 1920, has increased its earnings at a rate of 5.5 percent a year. At that pace, Merck's earnings would go from 83 cents in 1989 to only about $2 by 2005. That's a return of 12 percent, not 28 percent, in the last year (but still twice as much as the T-bond return). The average firm also has a lower P/E ratio than Merck, remember. No wonder investors pay more for growth.

Between 1950 and 2000, the average P/E ratio, as calculated by Value Line, was about 13, for an E/P of nearly 8 percent. Lately, however, P/Es have been rising (and E/Ps falling). The average P/E during the 1990s was 17, and from 1997 to 2000, it was 22. This rise, I believe, is perfectly reasonable, as you saw in Chapter 5.

Still, since the P/Es of industries and types of companies vary so much, it is clear that investors are valuing some earnings more than others. What kind of yardstick is it that measures the same bolts of cloth in different ways? For example, in June 2001, Sears carried a P/E of 11, and Wal-Mart a P/E of 42. Sears had a P/E-to-growth ratio of 1.2; Wal-Mart, 3.0. Which is the better buy? You simply cannot tell by looking at P/E or PEG. Superior investors require much more information—and *different* information.

The generalization about the P/E ratio, for now, is that it is wildly overrated as a good, all-in-one measuring instrument. The main reason is "E." Earnings are not as hard and fast as you might think. Companies have latitude in deciding whether to count certain revenues and expenses in this year or next; they can take massive writeoffs one year and then recover earnings (since the earlier writeoffs were too big) in another year. In short, they can *manage* their earnings to make them appear to rise in a pleasing fashion.

Earnings are more accounting device than solid reality. (For a complete rundown on earnings, see the next chapter.) The purpose of investing is to put dollars into your pocket either immediately or sometime in the future. Earnings do not always equal dollars in the pocket. Companies put their earnings to work in three main ways: They distribute them in the form of quarterly dividends to shareholders; they keep them to give to shareholders eventually; and they use them to make capital investments, in new or improved buildings or equipment.

Since 1920, according to Value Line, the average stock has had a dividend yield of 4.4 percent and an earnings yield of 7.5 percent, so a big chunk of earnings, more than half, was paid out as dividends. But lately, the size of that chunk has been falling (mainly for tax reasons; see Chapter 23), but the typical company still pays about one-third of its earnings out to shareholders on a current basis. Some of what used to go to dividends is now retained by the company to buy other companies in whole or part, to pay off debt or simply to pile up in the treasury for future use. For example, Microsoft, which earned $9.4 billion in the year 2000, had $32 billion in cash and short-term investments on its balance sheet on June 30, 2001.

Those earnings—in other words, the money that a company distributes to shareholders or *could* distribute if it wanted to—are frequently called "free cash flow." The rest of what a company earns each year is plowed back into the firm as capital investment. If that investment can, in turn, produce a big flow of cash, then it's the sort of company I want to own. But if a company needs the bulk of its cash flow just to keep up with the competition, then the company is less desirable. A good example of a firm with high capital requirements is Teradyne, Inc., the world's largest maker of sophisticated testing equipment for semiconductors. In a typical year, 1997, Teradyne had earnings of $1.14

per share but capital spending of 79 cents per share (you can get figures like these from Teradyne's own reports, from Value Line or from practically any other research service). That did not leave much for the stockholders. Teradyne pays no dividend and has a limited amount of cash. The good news is that it has practically no debt, but it's still not my kind of company since such a small portion of its earnings is left for shareholders.

Dell, on the other hand, had earnings in 1997 of 32 cents and capital spending of just 7 cents, which is one reason I love Dell. Another way of looking at this same phenomenon is by comparing Dell's annual earnings per share to its total capital invested per share: Dell's return on capital was 26 percent in 2001 compared with 10 percent for Teradyne. In other words, Dell pumps out cash on behalf of shareholders while Teradyne devours cash just to keep its business running on an even keel. But the cash that Teradyne spends for its expensive investments is not apparent from its earnings statement.

To complicate matters, some companies go on capital investment binges, using a substantial portion of their profits to improve their business in a once-in-a-lifetime, or once-in-a-decade renovation. Typically, the Washington Post Co., the firm with which we began this chapter, uses only one-half of its annual earnings for capital investment and another quarter or so for dividends. But between 1997 and 2000, as it moved into the Internet and the education business, the company earned a total of $20 per share and spent $19 on capital investments. As a result, return on total capital dropped from 20 percent to 7 percent over the period. Will the investment spending pay off? Shareholders can only guess.

It is clear, however, in the case of a consistent capital investor like Teradyne that earnings alone do not provide a useful measurement of success since such a large portion of earnings is gobbled up in improvements necessary just to keep the company competitive. This observation is a warning to investors: Don't put all your focus on the P/E ratio. It is not the be-all and end-all. Free cash flow is probably the best number of all to compare with price, but, frankly, it's not easy to calculate (though there are shortcuts, as you will see in the next chapter) and no final solution.

If nothing else, P/Es are convenient and they can be used for comparison between similar stocks. If I am faced with two companies that are close to the same in their businesses and performances but carry different P/Es, I will take the stock with the lower P/E. Compare, for example, AutoZone, Inc., the largest auto parts and accessories retailer in the U.S., and O'Reilly Automotive, with 702 auto parts stores plus substantial sales to mechanics. The businesses aren't exactly the same, but they're very close. During the late 1990s, their average annual cash flow increases (slightly above 25 percent) were about the same, and Value Line estimated that from 2001 to 2005, growth for both would be about 15 percent annually. Both are rated "B+" for financial strength by Value Line, and both have been roughly as volatile as the market as a whole (AutoZone's beta was 1.05; O'Reilly's, 1.0). But in June 2001, AutoZone traded at a P/E of 18 while O'Reilly traded at a P/E of 28. Here is a P/E anomaly that I would exploit, by buying AutoZone, not O'Reilly. AutoZone, very simply, is cheaper.

But such comparisons are exceptional; in most cases, P/Es are no help at all. Other popular valuation indicators have the same drawbacks. Each is almost a caricature of the status of a firm. The price-to-book (P/B) ratio, for instance, measures the price of a share against the net worth of a company (per share) on the balance sheet. But determining book value is an outdated concept in a world dominated by high technology and service industries. For Microsoft, human capital (the brains of employees, the collective memory involved in developing software over two decades) and the power of a network in which nine-tenths of personal-computer users have a Microsoft operating system are the major assets. Yet neither asset shows up on the balance sheet, which is full of things that aren't particularly important to a high-tech company, like real estate and machines. The average P/B ratio for the stocks of the S&P 500 index was 6.1 in June

2001, but variations are wide. AOL Time Warner, for example, had a book value of $37.15 while trading at $54, for a P/B of about 1.5, but Hewlett-Packard had a P/B at the same time of 3; Microsoft had a P/B of 13; AMR, the parent of American Airlines, 0.9; and Equifax, which sells marketing information, 10. For what it's worth (which isn't much), O'Reilly had a P/B of 3 while AutoZone's was 5.

But if not P/Es and P/Bs, then what? Surprisingly, a far less sophisticated ratio has proven far more valuable: price to sales. Yes, P/S! That's the number of dollars it costs an investor to buy a dollar's worth of a company's annual revenues. Hardly anyone pays attention to P/S, though I have heard favorable mentions by two money managers I trust: Kenneth Fisher (son of the great Phil; see Chapter 7), and David Dreman, author of *Contrarian Investment Strategy*, one of my favorite financial books.

But P/S received an even more important endorsement in 1996, when James P. O'Shaughnessy published an excellent technical work, *What Works on Wall Street*. With access to the massive S&P Compustat database on more than 10,000 stocks, he tested dozens of stock-picking strategies to find the methods that produced the best results during his study period, 1952 to 1994. Surprisingly, he found that, if you had invested only in the 50 stocks with the lowest P/S ratio each year, your average annual return over the period would have been 18.9 percent, compared with 14.6 percent for all the stocks in the Compustat universe and 14.7 percent for the stocks with the lowest P/E ratios. For fun, O'Shaughnessy also looked at the stocks with the *highest* P/S ratios. They're "toxic," he wrote, rising just 8.2 percent on average. Examining overlapping 10-year periods, he found that low P/S stocks beat the market an incredible 91 percent of the time.

The advantage of P/S as an indicator is that companies have a harder time dressing up their revenues than their earnings. Sales are sales, but profits can be influenced by subjective judgments, such as when to take writeoffs. Also, sales indicate a company's potential for earnings. If sales are rising but profits are stagnant, a good manager can bring costs into line. But if sales are stagnant, there is little hope. A good example of the joy of rising revenues is International Business Machines Corp. In the early 1990s, IBM's profits languished, but the company was still generating $65 billion in sales (triple the sales of Microsoft in 2000, by the way). IBM's P/S ratio in 1993 was less than 0.5. In that year, Louis V. Gerstner became CEO, and, through better management, turned the company around. Sales increased nicely, but profit margins soared. By 1996, IBM's P/S ratio had reached 1.1 as the stock price tripled. By 2001, IBM had tripled again, and the P/S was 2.0.

Still, P/S is no panacea. Since no one pays much attention to the number (except Value Line, thank goodness), you won't find it in the newspapers or cited by the TV pundits. You frequently have to calculate it yourself: Divide total revenues by total shares outstanding to get revenues per share; then divide that figure into price. If the result is less than 1, pay close attention. You may have a bargain stock. Still, P/S ratios suffer from many of the same problems as P/E ratios, including wild variations from industry to industry. Retailers, with low profit margins, will have low P/S ratios; Kmart Corp., for example, had a P/S of 0.1 in October 2001. But technical consulting and software companies, with high profit margins, have high P/S ratios. One of my favorite companies, Automatic Data Processing, typically carries a P/S of around 5. In the end, P/S is a blunt instrument. Use it to find a possible candidate for further study, not as a major arbiter.

For most people, treating investing as an art rather than a science makes the most sense. It is important to know about the differences between earnings and cash flow and about what constitutes book value, but, in the end, the best way to find a good company is to search for one that has consistently increased its earnings at a good clip and that seems to be in a good business with good management. You may be surprised to learn that the average rate of earnings growth for the past 80 years is only about 6 percent, which not coincidentally is roughly the same growth rate as the country's Gross Domestic Product (GDP), including inflation. If you find a stock whose earnings have been rising at 10 percent annually for a long time—good examples include Freddie Mac (mortgages), Automatic Data Processing (payroll processing), Target (retail chain), Danaher (tools), Walgreen (drugstores), Toll Brothers (homebuilder) and Fastenal (screws; see Chapter 39)—then you've really got something. And if you can hold that stock for a long time, the price today doesn't matter that much.

In the next two chapters, you will learn how to analyze income and cash-flow statements and balance sheets to find companies with the best prospects. For now, when you hear people jabber on about P/E or P/B ratios, the Secret Code advises that you pay little attention. If they ever did have much relevance, they don't any more.

CHAPTER TWELVE

COUNT THE CASH

AS A STOCK INVESTOR, you can do very well merely purchasing mutual funds and other professionally selected portfolios, but if you're serious about picking companies yourself, then you need to know the basics of financial statements.

While companies have to file statements every three months with the SEC using "generally accepted accounting principles," it's not at all difficult for them to deceive investors, at least for a few years. Most companies are honest and straightforward, but it can still be tough to get a clear, accurate picture of their finances just by reading the statements. Despite the drawbacks, you need to examine at least the rudimentary numbers before you buy.

But keep it simple. Concentrate on the annual figures only and compare them over the past few years. There are three statements that count: 1) income, 2) cash flows, and 3) balance sheet. I will concentrate on the first two in this chapter and the balance sheet in the next.

An annual income statement tells how much a company sold, in goods and services, over the course of a year ("revenue") and how much it spent to get those sales ("operating expenses"). Let's use ExxonMobil, the world's largest corporation, as an example.

Revenue is straightforward for most businesses. In Exxon's case, revenue totaled $233 billion in 2000. Operating expenses include the cost of making things or buying them from someone else (for Exxon, $108 billion in "crude oil and product purchases" comprised the single biggest item), the cost of selling them (advertising, paying a sales force, and so on), the cost of maintaining the business (general and administrative) and the cost of research and development.

Subtract operating expenses from revenue and you get "operating income" (notice that "income" in accounting terms is not sales, it's profit); in ExxonMobil's case, operating income totaled $24 billion in 2000, or about one-tenth of revenue. But operating income isn't a company's final profit. Other items have to be added and subtracted first. Added are interest and dividend income (from cash and bonds the company owns) and gains on the sale of investments or property the company owns. Subtracted are income taxes, interest expense (on debt the company owes) and losses on the sale of investments or property.

Also on the minus side are losses from the expense of shutting down operations, closing a subsidiary, discontinuing a product line or laying employees off, even if those expenses will be incurred out into the future. One of the underlying rules of accounting is that you have to subtract expenses the moment you know (or have a good guess) that they will happen. If the company's estimate of the cost of shutting down a plant, for example, proves too high, then it books the difference as recaptured revenue in later years.

Unusual revenue and expense items that come up during the year are called "extraordinary" or "non-recurring." They are, frankly, a headache for anyone trying to analyze an income statement, but there's nothing you can do but check the notes to the financial statements to find out what they are. If an item is truly non-recurring, then it should not enter into your analysis of the company. A legal judgment against a firm may deplete some cash, but it probably won't affect profitability in the future. What you want to know about a company, always, is what will happen next.

Exxon had an extraordinary gain of $1.7 billion because of "asset divestitures that were required as a condition of the regulatory approval of the Merger," according to notes to the statement. In other words, the company had to promise to sell off some subsidiaries at the request of regulators in order to get its 1999 merger with Mobil approved. Clearly, those sales were "non-recurring"; they won't happen regularly again.

After adding and subtracting all of the non-operating items, the company is left with "net income," also called "earnings." That is, the final profit. For 2000, ExxonMobil made $17.7 billion (or $16 billion before the extraordinary item)—more than any other company has ever made in history. (Citigroup was a distant second in 2000 with $13.5 billion in earnings.)

Total earnings are divided by the number of shares outstanding, and the result is earnings per share (or EPS), the number you hear about on CNBC or in the *Wall Street Journal* so much. ExxonMobil's EPS was $5.10, up from $2.28 the previous year. Or take another example, Biogen, the Cambridge, Mass., biotech firm, which had net income of $334 million in 2000. Divide that figure by 149 million shares in the hands of stockholders and you get $2.24 in earnings per share, compared with $1.47 in 1999 and 94 cents in 1998.

The growth of EPS is the single most important fact about a company but it's not the only fact. Biogen's earnings per share rose a spectacular 52 percent in 2000 (compared with 1999) and a spectacular 56 percent in 1999 (over 1998). As I noted in the previous chapter, the average company increases its earnings over long periods by only 6 percent annually. Why did EPS and net income increase so much for Biogen? Very simply because revenues increased—generally a good sign. (ExxonMobil's earnings doubled before the extraordinary gain from divestiture, and its revenues jumped 25 percent.) While businesses can fudge expenses, push them into another year, and add or subtract extraordinary items, they have a much harder time fooling with revenues. Sales are sales, and Biogen increased its sales from $558 million in 1996 to $927 million in 2000.

All of the figures I have cited from ExxonMobil's and Biogen's income statements are available on most financial websites, including AOL, MSN's MoneyCentral, Yahoo! and Bloomberg. But to get more detail, an investor usually has to consult a firm's complete Form 10-K, filed each year with the SEC and available on the Edgar database at www.sec.gov/edgar or in the company's annual report, typically online at the firm's website under "Investor Relations." More current, quarterly reports are called 10-Qs; you rarely need to worry about them.

Back to Biogen: By reading "Management's Discussion and Analysis" in the annual report, we find that the reason revenues are soaring is the success of a single drug, Avonex (also called Inteferon beta-1a), for multiple sclerosis. "Product sales from Avonex," said the report, "represent approximately 82% of the Company's total revenues in 2000 as compared to 78% in 1999." Revenues from royalties, another source of Biogen sales, actually declined in 2000, and "the Company expects to experience declining royalty revenues as a result of patent expirations."

Dependence on a single drug makes me nervous and, sure enough, just after I finished writing the first draft of this chapter, in June 2001, a Swiss drug company called Serono released a study that claimed that patients treated with its multiple-sclerosis drug "Rebif were less likely to suffer relapses than those on Biogen's Avonex." That report drove Biogen stock down from $67 to $54 in two trading days. Still, investors may have overdone their pessimism. The Rebif study is being contested, and, say several analysts, Biogen is a solid, well-managed company with more drugs in the pipeline. But the Rebif episode is a good example of what an income statement can teach an investor: With such a large proportion of its sales tied up in a single drug, Biogen was vulnerable.

Otherwise, Biogen's income statement looks clean and straightforward. So does that of Dell Computer Corp. Sales rose from $25 billion in the year ending Jan. 28, 2000, to $32 billion in the year ending Feb. 2, 2001 (companies can pick their own fiscal year, and retailers sometimes end a specific day of the week, in Dell's case the fourth Friday of the year). Net income for Dell increased from $1.7 billion to $2.2 billion over the same period. In other words, revenues rose 28 percent, and net income rose 31 percent—again, a sharp performance. A closer examination finds that Dell changed its accounting procedures in 2001 (a procedure that actually reduced net income, so it's nothing to be suspicious about). Dell helpfully offers a break-down of revenues by geography: In 2001, sales of $23 billion came from the Americas, $6 billion from Europe and $3 billion from Asia.

Similarly, Starbucks Corp., the coffeehouse chain (with 4,700 stores as of September 2001), divides its revenues among "North American retail," "Business Alliances" and "Other." And Siebel Systems, Inc., in 2000 took in $1.1 billion from software sales and $680 million from "professional services, maintenance, and other." Investors should keep an eye on the segments that are growing most (Asia in the case of Dell, alliances for Starbucks and professional services for Siebel) and consider whether the firm could run into roadblocks from competitors, regulators or simply customer demand.

I love digging into income statements, but it's a taste most investors lack, and luckily it's not required. Just check the rise in revenues over the past five years, making sure that it's steady and in the 10-percent range. Net income (and EPS) should be simi-lar. Then scan the statements for extraordinary charges and line-of-business details, like those alliances (for selling ice cream, for example) that are proving to be revenue-raisers for Starbucks.

———

But you aren't finished. Net income and earnings per share are accounting constructs; they aren't real money. What investors want from an investment is cash. Just as you might buy a rental condominium for the monthly income it throws off and the capital appreciation you get when you sell it at a profit, so all investors purchase stocks for the dollars they can ultimately put in their pockets. With stocks, the cash comes in the form of dividends (if any), capital gains (when you sell at a price higher than you bought), or the proceeds from a buyout by another company. Since, as a shareholder, you are a partner in a business, the flow of cash you derive comes from the success of the business in generating, not the earnings it reports to the SEC, but the cash that it gathers on your behalf. The difference can be considerable.

For example, if a company needs to make large investments each year in building new factories or buying new machines, just to keep up with the competition and earn a little more than it did the year before, then its trove of earnings gets plundered, and there isn't much left for the shareholders.

According to accounting conventions, a capital investment rarely counts entirely as an expense in the year it's made. In other words, if a company spends $1 million on salaries, that cost is immediately deducted from revenues, but if the company spends $1 million on a new building, only part of the cost is deducted the first year (say, $30,000), with the rest deducted over the useful life of the building, which might be 30 years. The part that is deducted each year is called depreciation, but the full capital outlay of $1 million is real money. It comes out of the company's cash in the year it occurs.

With that background, let's look at the statement of cash flows for Biogen. All cash-flow statements begin with officially reported net income, which then goes through a series of adjustments. For example, expenses that don't involve cash expenses are added back in. The main non-cash expense is typically depreciation and amortization (which is the same thing as depreciation but for financial assets). Remember that when a company like Biogen buys a building or a machine, the purchase price goes out the door immediately, but the asset is depreciated over time (in Biogen's case, "buildings and equipment are depreciated over estimated useful lives ranging from 30 to 40 and 3 to 10 years, respectively," according to a footnote). So depreciation is an accounting expense long after the money is already spent. In other words, it is no longer money out the door. For that reason, it is added back to earnings to show a company's true flow of cash. For Biogen, depreciation and amortization amounted to $39 million in 2000.

The cash flow statement adjusts income in other ways as well. All publicly held companies do their accounting on what is called an "accrual" basis, which means that they typically record the revenue from a sale when they send out the bill, not when they actually put the check in the bank. (By contrast, individual taxpayers file their personal Form 1040s on a cash basis.) As a result of accrual accounting, when accounts receivable rise, as they did in Biogen's case in 2000, then the increase gets subtracted from earnings in calculating cash (since that extra money has not gone into the bank yet). Similarly, when receivables fall, the decrease is added to earnings. With accounts payable, it works the opposite way: rising payables mean more cash, declining payables mean less cash.

Special one-time expenses can also add cash beyond the level of earnings. Biogen did not have such items in 2000, but another drug company I examined, King Pharmaceuticals, did. King's earnings included a $29 million "write-off of inventory." The reason, again, can be found in the footnotes: "The company received written notification from the FDA that it must cease manufacturing and distributing Fluogen, an influenza vaccine . . . until we demonstrate compliance with related FDA regulations." This is not good news since King had to take all the Fluogen (despite its clever name) off the shelves. Since Fluogen is now, apparently, worthless, the company has to record an expense immediately against its revenues, but, of course, no real money comes out of the company's bank account so, in cash-flow terms, the expense gets added back.

Financing activities, like increasing or reducing debt, have no effect (except in terms of interest) on an income statement, but they have a big impact on cash. Biogen repaid $5 million of its long-term borrowings (thus reducing cash), but, more important, it bought in $300 million worth of its own stock, reducing cash further. ExxonMobil used a big chunk of its copious 2000 earnings to repay a load of debt ($6 billion) and to buy its own stock ($2 billion).

During the same year, King was engaged in a more complicated restructuring, exchanging debt for equity. The company borrowed about $200 million in 2000, but it also paid off $600 million in old debt, so its cash, as result of these transactions, declined by $400 million. It also raised $387 million by selling stock, so the net result was about a wash. Also under the "financing acitivities" rubric are payments companies make in dividends to shareholders. Biogen and King, like more and more companies these days, offer no dividends, but ExxonMobil, with a dividend yield of about 2 percent, paid out nearly $7 billion.

The numbers to watch carefully on a cash-flow statement are the ones under "investing activities," especially purchases of property, plant and equipment. In Biogen's case, these capital expenditures amounted to $194 million in 2000, up from $83 million in 1999 and just $29 million in 1998. Such a dramatic increase can be a cause for concern. Does Biogen suddenly need to add new facilities because the old plant is out of date? How much more capital has to be invested over the next few years? A good rule of thumb is that, for a sound and steady company, the figure for annual capital investment ought to be around the same as for depreciation. ExxonMobil made capital "additions to property, plant and equipment" of $8.4 billion in 2000 and had depreciation and "depletion" (a kind of depreciation for mineral holdings) of $8.1 billion. But in Biogen's case, investment was five times greater than depreciation.

The bottom line for cash flow is an item called "net increase (decrease) in cash and cash equivalents." In Biogen's case, it was a decrease of $8 million—a trivial number for a firm with nearly $1 billion in sales. In other words, Biogen started the year with $57 million in cash in the bank. It ended the year with $49 million. Basically, Biogen in 2000 used all of its profits to invest in its future growth. It was an exceptional year, and the investment will have to pay off to justify the stock price.

By comparison, Dell Computer is a cash-generating demon, in large part because its business, selling computers by mail-order and over the Internet, does not require huge capital outlays. Plus, buyers typically pay up-front and wait while Dell builds their machines. In the three-year period from 1998 to 2000, Dell increased its cash by a total of nearly $4 billion despite spending $2 billion in investments in other companies. ExxonMobil, after its fantastic year, increased its cash by $5.4 billion, even after sending $14 billion out the door for dividends, debt repayment and stock repurchases.

The main reason to examine cash-flow statements is to find out how much "free cash," or as Warren Buffett calls the figure, "owner earnings," a firm generates in a typical year. Since nearly every year brings extraordinary events like expense write-offs, trades of debt for equity and the like, you should keep your eyes on just a few key numbers.

Start with earnings, then add back depreciation and amortization. This number roughly represents the amount of cash the company has generated. Subtract from it capital expenditures in a typical year. For Biogen, the three-year average was about $100 million, but its numbers are all over the lot, a disturbing situation that requires more study. For Dell Computer, capital expenditures rose over three years from $296 million to $401 million to $482 million—a more predictable progression and, happily, a rate almost exactly the same as the growth of net income.

In 2000, Biogen's net income was $334 million and depreciation was $39 million, so cash before capital expenditures was $373 million. Subtract $100 million as a typical (we hope) year of capital spending, and "owner earnings" or "free cash flow" was $273 million, or $1.83 per share; after adjusting for receivables and a few other items, it's about $2 per share. That is what Biogen is making in profits for its investors. The stock, on

June 30, 2001, was trading at $52. Let's assume that cash flow grows at 17.5 percent annually for the next 10 years (that's the estimate of Value Line for the next five years). By 2010, owner earnings will be about $10, a handsome annual return of almost 20 percent on an investment of $52, but 10 years may be a long time to wait.

Deciding whether to purchase Biogen is your own call, but it's a choice that depends on an examination of statements both of income and of cash flows. Too many investors rely solely on earnings per share, but, in the Secret Code, it's cash that counts.

CHAPTER THIRTEEN

FIND COMPANIES WITH SOLID ASSETS AND WITHOUT THREATENING DEBT

IF FEW INVESTORS take the time to read a company's statement of cash flows, even fewer read its balance sheet. Don't ignore it. In 1999, many high-tech companies were losing money—that is, their expenses were much greater than their revenues. But it wasn't until their balance sheets started to deteriorate that the firms' stocks started to drop sharply, and many of them filed for bankruptcy.

A balance sheet tells where a company stands at a given moment, usually the end of its fiscal year. There are two parts: assets, which are items of value that the company owns, and liabilities, which are obligations that the company owes. The two parts balance—that is, they add up to the same total. In the case of ExxonMobil, assets and liabilities in 2000 were each $149 billion. The item that makes assets and liabilities come out even is "shareholders' equity," or net worth. Take the assets (again, $149 billion, mainly in petroleum reserves and refineries), subtract the liabilities owed to people and institutions other than the shareholders ($78 billion), and you get what the shareholders themselves own ($71 billion, or about $20 per share)—their equity stake.

Let's look again at Biogen. On the asset side of the balance sheet on Dec. 31, 2000, the company had $49 million in cash and "cash equivalents" and $634 million in "marketable securities." It's always a good idea to check the notes to the balance sheet to find out what the company means by such terms. In Biogen's case, cash equivalents are investments like money-market funds and Treasury bills that "are highly liquid," maturing in three months or less. "Marketable securities" are also short-term, "principally corporate notes and government securities." Fine. Biogen, a company that had sales of $926 million in 2000, was sitting on a pile of cash and near-cash worth $682 million.

The other major assets, for Biogen and most other companies, are usually accounts receivable (the bills that Biogen's customers have yet to pay) and property and equipment. I like to be sure that accounts receivable aren't getting out of hand, indicating that some customers might be deadbeats and that the company could be inflating its sales figures by neglecting to write off the bad debt. Biogen's accounts receivable amount to $143 million; that's 15 percent, or about two months' worth of sales. That's not great, but it is acceptable. Be wary of companies that carry receivables amounting to 20 percent or more of their sales; they may have uncollectable bills on their books. (ExxonMobil had $23 billion in accounts receivable, or about 10 percent of annual sales.) Biogen's property is valued at $400 million, up from $240 million the year before. The footnotes show that the difference is "construction in progress," so Biogen is apparently adding a major plant. The notes show it's a "biological manufacturing facility in North Carolina."

The liabilities side of the ledger is more important. A company loaded down with debt might face bankruptcy since it has to meet high interest and principal payments even if profits fall as the economy slows or a product fails. There's no cushion. In Biogen's case, accounts payable plus accrued expenses (what the firm owes to its suppliers and to the tax authorities) total about $170 million. Debt is $47 million, and the notes indicate a term loan due in 2005 and a construction loan due in 2007. That's not onerous; interest payments are less than $5 million annually while net income (out of which interest is paid) totaled $334 million in 2000. The historical record shows that since 1996, the smallest profit Biogen has ever made was $33 million, or six times its interest obligation in 2000. Unless sales and profits decline dramatically, the balance sheet appears sound.

In all, Biogen has $1.4 billion in assets and just $325 million in non-shareholder liabilities. That leaves $1.1 billion in shareholder equity, or $7.38 for each of the 149 million shares. Shareholder equity is also called "book value," so, in mid-2001, the ratio of Biogen's price ($52) to its book value was about 7-1. The price-to-book (P/B) ratio used to be a formidable valuation measure, but, as I noted in Chapter 11, it is no longer much use. The overwhelming assets of many companies today reside in their human capital—the education, training and overall braininess of the people they employ—and human capital does not show up on the balance sheet. Peter J. Wallison of the American Enteprise Institute and Robert Litan of the Brookings Institution write that "estimates suggest that as much as 80 percent of the total value of the stocks in the S&P 500 index is based on intangible assets."

At a time when so many assets are intangible, investors should focus their attention on one asset and one liability only. The asset is cash. It's reassuring when a company has a lot of it, though buckets of cash raise a question: Why not give it back to the shareholders? At the end of 2000, Siebel Systems, a fast-growing Internet software firm that helps companies manage their relationships with customers, had cash and short-term investments of $1.2 billion (compared with sales of $1.8 billion). That sounds like a lot, but Siebel has been using its cash to buy companies like MOHR Development, Paragren Technologies and LivePage Corp., firms that help it bolster its own market position. Heavy cash balances in a young high-tech company make investors feel confident during an economic slowdown.

The single liability to watch is debt. Siebel had none at all. Similarly, Dell Computer had $5.4 billion in cash and short-term investments and just $509 million in debt. By contrast, Libbey, Inc., maker of glass tableware, had $1.3 million in cash and $161 million in debt.

Key questions with debt are when it's due and what the interest payments are. The notes to its 10-K show that, in 1998, Dell issued $200 million worth of bonds that are due in 2008 and pay 6.6 percent interest and another $300 million worth that are due in 2028 and pay 7.1 percent interest. None of this is worrisome. Far from it. Dell is a company generating $2 billion in free cash a year and paying less than $40 million in interest on its debt. Libbey, by contrast, had cash flow in 2000 of about $60 million and interest payments of $12 million. That's a decent gap, but it makes me nervous. If Libbey's earnings fall sharply, it might not be able to pay what it owes.

I have a strong bias against companies that are highly leveraged, which is a euphemism for being deeply in debt. A young firm, especially, should stay away from debt since its future stream of income for repayment is so volatile. Examples abound of telecommunications firms that got into trouble borrowing. Teligent, launched in a classy initial public offering in 1997 and headed by the former number-two executive at AT&T, never made a profit but managed to take on $1.2 billion in debt which it could not service.

Value Line offers a "capital structure" summary for each of the companies it examines, noting total debt, the portion due in five years, annual interest payments and the percentage that debt represents of total capital. There are no hard-and-fast rules, but a company should easily be able to cover its interest payments, and debt should represent no more than one-third of total capital (that is, the stock part of investment in a company should be at least twice the borrowed part). Nextel Communications, a wireless company, had long-term debt at the end of 2000 of $14 billion, representing 76 percent of capital; preferred stock, actually another form of debt, made up another 10 percent of capital. That's quite a load. Global Crossing, another telecom company, looked more sound at the time, with debt at 25 percent of capital (preferred was another 15 percent) and cash of about $1 billion. The only problem was that interest payments were running $450 million annually, plus $240 million for the preferred stock.

Absence of debt, however, is no guarantee of soundness in a business. Consider Priceline.com, which was launched in 1998 to sell airplane tickets over the Internet. Priceline, in mid-2001, had no debt and $143 million in cash. Unfortunately, the company racked up losses of $315 million in 2000 and was projected to lose $40 million in 2001. This is not the kind of company superior investors should own—debt or no.

In the end, balance sheets matter for the same reason that your own bank account, mortgage and credit-card debt matter. They determine your financial health, here and now. Things can change, certainly, but it's good to know that the company in which you are investing holds a cash cushion and lacks a debt threat.

CHAPTER FOURTEEN

NO ONE CAN "TIME" THE MARKET. DON'T TRY IT.

AFTER SEVERAL MISERABLE WEEKS during the summer of the year 2000, completely out of the blue, stocks turned around. In four days, the S&P 500 index, the benchmark for most money managers, rose 7 percent, and the technology-heavy Nasdaq rose a record 19 percent. European markets were up 8 percent; Asia, 11 percent; Latin America, 13 percent.

The news that evidently sent the markets higher was that unemployment was rising and economic growth slowing in the U.S., so the Federal Reserve might not have to raise interest rates as anticipated. But the cause was not important. Utterly unexpected turnarounds like this show why the winning strategy, always, is to buy good companies and mutual funds and to hold onto them. It's a strategy I like to call "Being There."

On average, stocks have returned 11 percent annually since the mid-1920s, but unless you are in the market—unless you're there—you can't benefit. You never know when, all of a sudden, the market will shoot straight up. A few years ago, Ibbotson Associates, the Chicago research firm, conducted a famous study that made the point dramatically. If you had invested $1 in the stocks of the S&P 500 in 1926, your stake would have grown to $1,114 by 1995 (including reinvested dividends). But if you had been out of the market during the 35 best months out of the 840 months in the period, then your $1 would have risen to only $10. In other words, 99 percent of the profits came in just 4 percent of the months. No one knows which months will produce those huge gains, but that doesn't stop investors from trying to guess, from "timing" the market. But timing is dangerous, for two reasons:

- First, you can't do it. The lure of timing causes investors to move to the sidelines when they shouldn't. Don't take my word for it. Here is what John C. Bogle, founder of the Vanguard Group, one of the largest mutual fund houses in the world, says about market timing: "After nearly fifty years in this business, I do not know of anybody who has done it successfully and consistently. I do not even know anybody who *knows* anybody who has done it successfully and consistently."

- Second, the payoff for accurately timing the market isn't worth the risk, as the Center for Investment Research at Charles Schwab & Co., the San Francisco brokerage firm, found in a study. Bryan Olson, a director of the center, concluded: "It's tempting to wait for the 'best time' to invest. But the best course of action for most people was to invest at the first possible moment, regardless of the level of the market."

Olson looked at four different imaginary investors. Each was given $2,000 on every December 31, starting in 1979. Investor A is a timer, who, incredibly, manages to put his money annually into the S&P at the end of the month that had the lowest monthly closing price of the year. Investor B simply puts his money into the S&P immediately, every Dec. 31, and just leaves it there. Investor C, who is a dunce at timing, purchases the S&P stocks at the end of the month that has the *highest* price of the year. (In the periods when they aren't in stocks, A and C buy U.S. Treasury bills.) Finally, Investor D simply buys T-bills. The market is too scary for him.

How did they do?

Investor A, the one with perfect market timing, has $387,120 at the end of 20 years. But Investor B, the buy-and-hold fellow, winds up with $362,185. Investor C, the poor timer, has $321,569. And the T-bill man, Investor D, has just $76,558.

The revelation here is that the timer with the hot hand (A) manages to make just $25,000, or 7 percent, more than Investor B, who merely shovels his cash into the S&P. So, even if you *could* time the market, your results would not be much better than buying and holding.

But what if you are convinced that there's a recession ahead? Shouldn't you pull out of stocks? Before you sell, remember that, after every downturn in this century, stock prices rose to levels substantially higher than before the fall. Between 1932 and 1987, there were 13 bear markets, defined as drops of at least 20 percent in the S&P index. A year after these declines hit bottom, the S&P had recovered an average of 46 percent. In the worst case, the gain was 21 percent; in the best, 121 percent. (See Chapter 27 for more on bear markets.)

Yes, there have been times when recovery was sluggish. In a column in the *New York Times* in April 2001, Jeffrey Madrick wrote that "stock prices plummeted in 1969 after the long and optimistic economic expansion of the 1960's. . . . And the market did not exceed its 1969 high again, discounted for inflation, until 1992. . . . In other words, if you had investments in the S&P 500 in 1969, it took 23 years to earn a positive real return from the movement of stocks. The 'long run' can be very long indeed."

There's a disingenuous sleight of hand at work here. Madrick refers to a "positive real return from the *movement* of stocks," that is to say, their prices, as reflected by the level of the S&P. But what investors want from stocks is *total return*, that is, price increases plus annual dividends. Total return is the benchmark all analysts use to measure the performance of a stock. Madrick conveniently drops dividends, which averaged 4.4 percent annually between 1920 and 2000. That makes an enormous difference.

Using Ibbotson data, I found that it took not 23 years, but *three* years, for the S&P to produce a positive real return after the sharp decline of 1969. More important, between 1969 and 1992, the 23-year period to which Madrick refers, the S&P returned 138 percent after inflation. Long-term Treasury bonds, again, according to my analysis of Ibbotson data, returned 79 percent. And short-term Treasury bills returned just 32 percent. Now, a return of 138 percent after inflation isn't very impressive for a 23-year investment, but it is, evidently, the worst stretch that Madrick could find. And it's nearly twice as much as bonds returned and more than four times as much as bills. Always remember that investing involves choice. You can't hide. You have to pick stocks, bonds or cash. There are indeed periods when stocks do poorly, but, during those periods, bonds often do worse.

Imagine you are gambling at a special kind of casino where, at roulette, the odds are massively in your favor. But you have had a run of bad luck and decide to switch to blackjack, where the odds favor the house. Does this sort of "timing" make sense? Of course not. Neither does market timing. Superior investors recognize a more profitable alternative: buy great companies and mutual funds and keep them.

NIX THE NASDAQ.
DO THE DOW.

DURING THE 1990S, Americans became obsessed with a number that very few of them had noticed before: the level of the Nasdaq Composite Index. The nightly news shows, which in the past had reported the closing price of the Dow Jones Industrial Average (if they bothered with stocks at all), were regularly reporting the Nasdaq, too. And no wonder. In June 1991, the index stood at 486. Less than nine years later, it had reached 5133. Then, suddenly, the Nasdaq collapsed. Within 13 months, it lost more than two-thirds of its value. Its luster was lost.

All to the good. The Nasdaq Composite is widely misunderstood. It is not the stock market but only a small and volatile part of it, the 5,000 companies listed on what used to be called the over-the-counter market. Superior investors would do well to ignore the Nasdaq and focus on the Standard & Poor's 500-Stock Index. Or, better yet, do the Dow.

The S&P is the benchmark against which most money managers measure their performance. It comprises roughly the 500 largest U.S. stocks, with about 20 names added and subtracted each year for bankruptcies, industry balancing and mergers. (For example, the S&P folks eliminated Chrysler from the list when it was bought by Daimler Benz, a firm based in Germany.) But I like the Dow even better. With only 30 companies, it manages to do just what the S&P does: track the performance of the market as a whole. While the S&P and the Dow differ from year to year, over longer periods their performances are remarkably similar. For example, from the start of 1990 to the end of 2000, the S&P rose 371 percent, and the Dow rose 377 percent.

The main point, however, is that neither of them is the Nasdaq. That index used to be composed of a diverse group of small-cap companies waiting to graduate to the New York Stock Exchange. But in recent years, the Nasdaq Composite has become dominated by high-tech firms, especially the huge ones: In mid-2001, just eight stocks out of about 5,000—in order of size, Microsoft, Intel, Qualcomm, Cisco Systems, Oracle, Amgen, Veritas Software and Dell Computer—accounted for one-third of the index's total value. Any sector (not just high tech, but finance, oil service, natural resources) will have a lot more volatility than the broader market, and a sector top-heavy with a few firms will be more volatile yet.

Volatility is not only scary, but it obscures performance. From June 2000 to June 2001, the Nasdaq bounced wildly between a high of 4275 and a low of 1639 while the Dow fluctuated only between 11,338 and 9389. In other words, the Nasdaq's low was 62 percent below its high, but the Dow's low was only 17 percent below its high. It is hard to pin the Nasdaq down, while the Dow follows a smoother, more discernible course. Think of the Nasdaq as a stock with a high of $43 and a low of $16 in the course of a year, while the Dow is like a stock with a high of $43 and a low of $36.

Smart investors should own portfolios that look like the Dow, not like the Nasdaq. The Dow, in a way, *incorporates* the Nasdaq through two of its 30 components—Intel and Microsoft, which were added in November 1999. The Dow includes two other high-tech stocks, both listed on the New York Stock Exchange: IBM (added in 1932, removed in 1939 and then added back in

1979) and Hewlett-Packard (added in 1997). Executives at Dow Jones, Inc., which owns the *Wall Street Journal* and *Barron's*, try to manage the index to reflect the economy as a whole—the intention of Charles Henry Dow, the investment manager who started it, first as an index comprising nine railroads and two industrial companies in 1884, then as a more comprehensive average in 1896.

Of the 12 stocks on the 1896 list, only one survives on today's Dow: General Electric (many of the others are obscure: Laclede Gas? American Cotton Oil? Tennessee Coal & Iron?). But several of the current components have impressive longevity. Coca-Cola, DuPont, Eastman Kodak, ExxonMobil, General Motors, AT&T, Procter & Gamble and United Technologies have all been on the Dow (sometimes under different names) for at least 60 years.

Most modern indexes, including the Nasdaq Composite and the S&P 500, use a system weighted by market cap. Each stock's impact on the movement of the index overall is determined by its stock-market value, or capitalization (a figure derived by multiplying a stock's price by the number of its shares outstanding). GE, at $485 billion in June 2001, had the largest market cap in the world, so it influenced the S&P the most at the time. Microsoft, at $355 billion, had a huge effect on the Nasdaq.

But the Dow is different. Its founder applied what's called a "price weighting" to the index. Add up the prices of all the stocks and divide by a special number that changes continually because of stock splits. Originally, the number was 30; by 2001, it was 0.15. In other words, when a Dow stock rises one point, it pushes up the entire average by about seven points. Of course, what makes this rudimentary system downright weird is that a high-priced stock has much more effect on the Dow than a low-priced stock, even though price alone does not reflect a company's size or importance. Thus, at a time when IBM and Intel had almost the same market cap, IBM, trading at $113 a share, had about four times the impact on the index of Intel, trading at $28. If IBM rises 4 percent in a day, it pushes the index up about

30 points, but if Intel rises 4 percent, it pushes the index up about 7 points.

The other quirk of the Dow is that it includes so many old-fashioned companies. Few with-it money managers make stocks like Minnesota Mining & Manufacturing or Caterpillar major holdings in their portfolios. It was not until 1999 that the Dow dropped such clunkers as Sears, Goodyear and Union Carbide and added market-cap giants Microsoft and Intel.

But despite its stodgy and anachronistic ways, the Dow really works! In August 1982, the Dow stood at 777. In October 2001, it was over 9,000—in less than 20 years, a 12-fold increase, or 20-fold including dividends. The Nasdaq has done well too, no doubt about it, but the ride has been terrifying. From June 1991 to June 2001, the Nasdaq rose 317 percent; the Dow, 266 percent. But, after accounting for dividends (the Dow's are much higher), the returns were roughly the same, and the Dow was far less volatile.

The Dow's performance has been a thing of beauty, and it is testimony to three truths about investing.

1. Dow components are chosen, in large part, because they have shown an ability to grow in the past and a likelihood to grow for many years into the future. As Warren Buffett wrote in one of his annual reports: "In studying the investments we have made in both subsidiary companies and common stocks, you will see that we favor businesses and industries unlikely to experience major change. The reason for that is simple: Making either type of purchase, we are searching for operations that we believe are virtually certain to possess enormous competitive strength ten to twenty years from now. A fast-changing environment may offer the chance for huge wins, but it precludes the certainty we seek." A good goal is to look for companies that will be thriving 50 years from now.

2. Buy-and-hold is a strategy that works. Over the past 60 years, only 33 changes have been made to the components of the index. In other words, the average stock was held more than 50 years.

3. Diversification is a necessity, but it can be achieved without a huge portfolio. Of the 30 stocks, two are in the telecommunications sector, three financial, four high-tech, two transportation, two retail, six manufacturing, five consumer products, one restaurant, two pharmaceuticals, one energy and two conglomerates. You can change the names, but, using that same blueprint, you can build a sound portfolio of your own. Or you can buy the Dow itself—most easily as the exchange-traded fund called "Diamonds" (DIA) on the American Stock Exchange.

Another alternative is to buy a Dow-like mutual fund. Only one exists, as far as I know: Pilgrim (formerly Lexington) Corporate Leaders. The fund was started in 1935, in the depths of the Depression, and the idea was to select 30 companies that would survive and thrive for the next 80 years. Until 2015, however, the components of the fund, which like the Dow, would be price-weighted, could not change unless a firm went bankrupt or was merged out of existence. The early records were lost, but if you put $10,000 into the fund in 1941, despite an initial 12 percent commission, you would have an incredible $6 million today. The fund now includes 26 stocks (23 survivors plus three spin-offs of original companies), including Dow components like ExxonMobil and Citigroup plus others like Union Pacific and Chevron. Again, despite the old-fashioned nature of the portfolio, its performance from 1991 to 2001, at an annual average of 13.3 percent, trailed the fund averages by just one-tenth of a percentage point. Since there is little real-life management required, Pilgrim charges investors an expense ratio of only 0.67 percent. The dissolution date has now been extended to 2100.

A more up-to-date version of both Corporate Leaders and the Dow is the Investec (formerly Guinness Flight) Wired Index Fund, which invests in the 40 New Economy stocks that comprise an index concocted by the editors of *Wired*, the high-tech monthly magazine. Not all of the fund's components are high-techs, however; top holdings include WorldCom, DaimlerChrysler, Microsoft, Walt Disney, Glaxo Wellcome (pharmaceuticals) and Wal-Mart. These are firms which, the editors believe, will prosper in the new economic environment. It's a good list, but I still prefer the Dow.

But the Dow isn't perfect. I have four complaints: 1) It doesn't have enough energy stocks. 2) It has too many traditional manufacturers. 3) It needs more consumer-oriented high-tech firms. 4) It should admit foreign-based companies with large U.S. subsidiaries. So, in the next round of changes (some fiddling is done, on average, every five years), I would add BP, plc, the British company that merged with Amoco, the largest domestic oil producer; AOL Time Warner, the world's largest media company; and Dell Computer, probably the most powerful e-tailer. I would delete International Paper (with a market cap of just $18 billion compared with $141 billion for AOL and $63 billion for Dell), Honeywell and one of these three: Caterpillar, Eastman Kodak or 3M.

But I am not in any rush. What the success of the Dow teaches us is that patience pays and that companies themselves evolve with the economy. There is no need, none at all, to change your portfolio frenetically. Be cool, says the Secret Code, and prosper. Here are the Dow components as of October 2001, with their symbols.

AT&T Corp. (T)

Alcoa, Inc. (AA)

American Express Co. (AXP)

Boeing Co. (BA)

Caterpillar, Inc. (CAT)

Citigroup, Inc. (C)

Coca-Cola Co. (KO)

Walt Disney Co. (DIS)

E. I. DuPont De Nemours & Co. (DD)

Eastman Kodak Co. (EK)

Exxon Mobil Corp. (XOM)

General Electric Co. (GE)

General Motors Corp. (GM)

Hewlett-Packard Co. (HWP)

Home Depot, Inc. (HD)

Honeywell International, Inc. (HON)

Intel Corp. (INTC)

International Business Machines Corp. (IBM)

International Paper Co. (IP)

J. P. Morgan Chase & Co., Inc. (JPM)

Johnson & Johnson (JNJ)

McDonald's Corp. (MCD)

Merck & Co., Inc. (MRK)

Microsoft Corp. (MSFT)

Minnesota Mining & Manufacturing Co. (MMM)

Philip Morris Companies, Inc. (MO)

Procter & Gamble Co. (PG)

SBC Communications, Inc. (SBC)

United Technologies Corp. (UTX)

Wal-Mart Stores, Inc. (WMT)

ALWAYS THINK
TAXES

WHAT COUNTS IN INVESTING is not how much money you make but how much money you keep. The difference is what you pay in taxes.

The U.S. Tax Code is a hodgepodge, built over nearly a century, with changes accruing in nearly every congressional session. It does have one major characteristic, however: It tends to penalize savings and investment and to encourage consumption. That's the opposite of how a rational person would construct a tax system from scratch, but it is a fact of life.

Start with $1,000 from your employer. Pay income and payroll taxes and put what's left in the bank. The interest you earn on your savings account gets taxed. Accumulate enough interest to make a stock investment. The company whose shares you own pays taxes, then rewards you with a dividend from what's left, and then *you* pay taxes on the dividend. Use the dividends to buy U.S. Treasury bonds, and pay taxes on the interest on them, too. Stash your earnings in an Individual Retirement Account (IRA) and pay taxes when you make your withdrawals after age 59½. Do you have anything left over for your heirs? If it's more than

$675,000 (a figure scheduled to rise in the years ahead), it gets taxed too.

It's so much easier just to take the $1,000, pay income and payroll taxes, and buy a new suit or throw a dinner party for your two dozen closest friends. That way, you get hit by the IRS only once.

Still, the tax code does provide three important forms of relief.

1. The capital gains tax on the rise in the value of your investment is payable only when you sell it. Also, even when you sell, the tax is only 20 percent (or 18 percent if you hold the shares for five years starting in 2001). By contrast, the tax on dividends, interest, and short-term capital gains (holdings of less than one year) is the same as the tax on your normal employment income: nearly twice as much as the capital gains rate for many investors.

2. Most bonds are taxed more heavily than stocks. An investor in the 31 percent bracket who buys a $10,000 Treasury bond that earns 6 percent interest will receive not $600, but just $414 [$600 × (1 − 0.31)] at the end of one year. The same investor, buying a stock that appreciates 6 percent will receive $480 [$600 × (1 − 0.20)] if he sells after a year. But if a stock investor simply hangs onto the gains, she pays no tax at all.

3. Interest on municipal bonds is exempt from federal taxes, and, usually, a muni bond issued by an agency in the state where you live is also exempt from state taxes. Muni bonds, however, almost always pay a lower before-tax yield than government and corporate bonds. The calculation to determine whether you should buy nearly riskless munis or Treasuries is simple: Take the interest rate on the muni and divide it by 1 minus your ordinary-

income tax rate. So, if a 30-year highly rated muni is yielding 5.1 percent (as a typical bond of this sort was in fall 2001), its "tax-equivalent" yield for someone in a 31 percent bracket is 7.4 percent [.051/(1−.031)]. If a Treasury is yielding less than that, then buy the muni—though you need to be alert to other pitfalls (see Chapter 44 for all the details).

The Secret Code advises you to build up capital gains and, if you do want to sell stocks, use losses in some shares to balance gains in others. That's not difficult when you manage your own portfolio of, say, 30 stocks. You will always have some losers among the winners. But such a simple tax-wise strategy is nearly impossible when you own mutual funds, which, by and large, are managed by people who don't particularly care about investors' tax situations, which vary widely, anyway.

Pre-tax returns are what count for nearly all mutual fund managers, not after-tax returns. And, since mutual funds are pass-through vehicles that confer liabilities on their shareholders rather than on the funds themselves, those shareholders often are faced with unpleasant surprises. A hyperactive manager who sells stocks with big profits and holds onto stocks with big losses can generate huge capital gains for shareholders even in a year in which the fund falls in value.

Consider Nicholas-Applegate Global Technology Fund. It fell 36 percent in value in 2000, but it saddled its shareholders with a capital gains distribution of $36 per share when the fund was worth just $77 per share.

A working paper authored by Joel Dickson, John Shoven and Clemens Sialm—three scholars affiliated with the prestigious National Bureau of Economic Research—demonstrated that "investors who fail to pay attention to after-tax returns [of mutual funds] may well end up considerably poorer." Another NBER paper discovered that investors are waking up to the importance of mutual fund taxes, and, as a result, "funds that place higher tax burdens on their investors . . . are likely to experience lower cash inflows than other funds with similar pretax returns but lower tax burdens."

It's about time.

Some mutual funds are responding by encouraging managers to limit their trading (and thus the capital gains they incur) and to try to sell losers rather than winners, but, ultimately, the best way for investors to manage their tax liabilities is to manage their own portfolios.

Of course, not all mutual-fund investments are taxable. Many government-blessed retirement investments—IRAs, 401(k) plans, etc.—are tax-*deferred*, meaning that you eventually have to pay Uncle Sam, but, in the meantime, your nest egg grows without being diminished by an annual tax bite. You just get whacked when you withdraw the money. Still, a simple rule is that deferring taxes helps build assets.

Anyone can start an IRA and contribute up to $2,000 per year. Some IRA investments are also tax deductible for low- and moderate-income Americans, but the rules change constantly, so check the IRS website or your accountant. If you choose, instead, a Roth IRA, named for former Sen. William Roth (R-Del.), you do not get a deduction but, if you meet the requirements (an income below $160,000 for couples, an investment held for five years, and a few other rules), you can withdraw money without any taxes at all. With a Roth IRA, most investors are betting that tax rates will be higher in the future. Is that a good bet? Frankly, I don't know.

What I do know is that the more you put into deferred long-term accounts, the better. Of course, I prefer stocks for the long run, but if you want to hold bonds, IRAs and employer-sponsored 401(k) plans are more tax-efficient than taxable accounts since the tax rate is typically 40 percent to 100 percent higher on bond interest than on stock gains.

The best that can be said for our convoluted tax system is that it encourages Americans to be long-term investors. If you hold a 30-stock portfolio for 30 years, it should (if history is a guide) rise in value by a factor of 20 or more. Except for dividends, which have lately been pretty insignificant compared to capital appreciation, none of that lofty gain is subject to tax until you sell. Occasionally, politicians do us a favor. This is a big one.

ALWAYS THINK INFLATION

INFLATION IS A GENERAL RISE in the level of prices. Economists debate its source, but it clearly lies in a combination of lax monetary policy (too many dollars being pumped out by the central bank), excessive government spending, and artificial constraints on production (that is, supply bottlenecks, often caused by regulation). But the causes shouldn't bother you. Inflation, while it's moderated in recent years, will certainly be with us always. You need to know its effects on your investments.

When prices rise 5 percent in a year, it takes $105 to buy what $100 could buy 12 months earlier. Another way to say this is that, in a year, the value of a dollar has declined to 95.2 cents ($100/105=0.952$). If that keeps up, then the miracle (or the nightmare) of compounding will deplete the value of a dollar to just a few pennies.

The average rate of inflation from 1970 to 2000 was 5 percent. At that pace, during a human lifetime, the purchasing power of a dollar will diminish to about 3 cents. Or look at it another way: In 2000, you had to make a salary of $100,000 in order to match the purchasing power of a salary of $23,000 in 1970. If you bought a bond that produced $10,000 in income a year in 1970, your interest checks would be worth only $2,962 (in 1970 purchasing power) in 2000.

During the 1990s, inflation dropped to an average of 2.8 percent a year. While that rate is a big improvement on the 1980s (5.1 percent) and the 1970s (7.4 percent), it is still damaging over the long run. At 2.8 percent, the value of a dollar falls by nearly half in 25 years and by about three-quarters in 50 years. And perhaps the 1990s were an anomaly. Look instead at the inflation rate between 1950 and 2000: it was 4.1 percent—enough to cut the value of a dollar by three-quarters in only 35 years.

The moral here is that, when calculating how much you will need in retirement, always remember the importance of purchasing power, not simple (or "nominal") dollars. What you want to know is how many trips to Europe or Big Macs or months of rent on a decent apartment you will be able to afford, not how many little pieces of paper with George Washington's picture you will have. Since dollars decline in value, it requires more and more of them to buy something. As a 40 year old, you may be able to build a nest egg of $1 million by the time you retire at 65, figuring that it will throw off $60,000 in before-tax income. By if inflation averages 4 percent, then the income will have the purchasing power of just $23,000 in today's currency in the first year of your retirement; after that, it just gets worse.

Occasionally, the value of the dollar will rise. Between 1926 and 1932, rampant deflation, mainly the result of the stock market crash and Depression, pushed down prices and, thus, increased the purchasing power of each dollar. In fact, there was average inflation of precisely zero for the 20 years through 1945. But over the next 55 years, the value of a dollar dropped to 11 cents, and it is inflation, not deflation, that is the modern condition. In 2000 you needed $970,000 to have the same purchasing power as $100,000 at the end of World War II. What did this mean for investors? Ibbotson Associates calculated that one dollar invested in a basket of large-company stocks in 1926, with dividends reinvested, rose to $2,587 in nominal terms by 2000. But in real, after-inflation terms, a dollar rose to only $266.

For the small investor, there are two good ways to defend against the ravages of inflation: 1) invest in stocks for the long run, and 2) invest in inflation-indexed bonds for the short run.

Inflation doesn't help stocks, but it does not hurt them as much as it hurts conventional bonds. The reason is simple: Stocks represent the value of a business, and, during periods of inflation, a business can usually raise its prices. Bonds, on the other hand, pay a rate of interest that doesn't change. Creditors cheer for inflation; lenders (that is, bond investors) dread it. When inflation strikes, your interest payments decline sharply in value as does the principal you get when the bonds mature.

During the worst five-year period for inflation in history (1977–1981, when prices rose an average of 10 percent annually), large-company stocks registered average returns of 8 percent a year; small-company stocks, 29 percent; long-term government bonds (including both interest income and price declines), *minus* 1 percent. This was no fluke. In the period of high inflation during and after World War II, large-cap stocks returned 13 percent, small-cap 25 percent, and Treasuries 3 percent.

Those are nominal returns. Let's look at what happened to purchasing power by analyzing inflation-adjusted returns during the worst inflationary period of the 20th century: 1973 to 1981. Long-term government bonds produced negative returns, after inflation, in eight out of nine years, and $1,000 invested in Treasuries at the start of 1973 was worth just $564, in 1973 purchasing power, by the end of 1981. Stocks did not fare too well either during the 1970s, but over this rocky nine-year period, they declined to $712 in 1973-dollar terms—26 percent better than bonds.

A frightening truth about investing is that you can't hide. Stash your money under the mattress and, based on the experience of the past six decades, you are certain to lose purchasing power. Yes, you can buy short-term Treasury bills, but history shows they stay ahead of inflation by less than one percentage point on average. Treasuries beat inflation by 2.2 percentage points, and stocks by 7.9 percentage points.

The second protection against inflation is a special kind of Treasury bond, which made its debut in 1997. The bond, which I will examine in detail in Chapter 46, is guaranteed to beat the Consumer Price Index by at least 3 percentage points a year if you hold it to maturity.

While pundits praise conventional Treasury bonds as "safe" investments, the truth is they provide no shelter from inflationary storms that will always be with us. (The worst-ever 10-year period for T-bonds, thanks to inflation, produced a loss of 43 percent.) While the tempest rains on stocks, too, they do much, much better.

CHAPTER EIGHTEEN ○

ALWAYS THINK EXPENSES

INVESTING ISN'T FREE. The companies that put sellers together with buyers, execute trades and do the bookkeeping need to make a profit. So do the companies that assemble and manage mutual fund portfolios, exchange-traded funds and unit investment trusts. So do financial consultants and brokers who give you advice.

While investing expenses can't be eliminated, they can be constrained. They have to be watched carefully, which is not always easy since financial firms do a good job of hiding expenses, or of making them seem lower than they really are. The best example of subterfuge can be found (though not easily) in mutual funds. Many years ago, mutual funds charged stiff up-front fees, or loads, which averaged 8.5 percent. It was a cinch to see what you were paying and it was discouraging. Today, most loads have been dropped for funds that investors buy directly by investors from fund houses like Vanguard, Fidelity and T. Rowe Price. If you purchase funds through a financial advisor, you may still pay a load when you buy or sell the investment, but more and more advisors are eliminating such obvious fees and instead are collecting their commission as a part of the annual expense ratio that fund houses charge. You may never know you're missing that expense ratio since it is directly deducted from the fund's net asset value. If your fund soared 15 percent last year, it actually soared even more, say, 16.5 percent, before expenses were taken out.

The expense ratio comprises several different kinds of costs that the fund passes on to investors: a management fee, which goes to the advisor who makes the stock (or bond) selections; an administrative fee, to pay for the fund's operations; and in some cases a 12(b)-1 fee, named for a clause in securities law, which defrays marketing and distribution costs (yes, you, the investor, are being charged for a mutual fund's advertising!). But the key is not where the money goes but how much it is.

Expenses are expressed as a ratio of assets. In other words, they're a percentage of your investment in the fund. Expenses, of course, are charged on all funds bought directly, and, at first glance, they don't look too onerous. Certainly, in the late 1990s, when stock funds were chalking up returns of more than 20 percent a year, expenses appeared modest. But look closer.

The average expense ratio for a stock mutual fund is 1.5 percent. Since the average return of a stock fund in a typical year, before expenses, is about 11 percent, then it's evident that the fund house is taking nearly 14 percent of your gains (0.015/0.11 = 0.136). But it's worse than that.

Say you initially invest $10,000 in a mutual fund. Your expenses the first year are about $150, perfectly reasonable, it would seem. But, as the value of the fund rises, so do your expenses. How much? The calculations are difficult because, in addition to the expenses themselves, you suffer "foregone earnings," that is, gains you would have achieved if you had invested the money that went to expenses. A few years ago, the Securities and Exchange Commission, under its investor-friendly chairman Arthur Levitt, posted a "mutual fund cost calculator" on its website at www.sec.gov/investor/tools/mfcc/mfcc-int.htm. You have to make some assumptions, of course, but the calculator is a valuable tool.

For example, I decided to find out the costs of two long-term investments in mutual funds. In both cases, I assumed an initial $10,000 investment and an annual rate of return averaging 11 percent over 30 years. In one case, my assumption was that the fund charged expenses of 1.5 percent; in the other, 0.8 percent.

For the higher-expense fund, the $10,000 investment grew to $145,471, which sounded spectacular until the cost calculator told me that expenses and foregone earnings totalled an incredible $83,452. (Imagine a fund advertising that fact: "Invest With Us Long-Term. We'll Take One-Third of Your Account as Our Fee.") For the lower-expense fund, the $10,000 investment grew to $179,903, or $34,431 more than the higher-expense fund. In other words, an expense ratio just six-tenths of a percentage point lower yielded a return that was 24 percent greater! It's just one more example of the power of compounding over time.

But won't the mutual fund with the higher expense ratio be better managed? Not necessarily. A study by Financial Research Corp. looked at the performance of the best mutual funds (those rated four or five stars by Morningstar) and found that "stocks that charge the lowest fees normally generate the highest returns over time." In fact, this study, and another by CD/Wiesenberger, discovered that the difference in returns between low-expense and high-expense funds is more than double the difference in expenses. One obvious conclusion is that the average low-expense fund is actually better managed than the average high-expense fund. Among funds with high ratings from Morningstar and low expenses are Vanguard Equity-Income, with an expense ratio of just 0.41 percent, and TIAA-CREF Growth & Income, at 0.43 percent.

When it comes to super-low expenses, look for index funds, which are managed not by humans but by computers that mimic the performance of indexes like the Standard & Poor's 500 or the Wilshire 5000, which encompasses all 7,000-plus stocks trading on the three major U.S. exchanges. For example, Vanguard Total Stock Market Index Fund, which tracks the Wilshire, carries an expense ratio of just 0.2 percent. Using the SEC calculator, I found that a $10,000 investment, growing at 11 percent annually, became $215,579 over 30 years, or about 50 percent more than an investment in an actively managed fund with an expense ratio of 1.5 percent. Total costs for the index fund were just $13,334.

But are index funds really as good as managed funds? Some are, some aren't, but from 1984 to 2000, a majority of fund managers failed to beat the S&P after expenses.

In 2001, Vanguard's 500 Index Fund, which tracks the S&P, was the largest mutual fund in the world (just ahead of Fidelity Magellan). It carried an expense ratio of 0.18 percent, the lowest for a major fund, but higher than the 0.12 percent expense ratio charged by Spiders, the ETF (or exchange-traded fund; see Chapter 3) on the American Stock Exchange under the symbol SPY, which does precisely the same thing. With Spiders, however, you have to pay a broker to buy the shares for you. But, as a rule, ETFs, which use an index approach to investing, have very low expenses and present an attractive alternative, especially to specialty mutual funds, like those in Fidelity's Select series, which not only charge high expenses but, often, front-end loads as well.

Commissions for buying individual stocks through a broker vary widely, from about $10 per transaction to 2 percent of the dollar-value of the shares traded. (A hidden trading cost is the spread between the "bid" and "asked" price on a stock—the difference, usually a few pennies for liquid stocks, between what the seller pays and what the buyer gets.) Higher commission charges generally mean better service, but not always. Much of the research that large brokerage firms used to offer as justification for high trading commissions can now be acquired free on the Internet at sites like MoneyCentral (particularly good), Yahoo!Finance, Bloomberg, Morningstar and SmartMoney. The main advantage of real live brokers is that they offer a line of resistance when the going gets tough. If a declining market panics you into selling, the broker at the other end of the line can calm you down.

Lately, more and more brokers are being compensated with a fee that amounts to a percentage (typically about 1 percent) of the assets in your account. Some firms allow you to trade as much as you want for free in return for this asset management fee; others charge a small commission. This new system puts the broker on your side. Her incentive, like that of traditional financial advisors who have long been paid the same way, is to build your assets, and the best way to build assets is not by churning the stocks and bonds in your account but by holding onto them through thick and thin. After all, research shows that investors who stay in the market do much better than those who trade in and out.

Bond funds generally have lower expense ratios than stock funds. Typical are T. Rowe Price California Tax-Free Fund, which invests in municipals from a single state, with an expense ratio of 0.56 percent, and American Century Bond Fund, with a mix of Treasury and other taxable bonds, at a ratio of 0.8 percent. Still, this is a big bite since munis typically return only 4 percent to 5 percent a year. You can buy individual bonds for a small flat fee from your broker or banker (but again, watch the spread between bid and asked prices) or when a bond is issued you can purchase it directly from the U.S. Treasury. Check out the surprisingly promotional Treasury Direct website at www. publicdebt.treas.gov/sec/sectrdir.htm or call 800-722-2673. Money-market funds, by the way, charge microscopic expenses.

One irritating rule in investing is that you don't necessarily get what you pay for. Vanguard's S&P index fund is precisely the same as Merrill Lynch's, but Merrill charges an expense ratio of 0.38 percent to Vanguard's 0.18 percent. A broker who charges $29.95 for a $10,000 trade may give you better service than one who charges $100. Unfortunately, investors need to study a bit. Use the SEC site and the Morningstar site (www.morningstar. com, which lists expense ratios) and ask a lot of questions.

Remember, an expensive broker who earns your trust is worth far more than a cheap broker who disappoints or offers slipshod service.

Andrew Tobias wrote in the first edition of *The Only Investment Guide You'll Ever Need*: "By and large, you should manage your own money. No one is going to care about it as much as you." In a later edition, he was even more emphatic: "Trust no one. You've got to take responsibility for your own affairs." I disagree. Practically everyone needs help—if only an admonition to stay calm in a market correction. Unfortunately, there's no Secret Code to finding a good advisor. It's like finding a good lawyer or doctor. Unfortunately, trial-and-error is the process that works best.

NEVER BUY
ON MARGIN

BY OFFERING their customers loans, brokers make it easy for them to borrow to buy stocks. Too easy. In fact, loans that use stock as collateral, or insurance against default, are a huge source of income for many investment firms. There's no one from whom it's easier to borrow than your broker. When you open an account, just ask for a book of checks. Write one, and you have a loan. Even simpler, open an account with $10,000 in cash and tell your broker to buy $20,000 worth of stocks. The broker has made you a $10,000 loan on the spot, no fuss.

Such a loan is called a margin account. Under rules set by the Federal Reserve Board's Regulation T, investors can borrow up to 50 percent of the purchase price of stock when they buy on margin. In other words, for $5,000 in cash, you can buy $10,000 worth of stock, although the smallest and riskiest stocks do not qualify for margin treatment and many firms set tougher limits than the Fed. Since you are taking out a loan, it has to be repaid with interest. Typically, margin rates are one to two percentage points higher than mortgage rates. The tricky part is the collateral. You have to maintain a minimum level of equity in your account. If not, your broker will make you fork over more cash through a margin call. Generally it works like this:

Say you buy 1,000 shares of Cisco when the price is $40 per share. Total investment value: $40,000. But you put up only $20,000 in cash and borrow the rest; that is, you buy Cisco on margin. You now have a $20,000 loan on which you are paying, let's say, 9 percent interest, or $150 per month. If Cisco rises, you can "pyramid," buying more shares on margin. But if Cisco falls, watch out!

Assume Cisco drops to $25 a share. Your 1,000 shares are now worth only $25,000. Since you have a $20,000 loan, your collateral is too close for comfort for your lender, the brokerage firm. So you get a margin call: sell some of your Cisco stock to raise cash and reduce the principal on the loan. Otherwise, your broker will sell you out of the position whether you like it or not.

If you do buy on margin, be sure you read the loan agreement you are making with your broker. Many investors don't realize that, in order to meet a margin call, their stock can be sold within as little as an hour without their being notified. TheStreet.com, an online news service, reported in 2001 that "the wave of margin calls that accompanied April's stock slides will spawn a significant increase in legal challenges against brokerages," but investors "historically have won relatively few arbitration claims based on margin-call disputes."

Be aware that if you hold shares for a decent amount of time, there's a good chance you will get a margin call. The Federal Reserve has a nifty margin calculator at www.tradeworx. com/sec/cgi-bin/tutorialmargin.cgi. By entering the amount you want to margin and the symbol for the stock, you can find the likelihood that you will get a margin call from your broker. The calculator assumes, for example, that if you bought 1,000 shares of Cisco at $40 (putting up only $20,000), you would get a margin call when the stock fell to $28 a share. I typed "CSCO" into the calculator and found a 20 percent chance of getting a margin call within one month, 31 percent within three months and 41 percent within a year. With Merck & Co., a less volatile stock, the chances were much reduced: less than 5 percent in a month, 7 percent in three months and 23 percent in a year. Of course, these figures are just guesses. If the market booms, you won't get a call at all; if it tanks, the call could come tomorrow.

Margin buying boosts your leverage. Forget about calls for a second. If you borrow $20,000 to buy $40,000 worth of Cisco, then, if the stock rises 50 percent in price, your $20,000 investment is worth $60,000. Pay off the $20,000 loan, and you have doubled your money (minus a little interest). But if the stock falls 50 percent, your stock is worth $20,000. Pay off the loan, and you are wiped out; your equity is zero. Leverage sounds beneficial (and fun), but it is highly dangerous.

The Secret Code for margin buying is simple: Don't do it.

In theory, margin buying makes sense. If the average stock returns 11 percent a year, and you can borrow at 9 percent, then there's a delicious two-percentage-point spread. Sure, in theory. But in practice, stocks are risky in the short term. Forget margin calls and just think of your carrying costs. Once every three or four years since 1926 the market has fallen in value. You could find yourself paying a great deal of interest before your stock gets its head above water.

But there is an easier way to understand why margin buying is dumb. The hard part of investing is weathering the volatility. You may have done your asset allocation perfectly, and you may have picked a great stock portfolio, but what you do during the inevitably volatile periods that follow—that's what really counts. Most investors have a tough time hanging onto their shares during the down periods; they panic and sell. Buying on margin increases leverage, which increases volatility.

Here are the numbers: The standard deviation of the Standard & Poor's 500-Stock Index is roughly 20 percent. Remember that means that, in two-thirds of all years, returns will fall within one standard deviation (or plus-or-minus 20 percentage points) of the mean average return of 11 percent annually. Thus, two-thirds of the time, returns for the S&P will fall between negative 9 percent and positive 31 percent. That's very risky, and standard deviation is far higher for individual stocks.

Margin buying at 50 percent effectively doubles the risk. Remember the example above: Buying Cisco on margin means that a 50 percent price rise becomes a 100 percent gain and a 50 percent price decline becomes a loss of your entire investment. Doubling risk brings standard deviation up from 20 percent to 40 percent. So now, in two-thirds of years your leveraged returns will vary from minus-29 percent to plus-51 percent.

If most investors have a tough time with the normal volatility of the market, how will they do with double the volatility? Not well at all.

I will admit, however, to using margin myself. I will occasionally write a check on my Merrill Lynch Cash Management Account when I don't have any cash on deposit. That's a margin loan. Also, if I really find a stock attractive, I may buy it even if I don't have enough cash. That's also a margin loan. But, in both cases, I pay the loans back quickly, in less than two weeks. I am a fairly disciplined guy, and even for me, margin debt is a temptation. Stay away!

NEVER SHORT
A STOCK

WHEN YOU BUY on margin you borrow money to purchase stock, but when you sell short, you borrow the stock itself. While margin accounts are normally a means of taking advantage of rising prices, short selling is a way to profit from declines. Both practices are far too risky for superior investors.

Although history shows clearly that stocks return an annual average of 11 percent, betting against the market has long been a popular pursuit especially when stocks are down. No wonder: Many investors have a penchant for doing whatever worked yesterday. The easiest way to win if stocks fall is a technique called selling, or going, short. Instead of buying 100 shares of Microsoft outright at $60 a share for $6,000 (going long), you borrow 100 shares from someone who already owns Microsoft and then sell those shares immediately for $6,000. You still have to return the borrowed shares in the future (that is, you are "short" those shares and need to make them up), but your hope is that Microsoft's share price will drop from, say, $60 to $50 in the meantime. If that happens, you go into the market and buy 100 shares of Microsoft for $5,000, return the borrowed shares and pocket the $1,000 profit.

But these details aren't important. Tell your broker you want to sell a stock short, and the result will be that you make a profit if the price falls and suffer a loss if it rises.

You can also buy shares in mutual funds that do the shorting for you. The best-known of these is probably the Prudent Bear Fund, managed by David Tice of Dallas, the man who blew the whistle in 1999 on what he claimed were fishy accounting practices at Tyco International, the London-based conglomerate. Tyco's stock quickly fell from $53 to $30, but the company was exonerated by the Securities and Exchange Commission, and in 2000 it was one of the best performers among large-cap companies, doubling in price. Tice's fund provides an excellent lesson in why short-selling is rarely profitable. While he spends nearly all his waking hours trying to find stocks that will go down, his mutual fund lost one-third of its shareholders' money during the five years ending in August 2001, at the same time the S&P 500 was more than doubling. Despite the sharp drop in the market that began in the spring of 2000, Tice's fund was the second-worst among the thousands tracked by Morningstar for total returns between July 1996 and June 2001. How tough is shorting stocks? Tice's firm lost 16 percent of its value in the second quarter of 2001, a period when the average stock fund rose 8 percent.

We can all have a bad quarter or two, but if you hold shorted stocks long enough, you are virtually certain to lose money—just as you would in Las Vegas, where the house has an edge of about 3 percent. In the stock-shorting game, the odds against you are 11 percent, plus borrowing costs. But what about using short-selling for the short term? In an interview with SmartMoney.com, Michael Sapir, chairman of ProFunds, which has three short-selling (or bear) funds, said, "Sometimes, we say the bear funds are funds you might want to date but not marry." That may sound like reasonable advice, but it's not.

When you jump in and out of stocks ("date" them), you are employing market timing (see Chapter 14). That is, you're guessing where share prices will go in the near future. Market timing, to put it bluntly, does not work since stocks move in what Princeton economist Burton Malkiel 30 years ago recognized was a "random walk." Today's knowledge is already built into today's price, and tomorrow's knowledge is unknowable today, so tomorrow's price is also unknowable today.

Still, short sellers can do well over short stretches. For the 12 months ending March 31, 2001, for example, the Prudent Bear Fund was up 53 percent. Rydex Ursa, a fund that shorts the S&P, was up 38 percent. Those figures look very good, but the bigger picture is just awful. Prudent Bear fell 34 percent in 1998 and 23 percent in 1999. Depsite the bear market of 2000–01, for the five years ending June 2001, Rydex Ursa produced an average annual loss of 7.6 percent, trailing the S&P by more than 21 percentage points a year! Both funds ranked in the bottom 2 percent of all mutual funds tracked by Morningstar.

But aren't there times when you just know that stocks are overpriced and headed for a fall? I have had such premonitions myself, I will admit, but I have not acted on them. Success requires three things: a far horizon, good diversification, and the discipline to stick to the buy-and-hold plan. Still, while I would discourage an investor from acting on intuition, I know it can be irresistible.

Even if you are convinced, however, that stocks are headed for a fall, don't sell short. Instead, satisfy your urge by investing in bonds; a nice short-term bond fixed-income fund will do just fine. Or put your money into Treasury bills or money-market funds. An investor who took such an approach during the five years ending in spring 2001 would have turned $100,000 into about $128,000. That's not too good but at least it beats turning $100,000 into $60,000, as you would have done with even a clever program of short-selling.

There is no denying that, when markets are down, selling short looks like the smart thing to do. A better approach can be found in a letter to clients from Gail Simons of the Westchester Group, a Tarrytown, N.Y., money management firm. First, Simons assures readers that, "though markets go down fairly often, they have historically never stayed down." Then she adds, with sympathy and wisdom: "It is only human to feel a lot of discomfort in a situation like this, and no one is suggesting that you shouldn't have those feelings. We are just suggesting that it is historically a mistake to act on those feelings."

So don't be tempted to sell stocks short. Don't think of investing as a game that tries to pick losers. Think of it as an exercise in partaking in the growth of the economy.

CHAPTER TWENTY-ONE

STEAL THIS FUND

ONE OF THE JOYS of investing is that stock picks aren't patented. In fact, mutual funds have to report their holdings at least twice a year to the Securities and Exchange Commission. That's really not enough, but it will do for our purposes. Part of the Secret Code is larceny. I want you to steal the selections of the best mutual fund managers. Or, more accurately, I want you to use the selections as a crib sheet, scrutinizing the stocks, studying the companies, then deciding on your own whether to buy them. When you are searching for good companies in which to become a partner, the best starting point is a good mutual fund.

Consider Selected American shares, a superb growth and income fund whose managers, Christopher Davis and Kenneth Feinberg, mainly buy large-cap stocks with small dividend yields (hence, the "income" in the category name). For the 10 years ending in September 2001, the fund returned an annual average of 15.4 percent, beating the benchmark S&P 500 index by 3.2 percentage points, an admirable achievement. Just as important, for our purposes, Davis and Feinberg are buy-and-hold guys. Their turnover averages about 20 percent annually, meaning that they hold the typical stock for five years, which is about four years longer than most funds. Also a good sign is that they are value hunters; they try to find overlooked bargains.

In examining a fund, I look for unusual stocks near the top of the list of holdings, as reported in the Value Line Investment Survey, the Morningstar website (www.morningstar.com) or the fund's own site (in this case, www.selectedfunds.com). On the Selected American list, I was surprised to find Sealed Air Corp., a packaging company, as the thirteenth-largest holding. At $3 billion, the stock's market cap is far lower than that of most of the fund's stocks. Among other things, Sealed Air makes padded mailing envelopes and the polyethylene foam that holds breakable things in place during transport. It's a very profitable company, but earnings don't rise every year—an intriguing stock that's definitely worth a closer look. Other intriguing stocks in the portfolio include UPS, Costco, and Household International.

I also admire the Torray Fund, run by Bob Torray, a longtime pension-fund manager who launched this, his only mutual fund, in the mid-1990s. Morningstar's analyst writes, "This is one of the best stock-picking vehicles out there. Using a buy-and-hold approach, it holds comparatively few names." Again, Torray's list is an excellent candidate for legal theft. Unusual among his top five holdings is Tribune Co., which owns the *Chicago Tribune*, *Los Angeles Times*, a half-dozen other large newspapers, 22 major-market TV stations, and the Chicago Cubs baseball team.

Tribune stock fell by nearly half between the end of 1999 and the middle of 2000, in part because analysts thought the company paid too much for Times Mirror Corp. That decline is just what bargain-hunting Torray tends to like. He's in for the long haul, and Tribune may have what it takes, despite the shakeout the Internet is causing in traditional media. Tribune has a strong balance sheet and, while the acquisition of the Los Angeles–based chain hurt Tribune's per-share earnings, the company appears to be bouncing back. If you're thinking of a media firm for your portfolio, Tribune—along with the Washington Post Co., Gannett and AOL Time Warner—makes a good choice.

Everyone's favorite crib sheet is the list of public companies whose stock is owned by Berkshire Hathaway, Inc., the holding company chaired by Warren Buffett. You can find it by going to Berkshire's website (www.berkshirehathaway.com). But don't be misled by Buffett's letter of greeting, which is actually a shameless sales pitch. "You probably know that I don't make stock recommendations," he writes, "However, I have three thoughts regarding your personal expenditures that can save you real money. I'm suggesting that you call on the services of three subsidiaries of Berkshire: GEICO, Borsheim's and Berkshire Hathaway Life Insurance Company of Nebraska." GEICO, of course, is the auto and home insurer, and Borsheim's is a jeweler. Their shares aren't listed separately on stock exchanges because Berkshire owns them all, just as it owns all of See's Candies (maker of delicious chocolate lollipops), Executive Jet, International Dairy Queen, Shaw Industries (carpets), Dexter Shoe and about two dozen others. But Berkshire does own big chunks of larger public companies in which you can indulge, including American Express, Coca-Cola, Gillette and Wells Fargo & Co. Those are listed in the annual report, but you have to plow through the financials to find them.

In 2000, Buffett purchased—again, whole—boring firms engaged in such endeavors as selling paint and bricks. That got me thinking: what about building-materials companies that the market has shunned? Leafing through Value Line, I found a firm called Ameron International, which makes protective coatings and lighting poles. From 1992 to 2000, the firm increased its earnings every year, with growth accelerating in the late 1990s. Its P/E ratio in mid-2001 was just 9, or about one-third the S&P average, and it had a dividend yield of 2 percent. Ameron is small ($600 million in sales), and it has a lot of debt ($141 million, or 40 percent of capital), but cash flow ($12 for a $60 stock) is exceptional. It could be worth buying.

What about the more obvious sources to plunder? Shouldn't you be gleaning advice from the recommendations of stock analysts at large investment firms whose picks are touted far and wide in newsletters, on the Web and on TV? Here, I am ambivalent. Many of these analysts have built-in conflicts of interest. They work for firms that make big money underwriting equity and debt offerings of corporations on which the analyst must then pass unbiased judgment. Can you imagine a Wall Street research shop issuing a "sell" recommendation on a company that's a big client of the firm's investment bankers? As SEC Commissioner Laura Unger put it, these firms have "blatant conflicts that [surround] the business of bringing shares to the public and then recommending them to investors."

A careful look at the actual performance of analysts however seems to belie these concerns. A study published in 2001 by four California scholars examined 360,000 separate pieces of advice from 4,340 analysts between 1986 and 1996, gathering recommendations of each stock into a consensus and then placing the consensus in one of five groups, from "1" (most favorable) to "5" (least favorable). (By the way, consensus ratings can be found on such websites as CBS.MarketWatch.com and Yahoo!Finance.) During the time of the study, the average annual benchmark return for the market as a whole was 14.5 percent, but the group "1" stocks returned an annual average of 18.8 percent while the group "5" stocks returned just 5.8 percent, with the other groups falling precisely in order. Even after controlling for risk and size, the researchers found that the highest-rated group beat the benchmark by 4.1 percentage points while the lowest-rated group lagged the benchmark by 4.9 percentage points.

These results, published in a peer-reviewed journal, are impressive. Rare, for example, is the mutual fund that can beat the Standard & Poor's 500-Stock Index, the market benchmark, by four points over 10 years. The researchers, however, are reluctant to advise that you follow the advice of the advice-givers. The reason is transaction costs. The composition of each of the groups changes when the consensus on a stock changes, so investors have to jump in and out of companies at an average rate of once every three months. Trading costs eat up profits. Also, the scholars found that some analysts do a lot better than others (ratings in publications like *Institutional Investor* and the *Wall Street Journal* point you to the superior ones) and that their most useful purpose is to keep you *away* from bad stocks rather than getting you into good ones.

The truth is, stock analysts do not provide what superior investors need: *long-term* selections. Instead, their advice lasts only as long as the next rating revision, which could occur in just a few months. Newsletters present the same problem. The most you can glean from them is an idea or two for further study. For that reason, I think the best letter of all is the Dick Davis Digest (www.dickdavis.com). It excerpts the top stock selections from other newsletters—30 or 40 per issue. But it also makes sense to find newsletters whose stock-picking philosophies are similar to your own. For nearly a decade, I have subscribed to Dow Theory Forecasts (www.dowtheory.com), founded in 1946 and head-quartered far from the madding Wall Street crowd in Hammond, Ind. The newsletter tends to keep stocks on its rec-ommended list for a long time: companies like Bristol-Myers Squibb, Nike, Wal-Mart and Johnson & Johnson. Often, Dow Theory will direct subscribers toward a stock that has suffered a setback for no good reason. A choice in the spring of 2001, for example, was medical-device maker Guidant. Finally, I am a constant peruser of Value Line (www.valueline.com), especially "model portfolios" (three packages of 20 recommended stocks each). In mid-2001, the long-term portfolio included several intriguing value-oriented ideas, including Dole Food, Sunrise Assisted Living and Elan Corp., an Irish drug company whose American Depositary Shares trade on the New York Stock Exchange.

But, in the end, the best source of good stock-picking notions remains the list of holdings of an excellent mutual fund. Consider Tweedy Browne American Value, run by a superb management team at a firm founded in 1920 by Forrest Berwind Tweedy, a leading practitioner of Benjamin Graham's philosophy. The fund outstripped the S&P with an annual average return of 14 percent for the five years ending in September 2001. A look at Tweedy's top stocks revealed some names I had never heard of, including Transatlantic Holdings, Inc., a large reinsurance company (that is, it insures the risks of other insurers), a stock which, according to Value Line, "offers a considerable amount of stability with little apparent risk." The stock fell sharply after the September 11 attacks but rebounded to above its pre-attack level within a few weeks. Just as important, I was surprised to find McDonald's high up on Tweedy's list. The fast-food chain has a gorgeous balance sheet, but many sophisticated investors abandoned it in the late 1990s, when it failed to increase profits at a rapid clip. If Tweedy Browne has faith, then McDonald's is worth a close look again.

In the end, superior investors have to make their own selections of individual stocks, but having excellent fund managers like Christopher and William Browne on your side can be awfully encouraging.

CHAPTER TWENTY-TWO

DON'T WATCH CNBC IN BROAD DAYLIGHT

AFTER SIX YEARS writing a twice-weekly financial column for the *Washington Post,* I decided to quit. My pieces tried to teach investors the fundamentals, but there was only so much to say. I had written 400 columns, and I was repeating myself. I was grateful to learn afterwards that my readers disagreed. They apparently liked to read over and over that they should buy and hold (it is a lesson not learned in one sitting).

The basic problem of financial journalism is this: Done well, it's not all that exciting. Television, however, needs to be exciting, otherwise viewers will change the channel and watch wrestling or Jerry Springer. So CNBC, CNNfn, Fox News and the rest try hard to make the stock market exciting, and, in the process, they often do investors a terrible disservice.

The ticker is the trouble. It dominates the programs, and sets the tone. Hour by hour, minute by minute, second by second, the anchors, reporters and analysts on the shows obsess about what the market is doing in the shortest of the short term ("we seem to have levelled off here on the Nasdaq over the past 15 minutes after falling in the first hour of trading"). They have to. The model, after all, is sports, and you can't imagine a sports announcer ignoring the score. But, of course, investing is not a short-term game, and the score at any moment means nothing. Instead, investing is a long-term process in which the superior players ignore the day and concentrate on the decade.

This is not to accuse the analysts of being dumb. They are not. In general, the level of financial talent on CNBC and the others is far superior to the level of political talent on the networks' nightly news programs. Neil Cavuto of Fox is the best interviewer on TV, period, and people like Lou Dobbs of CNN, Joe Kernen and Bill Griffeth of CNBC and Terry Keenan of Fox are smart and conscientious, but the medium is the message here, and the main message of financial shows is that you need to pay close attention to all the little ups and downs of the market—because it all means something, even if it is hard to say what.

Here is a typical dialogue from CNN's "Moneyline," May 11, 2001. Since "Moneyline" is an evening program that sums up the day's events, it is nowhere near as frenetic as the daytime shows, but it suffers from the same disease.

SUSAN LISOVICZ, REPORTER: The Dow and the Nasdaq closed with their weakest trading volume of the year, reinforcing investor uncertainty about the status of the economy and the mindset of the Fed. Willow.

WILLOW BAY, ANCHOR: Susan, it's fairly typical, though, isn't it, to see investors retreating to the sidelines before a Fed meeting?

LISOVICZ: Yes, it's absolutely true, but we've seen the backing and filling all week: a lot of hesitancy in the market this week [note two metaphors here: the market as backhoe and the market as person, taking on qualities in what the poet John Ruskin called "the pathetic fallacy," the illusion that things like markets react as though they were human beings] and that was underscored with the economic reports we got today. And one way you could really see it was in that low, low volume. Willow.

BAY: Susan Lisovicz at the Big Board. Thanks, Susan.

Of what possible use to long-term investors is this analysis? Zero. In fact, it is less than zero because its message is that they need to pay attention to things like Fed meetings, low volume, "hesitancy," and "uncertainty." Often, there is no decent explanation for the aggregate movement of the 7,000 listed companies that comprise the U.S. market, but that doesn't stop analysts from coming up with one anyway.

Flash back to May 18, 1995, a day on which the Dow Jones Industrial Average dropped 82 points, or about 2 percent, after rising in the previous six months by 700 points or nearly 20 percent. Why? Opined Ed Keely, manager of Founders Growth Fund: "The number-one worry is the sustainability of earnings and how strong the economy is." Peggy Farley of Amas Securities said that "profit-taking" was the culprit, while Dan Bernstein and Ross Waller of Bridgewater Associates, using a popular tautology, declared that the market fell "under its own weight." (Little did they know, but the market was embarking on the most powerful run in its history, with the S&P 500 index returning more than 20 percent in each of the years from 1995 to 1999.)

Despite the eagerness of analysts to explain short-term market movements, there is a good case to be made that such advances and declines are essentially random—but where does that leave poor financial reporters? With no story!

Trying to explain the ups and downs of share prices on a daily basis is as fruitless an exercise as trying to explain why a particular coin flip ended up heads or tails (it "fell under its own weight," guys). Investors should ignore the background noise and the fatuous explanations.

I know it's hard. The problem with stock movements is that they *look* like they're meaningful. In his famous 1973 book, *A*

Random Walk Down Wall Street, Burton Malkiel presented a chart that appeared to represent the daily activity of a nicely behaving stock. Actually, the points on the chart were plotted strictly according to the outcome of coin flips. "The persistence of this belief in repetitive patterns in the stock market is due to statistical illusion," Malkiel concluded. In other words, even chance events look as though they have meaning, thus providing a nice living to people on Wall Street called "chartists" or "technicians," who look for such patterns in stock movements.

In his book, *A Mathematician Reads the Newspaper,* John Allen Paulos takes Malkiel a step further, noting "the surprising number of consecutive runs of heads or tails" that result from prolonged random coin-flipping (you see the same thing at the roulette table, with red and black). If you flip a coin once each day for five or six years, he writes, it's likely that heads will enjoy a winning run for at least 10 days in a row. What a bull market!

"With these random clumping patterns in mind," writes Paulos, "think of the standard pronouncements of newspaper stock analysts. The daily ups and downs of a particular stock or of the stock market in general may not be as thoroughly random as these H's and T's are, but it's safe to say there is an extremely large element of chance involved. . . . One never hears of chance, however, in the neat *post hoc* analyses that follow each market's close."

Investing is tough enough without being led astray by the distractions of analysts looking so seriously at meaningless short-term price movements. What investors need to do is find good companies, buy them and hang onto them. So what financial journalists can do constructively is help us find good companies. Sometimes, CNBC and CNN offer interviews with analysts and corporate executives that provide insight into companies and industries. But rarely. Most of the analyst jabber is equally empty, concentrating on to-the-penny estimates of quarterly earnings. Here is a typical jargon-filled CNN excerpt from the "Market Call" show in the spring of 2001.

RHONDA SCHLAFFER, ANCHOR: Lehman Brothers is upgrading Dow component Johnson & Johnson to a buy from a market perform. . . . Joining us on the phone is David Gruber, the Lehman Brothers analyst who made the call on Johnson & Johnson. . . . Let's first talk about what you see going on with J&J that is causing you to raise the price target just a little bit.

DAVID GRUBER: Sure. There are two primary reasons why we raised our price target. We also raised our rating with a three market perform to a two buy rating. The first thing is, we see an improving competitive position with Procrit. . . . And secondly we see the potential for coded stents. In addition, the valuation was attractive. Our price target of $110 is a 27.5 multiple of the next 12 months EPS of $4. That is a 10 percent premium to S&P and a 9 percent discount to the pharma industry.

What does this mean? Do the folks at CNN really care whether their viewers understand? I doubt it. Again, the key is the scoreboard. If Gruber's upgrade moved the price of J&J up a little, then that's news; he's scored a touchdown, or at least a field goal, and CNN wants to talk to him. If you are an investor considering J&J (and I love the company), what can you glean from such a report? Perhaps you'll peer a little deeper into Procrit (which fights anemia), but whether J&J is a buy or "market performer" is of no concern to you. Instead, look closely at J&J's history, its balance sheet, its current earnings and its product line.

In fact, the best rule for daytime financial television is this: Don't watch it. The messages it sends are all wrong, and they focus your attention in the wrong direction. Instead of prices—the obsession of these shows—you should concentrate on businesses.

At the *Washington Post*, I once tried to persuade the business editor to stop running the stock tables, which stretch on for five or six pages. Run them on Sunday if you must. Anyone who really needs to know the price of a stock can get it online, but most people don't need to know, and they shouldn't be tempted to look. "If you aren't willing to own a stock for ten years, don't even think about owning it for ten minutes," Warren Buffett once wrote. So why look at the price every ten minutes? By the way, the *Post* still runs the stock tables.

CHAPTER TWENTY-THREE

GIVE DIVIDENDS
THE RESPECT
THEY DESERVE

DIVIDENDS GET NO RESPECT. In 2000, the total dividends paid by the 500 companies of the Standard & Poor's index fell by 2.5 percent, the first drop since 1991 and the biggest since 1951. The number of companies raising their dividends fell 12 percent, and, for the first time ever, more than one quarter of the S&P companies paid no dividend at all.

While the decline was dramatic, especially in a year in which companies raked in record profits, it should not have been surprising. Over the past few decades, managers have learned that most shareholders don't really care whether they get dividends or not. That's what the academic research shows, and no wonder. Dividends are doubly taxed: the corporation has to pay taxes on the profits that are the source of the dividends, and then the shareholder pays taxes on the dividends themselves. By the time all the taxes are paid on a dollar of a company's profits, it can become as little as 40 cents for the investor. But if the corporation *retains* the earnings, the shareholder pays no taxes until she sells the stock and then the federal bite is no more than 20 percent if shares are held a year or more.

In another popular detour around taxes, more and more firms began in the 1990s to "buy in" their own shares, that is, to use their excess cash to purchase stock from investors, thus reducing the number of shares outstanding and raising the proportion of the company that each share represents. For example, Schering-Plough, the drug company that makes the popular allergy-fighter Claritin as well as Dr. Scholl's foot aids, had 1.8 billion shares of stock outstanding in 1989 but only 1.5 billion in 1999. That move gave shareholders a big untaxed dividend. Even more dramatically, UST, Inc., maker of highly profitable, but obnoxious, smokeless tobacco products like snuff, reduced its shares during the 1990s from 218 million to just 167 million.

How do the shareholders derive a benefit from this kind of activity? Imagine that a company has 1,000 shares of stock outstanding and that it decides to use $5,000 from its treasury to purchase 100 shares owned by current stockholders. After the purchase, only 900 shares remain. If you owned 200 shares both before and after the buyback, then your proportion of the company would rise from 20 percent (200/1,000) to 22.2 percent (200/900). Your claim on future profits rises, and so does the value of your shares, but you did not have to pay current taxes on that increase (though you might eventually have to pay capital gains, of course).

Throughout most of market history, the typical company has given a little more than half the profits it's earned each year to shareholders in the form of quarterly dividends, keeping the rest to invest in its own business or to buy other companies. But in 2000, after a steady decline in the preceding years, the typical company gave shareholders less than one-third of its profits.

In the decades of the 1940s, the average S&P stock paid a dividend that amounted to 5.9 percent of its price. In the 1970s, this figure, called the dividend *yield*, fell to an average of 4.2 percent; in the 1990s, to just 2.6 percent. In 2000, the yield hit 1.1 percent, the lowest number since statistics on dividends began being collected, in 1825.

In the past, companies used dividends to attract investors to their shares, but, by the 1990s, dividends had become a sign of stodginess and weakness. Tech powerhouses like Microsoft, Oracle, Sun and Intel paid no dividends at all, even though they were piling up money from their operations. In mid 2001, for instance, Microsoft had no debt and $32 billion in cash.

Still, I like dividend-paying stocks. They provide income if you need it, they offer steady returns in tough times and they force companies to adopt strong management discipline in order to keep the payouts flowing (few events hurt a stock more than a dividend cut). While firms can manipulate their reported revenues and earnings through accounting shenanigans, they can't fake the cash they send out in dividend checks. Also, as Peter Lynch pointed out in his book *One Up on Wall Street:* "Companies that don't pay dividends have a sorry history of blowing the money on a string of stupid diversifications." One of the most famous mistakes of this sort was the disastrous 1976 acquisition by cash-rich Mobil of Marcor, the holding company for Montgomery Ward, the century-old retail chain. Ward's eventually went bankrupt.

The good news, however, is that "despite . . . overall declines, plenty of quality stocks still pay dividends," as Dow Theory Forecasts newsletter has pointed out.

For example, in September 2001, Bristol-Myers Squibb, a pharmaceutical company with record of strongly growing earnings, carried a yield of 1.9 percent, about half-again as much as the average stock. Philip Morris, the packaged goods, beer and tobacco behemoth, had the highest yield among the 30 companies of the Dow Jones Industrial Average: 4.5 percent. And, despite all those stock buybacks, UST had a yield of 5.6 percent.

Utilities, financials, and integrated oils are sectors whose stocks usually have the highest yields. Some of the best companies in these categories include KeySpan, natural gas, at 5.4 percent in September 2001; Citigroup, 1.4 percent; and BP (which owns Amoco), 2.5 percent. Real estate investment trusts (REITs) are required by law to pass 95 percent of their earnings through to shareholders, so they pay large but often fluctuating dividends. The Value Line Investment Survey has listed these solid stocks that pay handsome dividends: Kimco Realty, a REIT with a yield of 6 percent; Duke Energy (2.8 percent), a highly regarded electric utility; and BB&T Corp. (2.9 percent), a well-managed bank chain.

A stock's dividend yield is its expected annual dividend payments divided by its current price. A high yield can sometimes be the result of a low price, which means that high-yielding stocks are either bargains or cheap for a good reason. So be careful. For example, Value Line publishes a weekly list of the top-yielding domestic stocks, but the majority of the companies at the top (excluding REITs) typically rate well below average in quality. They may fail to pay the dividends they promise.

But, if the company is sound, a high yield is often a signal that the stock is a value (since the price is low relative to the payout). How do you know the company is sound? First, check its balance sheet. But, second, see if it has been increasing its dividends for a long time. Three of my favorite mutual funds specialize in stocks with records of boosting their payouts: Fidelity Dividend Growth, T. Rowe Price Dividend Growth and Franklin Rising Dividend.

The ideal company is a dividend-paying stock with a long-term record of increasing its profits and its payouts. With strong growth, even if the yield is low, your dividends will rise powerfully over time. A good example is William Wrigley Jr. Co., the world's largest maker of chewing gum, with brands like Doublemint, Big Red and Hubba Bubba. The stock was yielding 1.5 percent in the fall of 2001, with a payout scheduled to rise to 76 cents for the year, up from just 8 cents in 1984! Wrigley's earnings have risen in each of those years, from 16 cents a share to $1.45.

Or consider Merrill Lynch & Co. If you had bought $1,000 worth of Merrill stock in 1991, dividends that year would have totalled $26. In 2001, the dividends on that $1,000 investment were expected to total $136, for a dividend yield, in that year alone, of 13.6 percent on your original stake. If you had bought a corporate bond paying 8 percent in 1991, you would still be getting just $80 in interest checks today. If Value Line's projections for Merrill's growth are correct, within another 10 years, dividends will rise to more than $600, for a 60 percent yield on that 1991 investment in 2011 alone. By the way, during the 1990s, Merrill stock rose in price more than 10-fold.

Dividends put the power of compounding on an investor's side, with results that are truly incredible over time. For example, using newly developed data on New York Stock Exchange companies, a study by Ibbotson Associates found that $1,000 invested in 1824 in NYSE stocks rose to $395,000 by 2000. But if the dividends from those stocks had been reinvested in new shares over that period, then the $1,000 would have grown to $3.1 billion! Or take a more reasonable example: An investment of $1,000 in the S&P 500 at the end of 1970 grew within 30 years to $13,000 without dividends. But, with dividends, the $1,000 grew to $36,000.

Because of the effect of compounding, a growing dividend is more important than a high yield. Among the companies that have increased their dividends by an average of more than 15 percent and have had at least 15 straight years of dividend growth through 2000 are Automatic Data Processing, payroll services; Nucor, steel; Abbott Laboratories, pharmaceuticals; Golden West Financial, savings and loan; and Wal-Mart Stores, the world's largest retailer. Four major companies, Procter & Gamble, Minnesota Mining & Manufacturing, Johnson & Johnson and Genuine Parts, have each increased their dividends annually for at least 40 years. Tootsie Roll, one of the stocks that Kevin Hassett and I highlighted in our book *Dow 36,000*, has increased its dividends for 36 years in a row.

Dividend-paying stocks should not comprise your entire portfolio. You need to own businesses that retain their earnings to give them the flexibility for acquisitions and to protect them against downturns. But, especially if you hold dividend-payers in tax-deferred retirement accounts and instruct your brokerage firm to invest the quarterly payouts in more shares, these stocks should not be ignored. In fact, the Secret Code demands that they be loved and respected.

MAKE YOUR CHILDREN
AND GRANDCHILDREN
INVESTORS AT BIRTH

IN AUGUST OF 1998, a bright yellow check for $827.84 arrived for me from the First Chicago Trust Co. of New York. And "a story," as Damon Runyon once wrote, "goes with it." Forty-two years earlier, the heirs of Henry Ford sold 20 percent of their family auto company to the public, raising $641 million in what then was the largest stock issue of all time. My grandfather, Bertram Schiff, who had been a stockbroker, bought a single share for $64.50 and gave it to me for my ninth birthday.

Ford Motor Co. had its ups and downs over the next four decades, but the stock rose and split, again and again. At the start of 1998, I owned 22½ shares of Ford and was getting a yearly dividend of $37.80—an annual return of 59 percent on the original 1956 investment.

The company, however, found odd-lotters like me expensive to maintain, so it offered to buy us out. Tired of having to deposit six-dollar checks every three months and of having to report miniature dividends on my tax return, I accepted. So, in a typical American stock market tale, $64.50 grew to $827.84 in Ford stock. In fact, the return was even greater. In December of 1998, I got another check, for $297, the value of four shares of

Associates First Capital Corp., a Ford spin-off that I didn't even realize I owned.

I told this story to a group of teenagers at an inner-city summer program sponsored by the H Street Community Development Corporation in Northeast Washington, D. C., and the children were duly impressed. But they would have been bowled over if I had been smart enough to *reinvest my dividends* over the years, rather than using them to buy model airplanes, comic books and movie tickets. How much would I have had? Unfortunately, I don't have detailed records going back to 1956 on Ford, but I do have data on large-company stocks from Ibbotson Associates, the venerable Chicago research firm. These figures indicate that my original $64.50 would have grown to about $3,000.

Since 1956, this nation has been through seven recessions, several oil shocks, a decade of virulent inflation, a Cold War, two hot wars, a presidential assassination, a stock market crash, and unprecedented terrorist attacks. Ford itself suffered a terrible crisis as poor products, high gas prices, shoddy management and competition from Japan nearly sank the company. As recently as 1991 Ford had a loss of $2.2 billion. Ford stock certainly went through wild gyrations. As recently as 1996, it was trading lower than it had 10 years earlier. But through it all, long-term shareholders prospered—especially those who reinvested their dividends.

The lesson here, as I told the teenagers, is that the single most important factor in investing is time. It's not stock-picking and certainly not market timing (trying to guess the short-term direction of stocks). The trick, if you can call it that, is to buy a piece of a great corporation and become a partner in its growth over a long, long period. The H Streeters are lucky. At age 14 or 15, they can invest in a stock like Ford today and watch it grow by a factor of 100, if history is a guide, by the time they're in their mid-fifties.

But buying a single stock is a big risk. Long-term investors need diversification, lots of stocks in different industries (see Chapter 10). And you have to try to pick companies with bright future prospects: strong balance sheets, a history of good management and a taste for flexibility. You can help your kids and grandkids experience the magic of the markets by investing in companies they know and that are likely to have staying power. A good example is Walt Disney Co., which sends its shareholders certificates festooned with cartoon characters, or Hasbro, which also owns such brands as Playskool, Tonka, Super Soaker and Parker Brothers games.

Look for stocks that have strong brand names, a stable history and great prospects for the long term. You might want to consider the Coca-Cola Co.; William Wrigley Jr. Co., for the child you would rather see chew than smoke; Gillette Co., for the little shaver; or Fannie Mae, for the prospective home buyer. If you'd rather stick to the toy theme, Mattel Inc. or Toys Я Us are obvious choices.

Say that you buy your nine-year-old son $100 worth of stock, and that it returns an average of 10 percent annually. Over the first 10 years he holds the shares, they will grow in value by $160. Over the next 10, by $410. Over the next 10, by $1,070. And over the next 10, by $2,780. If you're able to invest more, you can contribute up to $10,000 each year tax-free to a custodial account for a child, under the Uniform Gifts to Minors Act. The stock then reverts to the child when she reaches majority (usually age 18). You might also consider setting up an E-IRA (education individual retirement account) to which you can add $500 each year, which grows tax-free. Check with a broker or accountant to make sure you qualify under the income limits.

Or set up your *own* education account. By contributing $5,000 a year to the purchase of stocks you will build an account for your child of $286,000 (again, assuming 10 percent annual growth) at the end of 20 years. When you buy stocks for kids, also be sure your brokerage firm sends them annual reports. Or set up a dividend reinvestment plan so that your child earns new shares (or fractions) each quarter instead of cash. Or, even easier, buy your child shares of Stein Roe Young Investors Fund, which sends special kid-friendly quarterly reports.

Finally, if you're helping your children invest, don't forget taxes. Ellen McLellan of Merrill Lynch & Co. in Washington points to an idea suggested by *Mutual Funds* magazine: setting up Roth IRAs for kids. Income that provides the cash to invest in a Roth is taxable; withdrawals, on the other hand, are tax-free in later life, when the rate should be higher. You can pay your child to mow the lawn or do the dishes, and the child can use the money to establish a Roth IRA account. Say your 10-year-old daughter puts $1,000 a year into an IRA (invested in a mutual fund that returns an annual average of 10 percent). By the time she is 20, she'll have accumulated $17,531. If she leaves the money there and never adds a cent, it will grow to $1,277,855 by the time she is 65. Even assuming inflation of 4 percent, that's buying power in today's dollars of $160,000. That's enough to buy an annuity (an insurance vehicle that provides a flow of income) that could beat Social Security (if Social Security is around then, anyway).

CHAPTER TWENTY-FIVE

IF YOU CAN'T SIT STILL, SET UP A "FUN-AND-GAMES ACCOUNT"

"MY FAVORITE TIME FRAME for holding a stock is forever," said Warren Buffett. I agree, but I also know that most investors can't sit still that long. There is something, perhaps the pressure of the media, perhaps plain old human impatience, that makes us all want to do *something*. For that reason, Benjamin Graham once suggested, only half-facetiously, that investors should switch out of stocks and into bonds every once in a while, and then back again—not because it is a strategy that works but because it satisfies a normal urge and it can't get you into enormous trouble.

I have a different solution. It's called the Fun and Games Account (FGA), a pot of money whose sole purpose is to allow you to play the market to your heart's content.

Here are the FGA's characteristics:

- It must be small, representing no more than 10 percent of the total funds you're committing to stocks.

- It must be completely walled off from your main investment account. Keep your FGA with an online broker, for example, and your long-term investment account at a full-service firm (or vice versa).

- **All taxes associated with the FGA must be paid from that account alone.**

- **It has to be funded with money you can afford to lose. Write a check or transfer the money electronically, and assume that the whole thing is gone. In fact, it may soon be.**

- **It should serve three purposes: to satisfy unquenchable urges, to provide some pleasant entertainment, and to offer a way to learn.**

Trading stocks is a diversion that should not be confused with actual investing. Trading is based on a faulty premise: that you can figure out which way stocks will move in the short term. No one can, but nearly every investor needs to go through the experience of discovering this lesson personally.

So trade to your heart's content in your FGA. At the end of a year, if your money holds out, compare your after-tax performance with that of your investment account and with the broad market. There are three reasons that it is highly unlikely your FGA will win: (1) trading, even at $7.95 a pop, cuts into profits; (2) taxes on short-term gains are steep, and 40 percent or more of your profits can go to federal, state and local governments; and (3) many amateur traders often sell and buy at the wrong time, as fear and greed overwhelm logic.

But go ahead. Try an FGA, online or otherwise. And, as long as you are having fun, do the wild and crazy things that never pay off for smart long-term investors. Here are some suggestions:

Buy momentum. The easiest plays for short-term investors are momentum buys—you purchase a hot stock that has been rising and sell it at the first sign that the move is over. This activity is similar to jumping onto a moving train and approximately as dangerous, but that's what an FGA is all about. To find out what's hot, simply check the list of new highs that appears each weekday in the *Wall Street Journal*. Buy the hottest of the hot. In 2000, traders buying momentum stocks learned just how deadly this stunt can be, but for those who are new to equity investing, I'll review the fortunes of just one of the big momentum plays of that year.

JDS Uniphase, a maker of fiber-optic communications gear, was a favorite of day traders. From $89 per share on Jan. 7, 2000, JDSU hit $140 on March 3. But by April 14, the stock had fallen to a more earthly $79. That party was *so* over, right? Not quite. Two weeks later, the stock was back up to $103 and it went on to reach $135 by July. But anyone who thought this issue had legs as a momentum play was disappointed again as JDSU finished the year at $42 per share. By September 2001, the stock was $6—down more than 90 percent in 15 months. JDS Uniphase is a wonderful company with leading-edge technology, but even the greatest firms can be terrible short-term investments.

Time the market. Try your hand at predicting the turns in the market as a whole. If you think the market will rise, then buy Spiders, which track the S&P 500 (see Chapter 3). Maybe you believe that next week the Fed will cut interest rates in a big surprise. Buy Spiders now. If you're right, sell and pocket your profit. If you're wrong, sell and take your loss. Or maybe you just have a hunch that the worst of a correction is over. Again, buy now and sell quickly.

Go to the dogs. You can also use your FGA for buying stocks that have been beaten down, in order to ride them up. Be aware that this can be a risky strategy for short-term online traders—sleeping dogs can lie for a long, long time before rising. In fact, some dogs will actually be put to sleep by customers and creditors. Pets.com may have looked to some traders like a screaming bargain after it fell from its offering price of $14 per share to $6 during one month in early 2000. Then when it fell to $2 per share, some people could see it as even more undervalued. A short time later, it was out of business. On the other hand, iVillage, an e-commerce site for women, looked like classic tech toast, burning investors as it plummeted all the way from a high above $100 per share in 1999 to a measly 66 cents in December of 2000. A dead woman walking, right? Well, investors who took the plunge at 66 cents a share watched the stock move back above $2 in February, tripling their money in less than two months if they sold at the right moment. By October it was back to 91 cents.

FGA plays, online or not, are not much different from gambling. As long as you remember that, you can have fun and learn something, too. Just don't confuse what you're doing with investing.

CHAPTER TWENTY-SIX

SYSTEMS DON'T WORK, BUT USE THIS ONE ANYWAY

WHEN I WAS IN COLLEGE, I fell in love with horse racing, specifically with handicapping, the psuedo-science of picking equine winners. I became convinced that somewhere there existed a system that would predict the outcome of enough races to make me a rich man. I became enamored of *The Handicapper's Handbook,* by Tom Ainslie, a wonderful writer with a sensible set of indicators which, he contended, would point to a thoroughbred's success. In the book, the author would analyze a race using a system that combined speed with pace, then, on the next page, would show the actual outcome, always an Ainslie victory.

Alas, life wasn't like that. While Ainslie's book helped me enjoy myself at the track—and not get into big trouble, it was no miracle cure. The truth is, a few gifted handicappers can make a living at the racetrack, but not by using iron-clad rules. Observant reasoning, the result of thousands of hours studying and watching, works better than systems. So it is with the stock market.

Stock-picking systems do not work. There is no formula that can produce sure winners, or at least enough winners to beat the Standard & Poor's 500-Stock Index, the benchmark. Investors have been trying to find such shortcuts to riches for years, but in vain. Still, while a stock system can't perform magic, it *can* be a useful addition to your Secret Code portfolio.

But before I tell you what I like about systems, let me tell you why they don't work. A stock-picking system requires a strategy that other people haven't caught on to yet since it has to exploit anomalies, or mistakes, in prices. Such situations can indeed occur, but they don't last very long. Soon, what economists call a no-arbitrage situation prevails, and the system's advantage disappears. Or to put it another way: As soon as everyone accepts that a strategy works, that strategy no longer works.

Most systems are discovered through backtesting—that is, by taking the formula and applying it to historical stock data. Since there are literally billions of possible systems, it stands to reason that some of them can be found to have worked in the past. Imagine, for instance, a system whose formula is a portfolio composed of every 30th stock listed in the alphabetical New York Stock Exchange tables: that is, stock No. 30 (Aaron Rents, Inc.), No. 60 (Air Products & Chemicals), and so on. Let's say that we backtest the system, and it turns out that the average returns are 6 percent over the past 75 years, well below the S&P average of 11 percent.

Well, toss that system out. Now, let's try again, with a system that picks every 31st stock: No. 31 (ABB ADS), No. 62 (Airborne, Inc.), etc. We backtest this formula and find that it gets a 20 percent return! Would you put such a system to work for the future? Of course not, since it has no rational basis. Yet, according to backtesting, it works, like the old saw about the winner of the Super Bowl determining the result of the presidential election.

Leslie Douglas, longtime partner in one of Washington's last independent investment firms, Folger Nolan Fleming Douglas, discovered a simple system with a seemingly rational basis that produced fantastic results for the first nine years he used it. The "Douglas Theory" involves buying equal amounts of the five Nasdaq stocks with the highest market caps at the start of each calendar year, selling them at the end of the year, then repeating the procedure. The system produced average annual returns of an incredible 47.9 percent from 1991 to 1999, compared with 18.1 percent for the Dow Jones Industrial Average, which the Douglas Theory beat in seven of the nine years. An investment of $10,000 in the Douglas stocks in 1991 became $251,800 by 1999, while, over the same period, $10,000 in the Dow became just $43,400 (the Nasdaq Composite as a whole rose to $108,900).

But the year 2000 was a disaster for the Douglas Theory. The five stocks—Microsoft, Intel, Cisco Systems, WorldCom and Oracle—lost 39.5 percent of their value while the Dow declined only 4.8 percent. Still, over 10 years, the average annual return for Douglas was 39.1 percent, compared with 15.8 percent for the Dow, a huge difference. The Douglas Theory needs more time. The five stocks for 2001 (the same as in 2000 but with Qualcomm substituting for WorldCom) trailed the Dow at midyear by four percentage points, but the system appears to have a reasonable foundation: that, among the tech stocks of the Nasdaq, big, solid companies are undervalued, perhaps *because* they are Nasdaq firms.

Even the best systems, those actually based on a solid investment rationale, can come up short. Take Dogs of the Dow, undoubtedly the most popular system in recent years. The simple formula, discovered in 1978 by a money manager named Michael O'Higgins, once beat the pants off the market. It works like this: At the start of the year, invest equal amounts in the 10 stocks with the highest dividend yields among the 30 stocks of the Dow Jones Industrial Average. At the start of each subsequent year, sell those 10 and repeat the process.

Between 1952 and 1996, Dogs of the Dow returned an average of 3.5 percentage points more than the S&P, an extraordinary performance. The Dogs system did not begin to receive widespread coverage in the press until the mid-1990s, but when it did, almost at once, the strategy started to falter. It failed by a wide margin to beat either the S&P or the Dow as a whole in every year from 1997 to 1999, then managed to finish slightly in the black in 2000, a year of losses for practically every index.

Between 1996 and 2000, the Dogs system returned a total of 50 percent while the S&P returned 88 percent. Variations on the Dogs theme haven't done much better. In 1995, The Motley Fool (www.fool.com), one of my favorite websites, invented the Foolish Four strategy, using four of the five lowest-priced Dogs, but in December 2000, the Fools gave up on it. Founding brothers David and Tom Gardner said they "doubt that the strategy will consistently outperform the stock market's average in the future."

I was never a fan of the Foolish Four, or of a simpler variant involving the five lowest-priced Dogs, mainly because I saw no rationality in the systems (the fact that a stock price is low in absolute terms is meaningless; Intel at $30 a share is not cheaper than the Washington Post Co. at $500), but I continue to like the traditional Dogs. It has a sound foundation: stocks that have high dividend yields are frequently undervalued because, by definition, a stock's yield is its annual dividend divided by its price. A high yield indicates either a high dividend or a low price. So, often the Dow's highest yielders are its cheapest stocks—hence, Dogs. A high yield can also indicate that a company is in serious trouble and might not make its next dividend payment, but since the Dogs comprise only Dow stocks, which tend to be responsible citizens with good balance sheets, the chances of their cutting or missing a dividend are low, though not non-existent.

Still, there are problems with the Dogs, the first being the no-arbitrage condition. Clearly, in the late 1990s, investors started catching on. Anticipating a surge of demand at the start of the year for Dogs stocks, investors simply started buying them earlier. Prices rose, so gains were not so strong over the next 12 months. My guess, however, is that the more recent performance of the Dogs may have deterred new investors, so it may start working again.

But even if it does, the Dogs system faces major obstacles. One is that it requires a lot of year-end selling; thus, taxes.

Another is that firms are putting less emphasis on dividends, again because of taxes, so a high yield may be indicative of almost nothing, certainly not bargain status. New Dow stocks Microsoft and Intel, added in 1999, pay no dividends at all, and financial firms, energy stocks, and industrials have come to dominate the Dogs. In fact, at the start of 2001, the list of Dogs was precisely the same as at the start of 2000: Philip Morris, Eastman Kodak, General Motors, DuPont, Caterpillar, JP Morgan Chase, International Paper, SBC Communications, ExxonMobil, and Minnesota Mining & Manufacturing. The average yield was 3 percent—or about twice that of the Dow as a whole.

According to an excellent website, www.dogsofthedow.com, the system returned an annual average of 17.2 percent from 1992 to 2000, compared with 17.8 percent for the full Dow and 17.0 percent for the S&P. Still, I am happy to recommend a system like the Dogs of the Dow to investors who can hold the shares in a tax-deferred account and who stick to the formula, reallocating every year.

Why should superior investors use a system that lags the market as a whole? The benefit of the Dogs is that it tends to keep you in the stock market with a diversified portfolio through thick and thin, and that's no minor achievement. Sure, owning a portfolio of all of the Dow stocks may be just as good, and I have no objection to such a route, but, with all its drawbacks, the Dogs is more fun. So far, I have found no other system that merits serious consideration, but I am keeping an open mind, especially about Leslie Douglas's Theory.

PART 4 ○

WHEN TO BUY,
WHEN TO SELL

CHAPTER TWENTY-SEVEN

BEAR MARKETS ARE FOR BUYING

WHEN STOCKS DECLINE, people get scared. Many, unfortunately, sell. In March 2001, for example, the Standard & Poor's 500-Stock Index, a good proxy for the market as a whole, dropped 13 percent. One result: investors pulled $15 billion out of U.S. equity mutual funds. That's the opposite of what they should do. Market declines, especially bear markets, provide excellent buying opportunities. And if you can't bring yourself to buy, then at least hold. You may not win in the short term (many stocks were lower in the fall of 2001 than in the spring), but you will in the long.

During the grinding 2000–01 bear market in technology, I was asked by the well-known CEO of a software company whether I thought stocks had bottomed. I told her I had no idea and that anyone who said he had an idea was either a liar or a fool. When you are in a bear market, you never know exactly when it will turn up. Never. In general, short-term prognostication is a ridiculous basis for investing. The best strategy, always, is to buy great companies and hold them in diversified portfolios for a long while. That means through good times and bad, since none of us knows when the bad times will turn good again.

What we can do in bear markets is look to history for reassurance. The stock market always falls in advance of an economic slowdown or recession (two consecutive quarters of declining GDP, something that happened nine times between 1946 and 2000). But it always recovers at a higher level. In other words, bear markets (defined as a decline of 20 percent or more in the S&P or some other broad index) end. As Mark Twain once replied when asked if it would ever stop raining: "Always has."

Between World War II and the start of the new millennium, there have been 11 bear markets in U.S. stocks, or roughly one every five years. Their patterns are remarkably similar. The median amount of time it took the market to fall was 17 months. The median for bouncing back from the new bottom to the previous top was 16 months. The declines for all but one of the bear markets were between 20 percent and 36 percent, and the bounce-back times for all but one were 19 months or less.

InvesTech Research looked at every bear market since 1932 and found even more encouraging statistics. Within six months of hitting bottom, the average bear rose 28 percent; within one year, it rose 46 percent. The weakest resurgence came during the 1946–49 bear market, when stocks rose only 20 percent from the bottom. Still, not bad.

Resilience is a primary characteristic of the U.S. stock market. Between 1929 and 1931, the market fell 61 percent, but over the next three years, it rose 94 percent. Since the Great Depression, the two worst calendar years in market history were 1973 and 1974, when S&P shares fell 37 percent. But over the next two years, they rose 70 percent.

A study by T. Rowe Price & Co. took a longer view in examining technology stocks. Between 1988 and 1995, a leading tech index had five declines of 13 percent or more. Within five years of each of those declines, the median recovery was 168 percent; the worst recovery, 51 percent.

Still, I don't put much faith in data regarding individual sectors like technology. Pieces of the market are far more volatile than the market itself. When we look only at the S&P or the Dow, we see that stability is dramatically linked to longevity. For example, the S&P declined in 21 of the 75 years between 1926 and 2000. But it declined in only two of the 64 overlapping 10-year periods between those dates. According to Ibbotson Associates, stocks beat bonds and Treasury bills in every over-lapping 20-year period since 1926 (i.e., 1926–46, 1927–47, etc.).

Even more impressive is the superior performance of stocks when inflation is taken into account. Stocks have declined in real, after-inflation terms in 24 of the 75 one-year periods since 1926, but Treasury bonds have declined in real terms in 29 of those years. Between 1975 and 2000, stocks were down six times, bonds down 10 times.

But, of course, there is no guarantee that stocks will always rise over the long run or that they will typically trounce bonds over the long run. The future is unknowable, but the past is an excellent guide. Based on 200 years of stock market history, it is a very good bet that stocks will outperform bonds. The longer you hold stocks, the lower the risk.

While there is no way to know when a bear market has ended, it stands to reason that buying when stocks are cheap is more productive than buying them when they are expensive. But maybe buying in a bear market is more than we can ask of an investor. Simply holding onto your shares is a worthy accomplishment in tough times. Still, the best way to insure that you will keep buying, even as the bear bears down on you, is to begin a program of extracting a certain sum from your bank account or your paycheck every week, fortnight, month or quarter. A 401(k) plan performs this magic automatically. When stock prices fall, you buy more shares. If you are pro-grammed to purchase $180 worth of General Electric stock every month, then, when the price is $60, you get three shares; when the price is $36, you get five. The same technique works for mutual funds.

Since investing, as Benjamin Graham teaches, is becoming a partner in a wonderful business, then the objective should be to accumulate as many shares in that business as you can. Lower prices allow you to buy more shares. So don't fear bear markets; instead, embrace them in a bear hug. That way, they can't hurt you.

CHAPTER TWENTY-EIGHT

MAKE A WISH LIST AND KEEP IT HANDY

ONE OF THE BEST PIECES of stock-market advice came my way many years ago from, of all people, my stockbroker. It is shockingly simple, and it works. Make a wish list, he said, of companies which you would dearly love to own but whose prices you consider too high. Keep it on a scrap of paper in your wallet, always. The list should include the names of 10 stocks and their desired prices. Make the prices low.

The idea here is to make the natural short-term volatility of stocks work in your favor. Benjamin Graham wrote a half-century ago that "the investor may as well resign himself in advance to the probability, rather than the mere possibility, that most of his holdings will advance, say, 50 percent or more from their low point and decline the equivalent of one-third or more from their high point at various periods in the next five years."

Graham may be understating the case. In mid-2001, Microsoft was trading at $73 a share, but in the preceding two years, it had been as high as $119 and as low as $40. General Motors was trading at $59, and over 12 months it had fluctuated between $76 and $48. Even a relatively tame stock like Pfizer had bounced in a year between $29 and $49.

Here's an example of what I call the Low-Price Action List (L-PAL) in action. Say you like AOL Time Warner. And why not? There's still a question of how well the pieces can be integrated, but the company has the potential to become the most powerful and profitable media company the world has ever seen, with both rich content and a spectacular delivery system over the Internet and through coaxial cables. But there's no doubt either that this is a risky venture. In mid-2001, at a price of $50 and a P/E ratio of about 70, AOL Time Warner probably lacked what Graham called a "margin of safety." But the stock had been as low as $32 and as high as $63 in the preceding 12 months, and the consensus among analysts was that the company could earn $1.50 a share for the year 2002. A price of $37.50 in 2001 would indicate a P/E of 25 based on projections for 2002. Sounds good, but why not knock off ten bucks more and put AOL on your L-PAL for $27.50?

Similarly, Walgreen is a company I have always wanted to own. It has perpetually seemed too expensive. At $44 and a P/E of 50 in March 2001, it was still no bargain, but at $34, it looked very attractive. So I put it on the list. Sure enough, in June, the stock took a tumble when it missed analysts' quarterly predictions by just a penny. It hit my L-PAL target, and I bought it. Another example: Cisco Systems had fallen from $70 to $15 by September 2001, hitting a low of $13 along the way. At $15, Cisco seems well-priced, but for my L-PAL I am looking for something more spectacular—say, $10.

Pricing stocks on your L-PAL is more art than science, but the rule is to keep going lower. It helps psychologically to cheer as the market falls. As Buffett once wrote, "Only those who will be sellers of equities in the near future should be happy at seeing stocks rise. Prospective purchasers should much prefer sinking prices." It's true that you may miss some great stocks if you follow the L-PAL method exclusively which is why you should reserve it for second-tier, rather than must-have companies. If you love Cisco at $15, then buy it; it may never see $10 again.

But if you want to own Cisco in large part because it is a bargain, then wait for your L-PAL price.

Also, it is important to keep up with the underlying businesses of your L-PAL companies. If Cisco is making management mistakes or if its price deterioration is caused by poor products or new competition, then scratch it from your list. If you don't, you could be stuck with a clunker because the only way this system will work is by making it an immutable rule that you have to buy, say, $5,000 worth of the stock as soon as the price hits your target. The Secret Code allows no fudging.

CHAPTER TWENTY-NINE

SELL ALMOST NEVER

IT IS MUCH HARDER TO KNOW when to sell a stock than when to buy one. For that reason, you should try to buy only stocks you think you will never sell. "Inactivity," Warren Buffett once said, "strikes us as intelligent behavior." Your goal in buying a stock is to own it forever.

Not selling has wonderful advantages.

1. You postpone paying capital gains taxes.

2. You have to make only one decision (to buy), rather than three decisions (to buy, to sell, and to buy back—or to buy something else instead).

3. You aren't tempted to do something stupid, like trying to predict the short-term direction of the stock's price.

Also, a no-sell strategy puts the awesome power of compounding on your side. In 1973, for example, Buffett bought about one-fifth of the Washington Post Co. for $11 million. In 2001, those shares were worth over $1 billion. In dividends alone, Berkshire received checks from the Post totaling $9.7 million in 2001, an annual return of 88 percent on the original investment! And, if Buffett wanted to sell his Post stock in 2001, he would have turned a very handy 9,000 percent profit over 28 years.

In the short term, the price of a stock can be determined by wild fits of emotion by investors. But, in the long term, it will be determined, in almost every case, by the actual performance of the underlying company. "Most of our large stock positions," Buffett said in an interview back in 1978, "are going to be held for many years, and the scorecard on our investment decisions will be provided by business results over that period, and not by prices on any given day." Benjamin Graham observed that in the short term the stock market is a voting machine, but in the long term it is a weighing machine. It measures reality.

Still, while holding stocks forever is an admirable goal, sometimes it isn't possible or even advisable. When is it time to give up on a stock?

The savviest comments I have ever read on the subject are found in *Common Stocks and Uncommon Profits* by Philip A. Fisher, whom you met in Chapter 7. Fisher wrote that "it is only occasionally that there is any reason for selling at all." Yes, but what are those occasions?

They come down to this: sell if the company has deteriorated in some important way. And Fisher is not talking about price! Like Buffett but unlike most small investors, Fisher rarely gets transfixed by the daily price, either high or low, of a stock he already owns.

When to sell? First, Fisher says it is absolutely necessary that an investor know why she bought the stock in the first place. You can't know when to sell unless you know why you bought. Typically, you should buy a stock because you like the management and the products and because you think demand will be strong and competition won't be bothersome. For example, as I said earlier, one of the stocks that I highlighted in my 1999 book, *Dow 36,000*, was Tootsie Roll Industries. Between July 2000 and

January 2001, the stock rose from $36 to $51. What would make me sell Tootsie Roll? Certainly not the higher price. Instead, I would sell if the business declines in some way.

Turn to Fisher: "When companies deteriorate they usually do so for one of two reasons. Either there has been a deterioration of management, or the company no longer has the prospect of increasing the markets for its product in the way it formerly did." In the case of Tootsie Roll, I would have to see a change in management that leads to some bad decisions that put the business in a decline. I would not sell simply because longtime CEO Melvin Gordon retired. As for increasing markets: I would have to see demand for candy fall, a strong competitor enter Tootsie Roll's niche, or some bad acquisition decisions made. The company, for example, has thrived by sticking to its knitting, making and selling strongly branded candy. If new managers decided to buy a baseball team or add soft drinks to the product line, I would get the yen to sell.

But the point is this: The decision to sell a stock depends on the fundamentals of the business, not on the short-term prospects of the economy (whether Alan Greenspan raises or lowers rates or other obsessions of myopic analysts) or on the passage of a tax bill and certainly not on a decline (or a rise) in the price of Tootsie Roll's stock.

The biggest mistake investors make is to sell because a stock is falling. If anything, that's usually a good time to buy: the shares are on sale. It is true that a significant decline in a stock price can be a signal that something, indeed, is wrong with the company. So don't ignore price movements entirely. For example, when Procter & Gamble stock fell 40 percent in just a few days a while back, investors were alerted that the company was having terrible problems raising prices of its products and increasing its earnings. It came as a shock to most shareholders. If you owned P&G, should you have sold in the spring of 2000, when the stock fell from $115 to $55 a share?

It was a tough call. My guess would be that P&G, with its fabulous brands and great distribution system, would get a new

CEO and get its act together. It did, but the recovery was a sluggish one. By September 2001, the stock was trading at $75.

My inclination, always, is to hold when it's a close call. But sometimes the case for selling is crystal clear. Owners of companies like Priceline.com and Lucent got a shock in 2000 when it became clear that their executives had grossly overestimated their companies' abilities to spin profits. In the face of gross management failure, dumping such stocks made lots of sense.

One popular selling technique is to put a "stop-loss" under a stock. The notion was made popular by a professional dancer and crossword-puzzle editor named Nicholas Darvas, who wrote a bestseller in 1960 called *How I Made Two Million Dollars in the Stock Market*. Using this strategy, you buy a stock at $50 a share and tell your broker to sell automatically when the stock breaches a level below it, say, $40. If you do this consistently, you will never lose more than 20 percent on any stock, unless it plummets through your floor on heavy selling. But a stop-loss system is foolish. It puts you at the mercy of the whims of Mr. Market, who sometimes, for no good reason, gets very pessimistic.

Say you have bought a house for $500,000. Imagine that interest rates rise, the economy slows, and real estate prices drop. The house next door, the same as yours, sells for $400,00. Is this a sign that you should put your house on the market now and take the 20 percent loss before it falls further? Of course not, but that is precisely the effect of stop-loss selling of stocks.

You can get badly whipsawed. Consider the case of Talbots, Inc., the preppy women's clothing chain. In mid-1998, imagine you bought the stock at $15 a share. Within a few months, it dropped to $12, so under stop-loss 20-percent rules you would have sold. But by the end of 1999, Talbots was trading at $27; by the end of 2000, at $54. Very few stocks go straight up, so while a stop-loss strategy for selling prevents big losses, it also prevents big gains.

Which brings up another popular strategy for selling: dump your stocks after they have risen. Many successful money managers follow this technique, setting a sell-target for every stock they buy. Such a strategy can work in the hands of an expert, but can a small investor follow it? Establishing a target, changing a target, selling when a stock hits a target and then buying later at a lower price and setting a new target—all of these steps require time-burning analysis and disciplined implementation.

In fact, what many small investors do is short-circuit the discipline. They sell stocks simply because they have made powerful moves upward. This is the don't-be-greedy school of investing. Many excellent companies that rise, keep rising. Look at Dell Computer: If you had invested $10,000 in the stock in 1992, you would have $120,000 by 1996. Time to sell? Why be greedy? Well, in the next five years, Dell stock returned 2,366 percent, boosting your original $10,000 investment to about $3 million.

Another misguided reason to sell is anticipation that stocks as a whole are about to fall. Trying to guess the highs or lows of the market is an impossible task. As Peter Lynch once put it: "Far more money has been lost by investors preparing for corrections than has been lost in the corrections themselves." History shows that markets decline before—and in the early stages of—economic slowdowns; then rise as the slowdown is coming to an end. After every recession, stocks have ended up higher. So why sell? It seems more logical to buy.

One good reason to sell is to maintain a reasonable allocation of assets. Say, for example, that you established a $100,000 portfolio in early 1996, with each stock representing 1/20th of your holdings at a cost of $5,000. Over the next five years, 18 of the stocks rise by 80 percent each (about average for the market), one stock falls in value by 60 percent; and the 20th stock is Dell, which rises by 2,300 percent.

Now, your portfolio looks like this: 18 stocks worth $9,000 each; one stock worth $2,000; and one stock, Dell, worth $120,000. The total portfolio, which started out at $100,000 five years earlier, is now worth $284,000. Very nice, but Dell represents 42 percent of your holdings, the doggy stock represents less than 1 percent and the others each represent about 3 percent.

This may sound like an extreme case, but, in modified form, it is the situation in which many investors found themselves in early 2000 after their tech stocks had boomed and their run-of-the-mill consumer stocks had stagnated. To be blunt: No stock is so terrific that it should represent 42 percent of a 20-stock portfolio. It's just too risky. You either have to sell some Dell along the way or add enough new money to dilute Dell's prominence. There is no formula for producing a good allocation of assets over time. Common sense and vigilance, basic tenets of the Secret Code, will do fine.

In general, however, the rule is to buy stocks as though you were going to keep them forever. You can't always do that, but long-term holding should be your goal. Don't forget that, with a diversified portfolio of 20 stocks or more, you will always have some losers, including big losers. Don't despair. Those losers will turn into winners if the companies retain their strong fundamentals, and if you have the patience and the courage to hold on.

PART 5 ∘

WHAT TO BUY

New Hanover County Public Library
Wilmington, NC

Automated Renewal number :910/798-6320
Renew by phone: 798-6302
renew online: www.nhclibrary.org
Please have your library card ready
Use www.libraryelf.com to help manage your account.
****

Check-Out Receipt

Title: The secret code of the superior
investor : how to be a long-term winner
in a short-term world / James K.
Item ID: 34200065O6782
Checked-out Date: 8/18/2009
Due Date: 9/8/2009 2:58:39 PM
Location: Main

Ask about upcoming Programs....
Libraries are more than just books!

CHAPTER THIRTY

INVEST IN PEOPLE, NOT STOCKS

ON OCTOBER 20, 1997, a bulletin flashed across my Bloomberg News terminal: Bank One Corp., the Ohio holding company which then owned 1,502 banking offices in 12 states, had agreed to buy First Commerce Corp. of New Orleans in a stock swap worth $3 billion. I quickly typed "FCOM" into the machine and then hit the "Equity" key. First Commerce was trading at $66.50, up $8.50 from the previous trading day. I did the calculation in my head. I had made a lot of money.

My success with First Commerce was the result of one of the best Secret Code strategies of all: buy stocks whose managements you respect, or better, revere. It's a bonus if that reverence derives from personal contact. Yes, it's true: With stocks, it is whom you know as much as what you know.

My own roots with First Commerce went back to 1972, when, as a 25-year-old newcomer to New Orleans with no track record and no assets, I received a $20,000 loan from the bank to start a weekly newspaper. Six years later, I sold the paper and went to work part-time for the bank's brilliant chief executive, a high-principled lawyer named Tom Rapier, who ran the company his own way, not worrying about quarter-to-quarter earnings, weeding out bad credit, expanding into new markets, keeping his eye on the larger prize.

Rapier was a big man, a chain-smoker with a weakness for veal-cutlet po-boy sandwiches, slathered in mayonnaise and doused with Tabasco sauce from an industrial-size bottle on his desk. He was philanthropic, intellectual and charismatic, and he taught me a lot about business and about people. In 1983, he died suddenly of a heart attack at age 50. After a brief succession struggle, he was followed by Ian Arnof, a 43-year-old Harvard MBA whose family owned a small bank in Arkansas. Arnof was as high-minded as Rapier, but he knew more about marketing, technology and finance in general. It was clear to me that, whatever happened in New Orleans (and the city soon fell on hard times as oil prices dropped), Ian Arnof could run a bank and, by means I could not possibly guess at the time, would make the company thrive. That's when I started buying First Commerce shares. I was investing in a person, Ian, even more than I was investing in a stock.

It was an important lesson. Learning about CEOs, to the extent that you can judge their character as well as their management ability, isn't easy. It's an opportunity that comes along only a few times in an investor's lifetime. Take advantage of it. Ian did not give me any inside dope, of course; he never told me when he thought the stock was cheap or when earnings would soar or when a merger was in prospect. But I got to know him well enough to decide that this was an excellent manager—and an excellent person. If I owned a bank, I would hire him to run it. And, as a shareholder, I *did* own a bank.

As the years passed, a pattern developed. Arnof, like Rapier before him, did not hesitate to sell bonds out of the bank's securities portfolio when interest rates rose. There was a distinct tax advantage to selling bonds at a loss and replacing them with higher-yielding ones. "Why don't other banks do this?" I once asked Rapier. Because, he said, selling such bonds meant reducing earnings in the short term even though it meant boosting earnings (by more) in the long term. Analysts might not understand, and the stock price could fall. But Arnof and Rapier did not care about the short-term stock price. Similarly, they aggressively wrote off potentially bad loans, again reducing their profits in the short term to buttress their balance sheet and increase their earnings in the future.

The ignorance of analysts and money managers was bliss to an investor like me. As First Commerce took its write-offs, the stock price dropped, and I bought more. By 1993, First Commerce stock represented about 15 percent of my total financial assets. That was a big bet for a single stock, and it would become bigger as the price rose. I was fully aware that I was banking heavily on First Commerce.

Financial deregulation was creating a favorable environment for regional banks, which became takeover targets. First Commerce, however, was doing some taking over of its own, expanding throughout the state and eventually becoming the largest bank in Louisiana. It had long ago established the broadest automated teller-machine network in a three-state region, and it had a strong credit-card division.

After doubling in 1991, the stock was languishing. Still, as a long-term holder, I wasn't worried. I used the dividends to buy more. In 1993, First Commerce was trading between $25 and $30 a share. When interest rates rose, it headed lower, eventually hitting $23. I bought more, content to wait, not for a buyout (since I was getting the idea that Arnof wasn't interested in selling) but for recognition by the market of what a powerful performer this bank was. I had owned First Commerce stock in my retirement plan for a decade, and I could easily own it for another decade.

Then, in early 1995, the stock began to rise. By 1996, it hit $40, and I was sorely tempted to sell. At 15 times earnings and two times book value (the company's net worth on its balance sheet), First Commerce was more expensive than ever in its history. It was, I thought, fully priced.

Selling is the most difficult part of investing (as the last chapter explained), and simply believing a great company is overpriced is no reason to dispose of it. I would have sold if Arnof had left First Commerce or if the company had made a bad mistake or if the competitive situation had drastically changed (the bank had only one serious competitor in the state). But selling because a stock seems expensive is not a good idea for a long-term investor.

First Commerce burst through $40 and $45, all the while paying handsome dividends and, then in late July of 1997, it burst through $50. Here was a price that was truly absurd. After much hesitation, I sold half my holdings two months later at $56. I had quadrupled my money, and I thought it was time to call it quits.

Why sell only half my stock? The truth is that I wasn't sure of myself. Maybe, I reasoned (as it turned out, correctly), the market knew more than I did. Also, I wasn't enthusiastic about other assets; I didn't know where to put the proceeds anyway. Also, Ian Arnof had taken me this far; I felt I should stick with him.

Of course, I never should have sold *any* of my First Commerce. A short time later, the company was purchased in an exchange of 1.28 shares of Bank One for every one share of First Commerce. With Bank One trading at $53.63, a share of First Commerce was suddenly worth $68.64. I didn't wait for the swap. As soon as the bid was announced, I sold out at a slight discount—$66.50, at a price-to-earnings ratio of 21, or nearly three times the P/E average of the early 1990s.

Ian Arnof stayed with the bank for a few years, then went off to California. He remains a close friend, a living exemplar of a wonderful investing strategy, employed to great effect by the best of the venture capitalists: It's called backing *people*. It worked for me the one time I tried it. I may never get another chance, but I'm still looking.

CHAPTER THIRTY-ONE

INVEST WITH YOUR HEART AS WELL AS YOUR MIND

THERE ARE TWO WAYS to invest with a social conscience: 1) Make as much money as you can, no matter where you find the opportunities (among sweatshops, tax cheats, nature's despoilers) then use your gains for ethical ends, or 2) Put your money to work only in institutions that are ethical themselves, even if the gains are lower.

In recent years, the second alternative has become more and more attractive. With a little help, it's now easy to invest in companies that do well as they do good. In fact, many ethical companies do *better*. The Domini 400 Social Index, which tracks the performance of stocks fit for socially responsible investing (or "SRI," as the acronym goes), returned an annual average of 18.9 percent during the 1990s, compared with 17.4 percent for the S&P 500, the U.S. benchmark.

A worldwide measure, the Dow Jones Sustainability Group Index, includes about 200 large-cap stocks from 33 countries and 64 industry groups that "create shareholder value by embracing opportunities and managing risks deriving from economic, environmental and social developments." Since its advent in 1994, this index, too, has run slightly ahead of the global averages. Among the companies in the index: Nestle of Switzerland; Norsk Hydro, Norway; Toshiba, Japan; Volkswagen and Bayer, Germany; Groupe Danone, France; and Nortel Networks, Canada.

No wonder this kind of investing has become so popular. You can have your social conscience and profit, too. A survey in 2001 by the Social Investment Forum, an SRI advocacy group, found that "more than $2 trillion is invested today in the United States in a socially responsible manner," or 13 percent of the $16 trillion under professional management. In another study, the UK Social Investment Forum found that 59 percent of British pension funds, representing 78 percent of total assets, incorporate an SRI approach in their investing strategies, as do private money managers around the world.

As of spring 2001, some 100 U.S. mutual funds were taking an SRI approach. Most of them were small, but 16 funds had over $100 million in assets, and 14 received high ratings from the major research houses (four or five stars from Morningstar or an "A" or "B" from Lipper, another fine research service). The oldest SRI stock fund, Dreyfus Premier Third Century, started in 1972, had $1.2 billion in assets and an annual average return of 19.3 percent for the five years ending in 2000—one percentage point better than the S&P. An excellent source for details about SRI funds is the website www.socialfunds.com.

Calvert Group, Ltd., the largest SRI family, has 16 separate funds, including some that feature bonds and international stocks. Substantial fund houses like Vanguard, Neuberger & Berman and TIAA-CREF all have SRI funds.

I have often wondered, however, why an investor would cede his ethical stock choices to a professional manager. Most funds have their own, often-vague criteria for the "screens" they use to keep tainted companies out of their portfolios. Some funds ban companies that do animal testing; others bar gambling stocks; others, companies that make weapons. Nearly all disqualify firms that sell cigarettes.

But what are we to make of this SRI statement from one of the best of the funds? "In general, Parnassus looks for companies that respect the environment, treat their employees well, have effective equal employment opportunity policies, good community relations and ethical business dealings." An investor has to trust Jerome Dodson, manager of Parnassus and a former foreign service officer, to decide. Dodson's top holdings, by the way, are Freddie Mac and Fannie Mae, providers of financing for home mortgages. Other choices: LSI Logic and Genuine Parts.

My preference is to make the SRI stock choices myself, using the lists of holdings of funds like Parnassus for gleaning ideas, but there are alternatives.

For the past 15 years, Sacha Millstone, a senior vice president in the office of Raymond James & Associates in Washington, has become one of dozens of financial advisors who specialize in finding SRI investments for their clients. Environmentally friendly companies have always been popular, she says, but lately there is "a lot of concern about how goods are manufactured around the world." Clients don't want to invest in companies that abuse workers.

Public information on the Internet abounds, but there is no single list, nor should there be, in an area where subjectivity reigns. The Corporate Responsibility Newswire (www.csrwire. com), for example, runs copious stories about the good deeds of businesses: "Crest Kicks Off Partnership with Boys and Girls Clubs to Improve Oral Health," "7,800 Trees Planted at Sutton Lake" (by CP&L, a subsidiary of Progress Energy).

Millstone subscribes to a commercial research service called Socrates, offered to financial advisors by KLD & Co., Inc., the top consultant in the field. In a typically extensive report on Merck & Co., Socrates lists the corporation's charitable endeavors, pointing out that women make up 32 percent of the firm's managers, that Merck offers 26 weeks of family leave, that it provides discounts on HIV drugs to poor countries and that a magazine gave the firm top marks for its treatment of disabled employees. On the other hand, the report noted that Merck has no minorities among its top eight managers and that it had to pay a fine for air pollution.

But what really counts in socially responsible investing? In my own view, the issues raised by Socrates pale before Merck's most important ethical achievements—saving lives and curing illnesses by developing new pharmaceuticals.

Some investors might be surprised to see Cisco, Microsoft and Intel leading another popular SRI average, the Broad Market Social Index. Each of these firms has a reputation as a super-tough competitor, sometimes accused of bullying smaller firms. Is such conduct socially irresponsible? I don't think so, since rough-and-tumble competition is ultimately beneficial to consumers, but I can understand that other investors might disagree. (The Justice Department under President Clinton believed that Microsoft's conduct was not just unethical but illegal, and it prosecuted the company on antitrust charges. As I complete this book, an appeals court has reversed a key part of the ruling against the software company.)

But the truth is that the main reason that SRI stocks perform so well is that they are not much different from other stocks. KLD & Co., which manages the Domini 400 (the "D" in the firm's name stands for "Domini"), has excluded the obvious firms like Philip Morris Cos. and Lockheed Martin (another company that in my book is socially responsible, protecting us from threats to our national and personal security) but the top holdings are similar to those of many other large-cap funds.

In 2000, only two of the 400 stocks were eliminated from the index for transgressing ethically: Marriott, for gambling, and Alcoa, for military contracting. Through the first half of 2001, only one stock had been booted: Wal-Mart Stores, for unspecified "international labor controversies." Of course, some investors might have barred Wal-Mart from their own lists earlier for squashing small-fry competitors or homogenizing rural America. In the SRI game, personal judgment is what counts.

And, thanks largely to the Internet, investors have the tools to decide whether a stock meets their own moral standards.

A sound portfolio can easily afford to eliminate stocks an investor might find ethically questionable. In fact, investing is one of the few endeavors in which exercising a social conscience costs nothing except the time to do the research to find the baddies.

CHAPTER THIRTY-TWO

VALUE OR GROWTH?
BOTH

IN APRIL 2000, Deutsche Banc Alex. Brown, J.P. Morgan & Co. and several other fancy investment banking firms brought out an Initial Public Offering for a company whose humble business has been the making and selling of doughnuts. The company was Krispy Kreme, founded in 1937 in Winston-Salem, N.C. Through its 185 stores in 30 states, mainly found in the Southeastern U.S. but also gracing such venues as Penn Station in New York, it was producing 1.8 billion hyper-sugary dough-nuts a year, including the "Hot Original Glazed" and the "chocolate-iced custard filled." The surprise was that, just as high-tech stocks were taking a dive, Krispy Kreme was soaring. In fact, its management decided that it had outgrown the Nasdaq after barely a year, and the stock moved over to the tonier New York Stock Exchange. Some investors were thinking that Krispy Kreme Doughnuts, Inc., might battle it out with Starbucks as the hottest restaurant chain in America.

In a little over a year, Krispy Kreme underwent two 2-for-1 stock splits. A $10,000 investment was worth about $40,000. Since the company's earnings for the preceding 12 months were a mere 32 cents, its P/E ratio was over 100 (compared with 27 at the time for the average S&P stock), and its price-to-book ratio was 14 (compared to 6 for the S&P). Investors were paying for the excitement of a high-flying stock, but their enthusiasm might well have been sensible. After all, the analysts who covered the stock (and there were only five) were estimating that earnings would grow faster than 25 percent over the next year, and among buyers of the stock were such highly regarded growth funds as Putnam Voyager II, Fidelity Contrafund and USAA Aggressive Growth.

Krispy Kreme, its sales tripling to $360 million in five years, is a classic growth stock, that is, a stock whose earnings are moving up smartly and whose valuation, as measured by price-to-earnings and price-to-book ratios, is in the stratosphere as well.

In recent years, most growth stocks have been in fields such as computer software, biotechnology and energy, but the sector doesn't matter. It is the rapid rise in earnings and, typically, an even more rapid rise in price, that characterize a growth stock readily identified by its high P/E and P/B ratios. Consider, for example, Cognizant Technology Solutions, which develops software for financial-services and health-care companies. Despite the tech slowdown, Cognizant's earnings jumped from $1 million in 1997 to $11 million in 1999 to an expected $25 million in 2001. Sales octupled in four years. In June 2001, Cognizant was trading at $39 a share, for a P/E of 40 and a P/B of 9. According to the analysts at Value Line, the company should increase its earnings at an average annual rate of 40 percent for the next five years. Yes, Cognizant is a rip-roaring growth stock.

The opposite of growth, in the investment lexicon, is value. A classic value stock is Suiza Foods Corp., a Dallas-based distributor of milk, dairy products and bottled water. From 1999 to 2001, Suiza traded at a P/E of between 10 and 13, meaning that investors were willing to pay about one-fourth as many dollars for each dollar of Suiza's earnings than they were willing to pay for each dollar of Cognizant's. Suiza's price-to-book ratio was about 1.5, meaning that its market value was nearly the same as its value on the balance sheet. Suiza has been increasing its earnings, but slowly, an average of about 8 percent a year between 1998 and 2000. Also solidly in the value category is Abitibi-Consolidated, maker of newsprint and other wood products, headquartered in Quebec. In June 2001, the company traded at a P/E of 7 and a P/B of 1.6—in both cases about one-fourth the S&P average. Earnings per share were rising at a sluggish pace and threatened to decline in the year ahead.

There they are: growth and value. Most research firms that classify mutual funds, such as Morningstar and Lipper, use these rubrics to classify the styles of managers, and whenever I give a speech the issue of growth vs. value (which do I like more?) almost always comes up in the question-and-answer session.

The assumption is that an investor has to choose between fast-growers that may be overpriced and slow-growers that appear neglected. That choice dictates the investor's primary style, according to this analysis. So, each investor has to take a stand. Which is it for the superior investor, then: growth or value?

There is really no good answer, but that's mainly because it's not the right question. In fact, there is no more tiresome and distorted debate in the annals of investing than the one about growth stocks vs. value stocks. Obviously, smart investors should try to select stocks with both characteristics. The ideal purchase is a company with high earnings growth but a low P/E. It is not easy to find such companies, but what you *can* find are companies which are priced as value stocks today (because they have temporarily sluggish earnings or because they are in an industry that is out of favor) but which are likely to become growth stocks tomorrow. In other words, look for value stocks that will turn into growth stocks. A good example of such a company is Quest Diagnostics, the nation's leading provider of testing services for physicians, which traded at a P/E of 20 in 1998 and a P/E of 58 in mid-2001. Earnings per share soared from 89 cents to over $3, and the stock rose by a factor of 10.

But this debate is not a debate at all. History shows clearly that the best way to make a lot of money in the stock market is to buy stocks like Quest when they are cheap. (Duh!) In other words, value is valuable when value stocks grow. A value stock that does not grow is not worth owning. For example, during 2000 Stanley Works, a company that sells nearly $3 billion worth of hardware a year, traded at an average P/E ratio of 12, or less than half the P/E of the market as a whole. But Stanley has been trading at a low P/E for a long time and for good reason. During the decade of the 1990s, its earnings and revenues rose at an average rate of just 3.5 percent annually. Between 1995 and 2000, Stanley, which pays a nice dividend, returned a total of just 34 percent or one-third the rate of the market as a whole. Value alone is unenticing.

But not every low-priced stock should remain that way. In a recent study, Ibbotson Associates used the Fama-French database, which divided the stocks of the New York Stock Exchange each year into two equal groups: value (for those with low P/B ratios) and growth (for those with high). One dollar invested at the start of 1928 in large-cap value stocks (and then reinvested in such stocks each year) became $5,170 by the end of 2000; one dollar similarly invested in growth stocks became $1,017. Quite a difference.

Average annual return for large-cap value stocks was 12.4 percent; for small-cap value, 14.2 percent. The equivalent numbers for growth stocks were just 10.0 percent and 9.4 percent. Large-value beat large-growth in six out of eight decades. Still, you don't get something for nothing. Value stocks, according to Ibbotson, were more volatile.

Research also reveals strong cycles in which one type of stocks outperforms the other. Growth dominated during the last half of the 1990s. But, writes Anthony M. Maramarco in a letter to clients of David L. Babson & Co., a Cambridge, Mass., investment management firm, "Value investing has made a remarkable and, in the opinion of value managers, a long overdue comeback since the tech-heavy Nasdaq index peaked at over 5000 on March 10, 2000." In the year 2000, value beat growth by 30 percentage points.

It was satisfying vindication. Writing on the Morningstar.com website, Russel Kinnel reminded readers of the vituperation heaped onto value-stock mutual funds like Longleaf Partners in the late 1990s, when growth was king. Just check out the Morningstar chat pages from the past. A typical unhappy investor wrote on Nov. 11, 1999: "I, too, have been invested with LLPFX [Longleaf Partners] since 7/95. I was told it was an excellent fund. I also made the mistake of putting my children's college fund with them in May. They have lost 17% of their funds. I will be following you out of this over-hyped fund." But, over the 12 months ending June 30, 2001, Longleaf returned a whopping 25 percent, compared with a loss of 17 percent for the Standard & Poor's 500-Stock Index, the U.S. benchmark. Waste Management, Marriott International and General Motors were the fund's top holdings, representing a 30 percent of its highly concentrated portfolio. All three qualify as solid value stocks, carrying P/E ratios below the S&P average. GM, which rose more than 20 percent during the first half of 2001, had a P/E of 14 and a P/B of 1.2.

In fact, nearly all big value-stock mutual funds, which suffered during the late-1990s, shot up in 2000 and the first half of 2001. Among the best performers: Vanguard Windsor, American Funds American Mutual, and Dodge & Cox Stock. During the first four months of 2001, the average growth-stock fund lost 17 percent, according to Lipper, Inc., but its value analog gained 1 percent.

Does this mean you should jump out of growth stocks and into value stocks whenever you detect a shift in cycles? Absolutely not. I am perfectly content to buy a company when it is in the value stage, ride it to growth and then keep riding it forever. The old rule applies: buy great companies and hold onto them.

There are two lessons for superior investors when it comes to value and growth. First, as Maramarco puts it, "Portfolios should be rebalanced regularly so that one style does not become an outsized percentage of assets." In other words, you should own some growth stocks and some value stocks though most of your new purchases should be of value stocks that you expect to turn into growth stocks. Second, and far more important, the market moves in fits and starts. Stocks bought in their value stage become growth stocks, but the transformation does not necessarily occur overnight.

In a column in the *Washington Post* back in 1996, I coined the phrase "branded wallflower" to describe a stock that has a powerful brand name but that no one seems to like. At the time, I highlighted Merrill Lynch & Co. as a "perfect example." Over the next five years, adjusted for splits, the stock rose from $15 to $66, more than triple the rate of increase of the S&P. Not all branded wallflowers metamorphose into such beautiful belles of the ball. And Merrill Lynch may *still* be a value stock. In mid-2001, it was trading at a P/E of 15—a little more than half the S&P average. The reason its P/E remained low over five years is that its E (earnings) rose so fast.

Where to find branded wallflowers? Again, you can plunder the choices of experts. For example, Morningstar publishes a list of 29 "blueblood blue chips," large companies with stellar records of earnings growth, relatively low prices (P/Es under 30) and dividend yields of at least 0.5 percent. (A decent yield is often a characteristic of a branded wallflower since high yields are signs of low prices.) While not all of these bluebloods are cheap enough to be true wallflowers, some hold interest: American Express, the leader in travel and related financial services; ExxonMobil, the top integrated oil company; Telefonos de Mexico, the telecom powerhouse; and Wells Fargo, the California-based bank. Each of these companies has a magnificent brand name, built over decades and, at least at this time, was underappreciated by the market.

Or look at the holdings of a top value-oriented mutual fund like Dodge & Cox Stock: Bank of America (with a P/E in mid-2001 of 13) and Chevron (with a P/E of 10) certainly appear to be branded wallflowers. So do Albertson's (P/E of 16), the venerable grocery chain, and Sara Lee (P/E of 14), maker of Hanes hosiery and those frozen baked goods. Both are holdings of the second-largest value fund in the country, American Funds Washington Mutual. Another fine fund, AIM Basic Value, which returned a cumulative 70 percent for the three years ending June 2001 (58 points more than an S&P index fund), owned such branded wallflowers as Equifax, the giant information-gatherer and processor (and a longtime favorite of mine), at a P/E of 13, and Parker Hannifin, the world's largest diversified manufacturer of control systems for businesses, at a P/E of 12.

One rule of thumb in the game of finding growth-and-value stocks is to seek companies with a P/E that is lower than their expected annual rate of profit growth for the five years ahead. A stock with such characteristics, as of May 2001, was Arrow Electronics, the world's largest distributor of electronic components and computer products. Trading at a P/E of just 9, it was expected to increase its earnings by 25 percent annually for the coming five years, according to Value Line. Of course, earnings estimates are just educated guesses, but this one leaves plenty of margin for error.

CHAPTER THIRTY-THREE

SOME OF THE BEST STOCKS ARE RIGHT UNDER YOUR NOSE

IT WAS PETER LYNCH, the best mutual fund manager of all time, who set out the theory that you don't have to be a professional to select stocks. "Any normal person using the customary 3 percent of the brain can pick stocks just as well, if not better, than the average Wall Street expert," Lynch said in *One Up On Wall Street,* the bestseller he wrote after leaving Fidelity Magellan.

In contending that anyone can do it, Lynch was being too modest and a bit disingenuous. He knows very well that it was his innate talent and hard work (backed by a good Fidelity research team) that produced stock-picking the world had never seen before. During his tenure, from 1977 to 1990, the broad market roughly tripled, so a $1,000 investment became $3,000. But at Magellan, a $1,000 investment became $28,000. Don't tell me that an amateur can do nine times better than the S&P over a long stretch on his own, or even four times better.

Still, Lynch has a point. In some ways, amateurs do have an edge on pros. First, mutual fund managers face demands that individual investors don't. They have to produce a sterling record every quarter (or at least every year) to attract new investors, so they don't have the luxury of focusing only on the long term. Second, if they are successful, they will have huge amounts of money to move around, and their own buying and selling can cause big price fluctuations, so they can't concentrate their portfolios in only a few, or even 30, stocks the way that small investors can. Finally, fund managers have to look like they are doing something. They can't buy and hold, purchasing a bunch of great companies, slapping their hands and saying, "That's done!"

But Lynch's larger message is the important one for superior investors: You can find great stocks by keeping your eyes open. They are right under your nose. "I began my search for new selections in the usual fashion," he wrote in 1993 in *Beating the Street*, "I headed straight for my favorite source of investment ideas: the Burlington Mall." In his earlier book, Lynch told the story of one of his greatest discoveries: Hanes, the hosiery maker. He invested in the stock after his wife pointed out that everyone in the grocery store was buying pantyhose in new, graceful, convenient egg-shaped containers (L'eggs!). Such choices, he writes, are based on "common knowledge," as opposed to the specialized knowledge that professionals glean from expensive research. Other valuable Magellan discoveries: "Taco Bell, I was impressed with the burritos on a trip to California; La Quinta Motor Inns, somebody at a rival Holiday Inn told me about it; Volvo, my family and friends drive this car." And so on.

I had my own Lynchian epiphany a few years ago at a refreshment stop along Interstate 95 between Baltimore and Wilmington. There, in the quintessential middle American venue, was a long line of just plain folks—of varied races and national origins—waiting in line patiently to buy an expensive cup of Starbucks coffee and maybe a two-dollar cookie. Right next to them was a stand offering Maxwell House with no queue at all. Before that experience, I had naively believed that Starbucks was a limited upscale urban (or slightly suburban) coffeehouse phenomenon. As Michael J. Weiss wrote in his book on marketing and demographics, *The Clustered World*: "Visit Walnut Creek, California, on a Saturday morning, and the busiest area in town is the Countrywood Shopping Center around Noah's Bagels and Starbucks Coffee." Yes, but the Maryland House was busy, too! And not with Walnut Creek types, but with Glen Burnie types. I suddenly realized that Starbucks had the potential to serve a mass McDonald's-style market, and, after looking at the company's numbers, I bought the stock. From the end of 1997 to mid-2001, shares tripled in value as the company boomed. When it suffered mild setbacks (by launching a retail website, for example), I bought more. Starbucks has now built such a strong brand that it is licensing coffee ice cream, placing its product on United Airlines flights and selling new products like Frappucino. As of July 1, 2001, Starbucks had 4,435 stores, and it's opening new ones at a rate of better than 1,000 a year; only 20 percent of all stores are outside of North America. Better yet, Starbucks is increasing same-store sales at a 10 percent annual clip. Total revenues, from a standing start in 1991, now exceed those of Wendy's International, and, despite the expenses of opening new stores, so do profits. As for potential, consider this: McDonald's has 29,000 restaurants, and more than half are outside the U.S.

Another successful hunch of mine was Williams-Sonoma, whose trendy, high-priced culinary products I have been happily buying since the early 1980s. The company also owns Pottery Barn, Hold Everything and Chambers, which sends catalogs featuring nice towels. In a column in September 1994, I used the stock as an example of how small investors can conduct their own research. I loved the products, the company's financials were sound, and the price was right. The only sour note was sounded by Dan Sullivan, a California analyst, who told me that, even though he gave the stock his highest ranking, "I wouldn't recommend buying Williams-Sonoma now because we feel we are in a bear market."

With due respect to Sullivan, who edits a good newsletter called The Chartist, that's the worst reason I have ever heard for not buying a stock. Superior investors are concerned with the business, not with someone's guess about the economy or the direction of the stock market. In fact, Sullivan was wrong about the market. Within a year of our interview, the S&P had risen 26 percent; within three years, it had more than doubled. And he was wrong about Williams-Sonoma, which I bought (adjusted for splits) at $12 and was trading at $39 by June 2001.

Of course, it is much easier to find companies like Hanes, La Quinta, Williams-Sonoma and Starbucks, which are in grocery stores or malls or off the highway, than to find companies that sell sophisticated software or air-conditioning compressors or truck parts. But there are more obscure stocks that investors have no excuse for missing. Consider the dentist who invests in a company that makes fiber-optic transducers because a patient has given him a hot tip but neglects a firm like Dentsply International, which supplies him with root-canal instruments and x-ray equipment for his own work. Dentsply is my idea of a nearly perfect company. It has increased earnings every year since going public in 1987. Its dividend, first declared in 1994, went from 4 cents to 27 cents in seven years. It had an average annual earnings growth rate of 25 percent during the 1990s and, according to analysts, expected growth of 13 percent a year from 2001 to 2005. It has price volatility that is one-third below average, heavy employee ownership, just enough competition to stay sharp but not too much to drive down profits, and it has demographics on its side.

In a possibly obnoxious way, I frequently ask my dentists and doctors, people I meet at dinner parties, plumbers, car salesmen, colleagues, etc., about the best companies in their own fields. Who is your toughest competitor? Does someone have a great new product? How's business? Of course, as a journalist, I had an advantage. I found one of the most successful stocks in my portfolio, the Apollo Group (see Chapter 38), which runs a highly profitable chain of for-profit universities, when I went out to Arizona researching an article about new trends in education.

But you can get ideas looking at ads in magazines, buying a new suit or talking to the IT manager at your office.

Still, understand that a good idea is not tantamount to a good investment. An example is Amazon.com, launched in 1995 as an online retailer of books. Early users quickly understood that Amazon gave them a wonderfully efficient and comfortable buying experience, often better than a real-life bookstore. They might have been smart enough to buy the stock at its Initial Public Offering on May 15, 1997, at $18. Within a year and a half, 100 shares became 1,200 through splits, and the stock hit $113. So an IPO investment of $1,800 turned into $135,600 in 18 months. Not bad. But if you bought Amazon because you liked the idea, you may not have noticed that, at the dawn of 2000, the company was nowhere close to proving itself as a business. The market soured on the stock, and it was trading at $8.50 in early September. Ground-floor investors, nevertheless, were sitting on a profit of about 500 percent, but people who bought shares after mid-1998 lost money, in many cases, a bundle of money. The Amazon story reminds us that performance, not just first impressions, really counts.

A more stable high-tech business that I found under my nose was Dell Computer. I had bought a computer over the phone and the salesman talked me into purchasing all sorts of accessories, including a scanner that I still haven't unwrapped two years later. Dell understood how to sell consumer technology far better than a brick-and-mortar competitor, and it had a beautiful balance sheet and income statement, to boot (see Chapters 12 and 13). So I bought stock and became a satisfied customer in both senses.

The computer business, however, is not an easy sector for making money. In his book, Lynch says that he bought Apple Computer because "my kids had one at home and then the systems manager bought several for the office." Well, I was an early Apple enthusiast, too, but I'll bet there aren't many Apples sitting on the desks at Fidelity today. A monumental business mistake by Steve Jobs limited software applications (not to mention hardware alternatives), and Apple, despite a huge headstart, ended up a niche player. The stock peaked in early 1991 at $36 (adjusted for splits), just after Lynch retired. It steadily declined to $6.50 by 1997, then revived when Jobs returned with new products like the iMac. But in September 2001, shares were still 50 percent below their level of 10 years earlier.

The point is that you should use the Lynchian under-your-nose strategy as a starting point, a tip sheet. Then, do the research. The payoffs can be gigantic, but you have to be alert.

In 1993, did I notice that something spectacular was happening at Safeway, Inc.? That the stores were getting cleaner, better-stocked, more efficient, that dowdy urban outlets were being shuttered and that the competition was peeling away? I did. But did I consider Safeway as an investment? I did not. The stock shot up 20-fold in eight years.

In 1990, did I pay attention to an excellent outsourcing supplier called Paychex, which was handling the payroll processing at the Capitol Hill newspaper that I partly owned, saving thousands of small businesses like mine lots of money and lots of headaches? I did. But did I consider Paychex as an investment? I did not. The stock split eight times over the next decade, and a $10,000 stake rose to $750,000.

The moral is to think of becoming a partner in every superb business you run across. The joy of investing is that, for a price, you can own a piece of practically anything. So stay alert.

CHAPTER THIRTY-FOUR

OWN COMPANIES, NOT COUNTRIES

FOR DECADES, a key rule of investing was to diversify internationally. The reason was simple. When stocks in some parts of the world perform poorly, stocks in other parts of the world perform well. In other words, international markets were not closely correlated. As a result, owning a strong dose of non-U.S. stocks provided balance for a U.S. portfolio, and vice versa. The bottom line was that, with international diversification, investors could get returns almost as high as with an all-U.S. portfolio, but with considerably lower risk.

The statistics were convincing. A study by Sanford C. Bernstein & Co. found that between 1970 and 1995, U.S. stocks significantly outperformed non-U.S. in 12 calendar-year periods while non-U.S. outperformed U.S. in 12 years as well; in only two years were returns about the same. T. Rowe Price, the Baltimore mutual fund house, looked at the 10 major stock markets between 1980 and 1999 and found that the U.S. was number-one in only one of those years (1982) and that no country was on top more than twice except Hong Kong.

I chanted the mantra myself. As recently as 1997, in a column in the *Washington Post,* I was quoting the Price line: History showed that U.S. stocks alone were risky, but as more foreign stocks were added to the mix, "the portfolio's returns increased, but the degree of volatility, or risk, actually declined." The optimal risk/reward allocation, Price researchers found, came with a portfolio that was divided this way: 70 percent U.S. stocks, 30 percent foreign stocks.

But something changed. During the first six months of 2001, the U.S. market, as represented by the Standard & Poor's 500-Stock Index, was down 7 percent. At the same time, Britain's FT-SE 100 was down 9 percent; Germany's DAX was down 7 percent, and Japan's Nikkei's was down 8 percent. Of course, half a year does not a trend make, but in 2000 as well, world stocks moved together. For example, the average large-cap growth mutual fund fell 16.3 percent in 2000 while the average international fund fell 15.6 percent.

More important, a study by Robin Brooks and Luis Catao for the International Monetary Fund looked at the performance of 5,500 stocks in 40 markets over the period 1986–2000. The economists found that the correlation between changes in American and European stock prices had risen from 0.4 in the mid-1990s to 0.8 in 2000. In other words, the movements of U.S. stocks could explain 80 percent of the movement of European stocks, compared with just 40 percent a few years earlier.

Is this a fluke? If not, the convergence has two important implications for investors: First, geographic diversification won't offer much protection against volatility. In a year in which U.S. stocks are down sharply, foreign stocks will likely be down sharply as well. Second, the old "foreign" and "domestic" categories for companies themselves are becoming far less meaningful.

After all, how do you characterize a company like Canon, Inc., which sold $26 billion worth of business machines and cameras in 2000? Canon is based in Tokyo, but it sells only 29 percent of its products in Japan, 35 percent in Europe and 35 percent in the U.S., Canada and South America. Plants are in Japan, Europe, the U.S. and Southeast Asia, and foreign shareholders own 26 percent of Canon's stock, with about three-quarters of that in American hands.

An even more extreme case is Nokia, the cellular phone maker. In 1987, Nokia derived 40 percent of its revenues from its home country of Finland, 45 percent from the rest of Europe and only 15 percent from elsewhere in the world. But by 2000, sales had risen 12-fold, and only 2 percent of revenues came from Finland, 50 percent from the rest of Europe, 23 percent from Asia, 18 percent from the U.S. and 5 percent from the rest of the Americas. Even more dramatic was the change in Nokia's shareholder base. In 1994, only 15 percent of the company's stock was owned by Americans, with 60 percent held by Finns. By the end of 2000, those figures were almost precisely flipped, with 1.5 million Americans owning 55 percent of Nokia and 110,000 Finns owning 11 percent. Nokia's ADRs (American Depositary Receipts, which trade on U.S. exchanges and are a popular way to hold foreign shares) were the 10th most actively traded stock of any sort on the New York Stock Exchange in 2000, ahead of such giant U.S. firms as AT&T, ExxonMobil and Pfizer.

Or consider Unilever, the consumer-products company based in Rotterdam and London, which does business in 90 countries. One-third of Unilever's shareholders are American and one-fourth of its sales are generated in the U.S. with brand names such as Dove soap, Hellman's mayonnaise and Calvin Klein perfume. Is Unilever foreign? And what about Coca-Cola, which earned 68 percent of its profits in 2000 outside North America?

Mounting international mergers, the tendency of large companies to list their stocks on several global exchanges, and the increasingly free flow of capital have meant, as *The Economist* magazine recently put it, that "the health of a market's home economy may matter less than it used to." Then again, the health of that economy seems more and more tied to the health of other economies anyway with free trade and a global convergence of both political systems and corporate management styles. In the stock market, for better or worse, it's getting to be one world.

More and more, the managers of worldwide-stock funds don't make geographic distinctions. Jean-Marie Eveillard, the manager of First Eagle Sogen Global Fund, whose mandate allows the purchase of stocks and bonds anywhere on the planet, told me that "the differences between U.S. and non-U.S. companies are a lot less than they used to be." Not only are the businesses getting more similar in their global scope, but European and even Japanese companies are becoming more transparent for investors and more eager to please shareholders.

"I started in Paris 40 years ago," Eveillard said, "and I can tell you . . . a lot of progress has been made, at least for the large European and Japanese companies, or Asian in general, with public information. And in terms of availability of management to talk strategy with shareholders: With the Philipses and Unilevers and Bayers and Sonys and Matsushitas of this world, they are just as available as the General Electrics and Procter & Gambles."

Even managers of funds that specialize in U.S. stocks have been buying more international shares. You can hardly get more American than a fund called "American Funds Investment Co. of America" (the sixth-largest fund in the U.S.), but among its top 25 holdings are Royal Dutch Petroleum, Nokia and AstraZeneca, the global pharmaceutical house, formed in a merger between Swedish and British companies. Oppenheimer Total Return, another U.S.-stock fund, had, among its top 14 holdings, three foreign-based stocks: Tyco International, based in Bermuda with headquarters in London; News Corp., based in Australia; and Nortel, Canada. In mid-2001, the average U.S.-stock fund had 5 percent of its assets in foreign stocks.

Another phenomenon emerged in a study I undertook in late 2000 at the request of Citibank and the Organization for International Investment. Noting that foreign companies had been investing heavily in the U.S., opening plants, employing 6 million workers and pouring more than $300 billion in new capital a year into businesses here, we decided to look at the other side of the coin. First, we compiled a list of the 100 publicly traded non-U.S. companies that had the most sales in the U.S. through their American subsidiaries. The list, headed by DaimlerChrysler, Honda Motor Co. and BP, plc, included firms from 15 different countries in all business sectors. Then, we found the proportion of the parent company's stock that was owned by U.S. individual and institutional investors. The result: a remarkable 20 percent. Americans owned more than 30 percent of 22 of the companies, including Jefferson Smurfit of Ireland and the Netherlands, paper products; Invensys of Britain, construction; and Michelin of France, tires.

We called this group of companies the "Reciprocal 100" since they represented a two-way flow of capital: American investors bought foreign shares, and foreign companies invested in America. Next, we looked at the returns of the 100 stocks—67 of which traded as American Depository Receipts, easily accessible to investors on U.S. exchanges—from the end of 1995 through the end of 2000. Again, a surprise: the Reciprocal 100 returned 143 percent, compared with just 34 percent for the stocks of the Morgan Stanley Capital International (MSCI) World index, which does not include U.S. stocks, and 114 percent for the S&P 500. Do these stocks have something special that would justify such high returns? Perhaps it is their ability to operate beyond their borders, driven by the necessity of lacking the world's largest market but having to sell into it. At any rate, these companies, among them Sweden's Skandia (insurance), Germany's BASF (chemicals), France's fast-growing Vivendi (water utilities, media) and Japan's Sony (consumer electronics) should be attractive to superior investors, who should buy such stocks not because they are "foreign" but because they may be "best of breed," excellent firms within their own business sectors.

In fact, at a time when international diversification seems to mean so little, why own foreign stocks at all? No longer is it fool-ish to own an all-U.S. portfolio if domestic companies are what you know. But that kind of chauvinism can be dangerous in a new way. If you want an auto company in your portfolio, it makes little sense to look only at the two U.S. manufacters, GM and Ford. Broaden your search to Honda, DaimlerChrysler, Volkwagen and Toyota. And, even in a more globalized investing world, Japan may require special treatment. According to T. Rowe Price, Japan's correlation to the U.S. over the past 30 years has been only about half that of Europe, and, in recent years, there's been little change. So buying a few Japanese companies just because they are Japanese still seems a good idea.

What about emerging markets such as Latin America, Eastern Europe and Asian countries like India, Malaysia, Thailand and Singapore? They remain far less correlated to the U.S. than developed markets, but, again, you should pick companies, not countries. The key in choosing such stocks is something called corporate governance, the matter of shareholder-friendliness of companies that issue shares.

In early 2001, CLSA Global Emerging Markets, a Hong Kong–based subsidiary of Credit Lyonnais, the French financial giant, issued an extensive study of corporate governance in developing nations. It looked at 495 companies and examined 57 factors. Transparency (that is, the ease with which investors can figure out what is happening in the business) was a key element of the study, but the overall focus was on integrity and responsiveness to shareholders. CLSA gave high marks to firms that gave investors copious information, that stuck to a few core businesses and that were run for the benefit of small investors not managers or large owners.

"Corporate governance pays," the study concluded. Over the five preceding years, the total average return for the 100 largest companies across emerging markets was 388 percent, but the companies that finished in the top one-fourth of the CLSA survey for corporate governance returned an average of 988 percent.

The top-rated companies that were also recommended by CLSA as "buys" were, in order, Infosys (India), Singapore Airlines, CLP (Hong Kong), Singapore Press Holdings, Stanbic

(South Africa), TSMC (Taiwan), Nedcor (South Africa), Ambev (Brazil), Cemex (Mexico), ST Engineering (Sinagpore), Modelo (Mexico), Legend (China) and Embraer (Brazil). The surprise was that, even in markets known for a lack of transparency like India, Brazil, Hong Kong and Mexico, some companies stand out as offering shareholders a fair deal. (Cemex, by the way, is a good example of a Reciprocal 100-style company, though just a little too small to make the cut. It now sells as much cement in the U.S. as in Mexico, and about half its shares trade here as ADRs.) The fact is that, whatever a nation's laws, honest management shapes companies.

The highest-scoring company, Infosys Technologies, Ltd., is a consulting and software firm with a market capitalization of $10 billion. Infosys is based in Bangalore, India, and its shares are traded in the U.S. as ADRs. Its website (www.inf.com) is a model of the high-information, low-hype style, and its chairman and CEO, N.R. Narayana Murthy, who gave the 2001 commencement address at the Wharton School of the University of Pennsylvania, has the right idea about corporate governance: "The primary purpose of corporate leadership is to create wealth legally and ethically. . . . The *raison d'être* of every corporate body is to ensure predictability, sustainability and profitability of revenues year after year."

A company like Infosys should be judged against other U.S. software firms, not against Indian breweries or banks, the old style of choosing foreign stocks. The point is that, while chauvinism may now be acceptable in portfolio-building, a superior investor keeps an open mind about companies based in other parts of the world. After all, as Price's research department notes, none of the 10 largest steel companies, electronics companies or appliance companies is based in the United States. In 1970, U.S. stocks represented two-thirds of the world's market capitalization; in 2000, the figure was just shy of half.

But then again, you couldn't be a parochial investor if you wanted to be. Nearly all the world's great companies—General Electric and Siemens, Diageo and McDonald's, Microsoft and

SAP—are global in sales, employees and shareholders. The only drawback is that, paradoxically, a smaller world for businesses is a more volatile world for stocks. It's not as easy as it used to be to dampen that volatility just by owning foreign—or should I write "foreign"?—markets.

CHAPTER THIRTY-FIVE

DON'T INVEST IN THINGS. INVEST IN BRAINS.

BETWEEN 1978 AND 1980, while the price of an ounce of gold was quadrupling to $800 and silver was soaring from $5 to $80, I figured it was my constitutional right as a red-blooded American in my early thirties to speculate (I called it "invest") in precious metals. My own belief was that these metals were going to keep rising, but my preferred method of speculation was not to buy futures—that is, pay a small amount now for delivery of a load of gold several months down the road—but instead to purchase "call" options on the stocks of mining companies. Both approaches use leverage to boost profits but also losses. I knew that with futures, I could end up losing more than my initial investment (the price could fall so rapidly that I would not be able to "cover," or get out of my obligation) while with options I would merely see my investment fall to zero, at worst.

The first few options I bought were in Homestake Mining, a San Francisco–based gold producer with a rich history. I can't remember the prices, but in mid-2001, for 50 cents, you could buy an option, that is, the right, to purchase one share of Homestake in January 2002 at a price of $10. Shares of Homestake in June 2001 were trading at $7, so essentially you were betting that within six months the stock price would rise by at least $3 (or more than 40 percent). If it did not, your option would expire worthless. But if the price went to, say, $12, your 50-cent investment would produce $1.50 in profits ($12 − $10 = $2; then subtract the 50 cents).

I do remember that my first investment in options started as a big success. With millions of ounces of proven reserves, Homestake was zooming upward with the price of gold. I quickly doubled my money, and decided to sell half of my options to be sure that I would preserve my principal. That was a good move, since the rest of my options crashed to zero by expiration. I learned a quick lesson: investing in gold-stock options, like investing in options of any sort, was a sucker's game. Leverage makes volatility extreme. It is impossible to know when to get out. You are whipsawed as prices plummet, then rise, then plummet, then rise. That's their nature, and it's why superior investors simply buy good companies and hold them for the long term. Finally, options and futures investing involves lots of trading and lots of commissions. Amateurs almost never win.

But what about gold stocks alone? Or, more broadly, what about investing in companies whose livelihood is tied to their ownership of precious metals, or natural resources of any sort? That's a longer and more interesting story, although the conclusion is much the same.

During the first half of 2001, while stocks around the world were losing about one-tenth of their value, one glittering sector was rising sharply: precious metals. Newmont Mining was up 22 percent in six months; AngloGold, Ltd., a South African company whose American Depositary Shares trade on the New York Stock Exchange, was up 21 percent; and Homestake jumped an incredible 60 percent.

Meanwhile, at a time when most growth-fund managers were thrilled to limit their losses for the first half to 5 percent, mutual funds that specialize in precious metals, including Fidelity Select Gold, Vanguard Precious Metals and Franklin Gold and

Precious Metals, were scoring double-digit gains, and four precious-metals funds (including USAA Gold) made the *New York Times* list of the top 10 mutual funds of all sorts for the 12 months ending June 30, 2001.

It wasn't just gold and silver miners that were doing so well. Companies that specialized in extracting, harvesting, collecting or refining almost any commodity were thriving. "Basic resources" ranked second, behind autos, in stock performance among the 18 global sectors tracked by Dow Jones.

It was a time when many investors were kicking themselves because they didn't have precious metals or other commodity stocks in their stock portfolios.

But I was not among the self-flagellants. Over the years, I have grown to loathe commodity stocks, especially gold and silver. There is not the slightest reason to own them. In the past, there might have been a minor justification for buying such companies, or the metals themselves, as a hedge against inflation, but the Treasury Inflation Protection bonds that made their debut in the late 1990s (see Chapter 46) work much better, guaranteeing a real interest rate of 3 percent to 4 percent annually plus the increase in the Consumer Price Index.

There is a simple reason to stay away from gold stocks and their ilk. When you buy them, you are betting on commodities, on things. When you buy shares in a more conventional software firm or retailer, on the other hand, you are betting on people or, more precisely, on the human imagination, and that's the force that has powered the world economy for the past two centuries. Gold, silver and copper have been around forever, but it is only human capital, unleashed in a society that values competition and property rights, that creates true widespread wealth.

A quarter-century ago, some economists were arguing that commodities—gold, oil, water, copper, grains—were inevitably growing scarcer. Their prices would rise as the population put more strain on the limited supply, and, eventually, many of these commodities would be used up, disappear. That did not happen. Instead, in continuous efforts to cut costs, businesses have brought better management and better technology to bear, replacing some of what they used to require from mines, fields and farms. Plastics, synthetic fibers, glass wires, silicon, food flavorings and more—these have served to drive down the prices of commodities.

Gold was $442 an ounce in June 1981; it was $271 an ounce 20 years later. Silver dropped over the same period from $9.65 an ounce to $4.43; soybeans, from $7.07 a bushel to $4.38. And those figures don't even count inflation, which depleted the dollar to about one-third its 1981 value, so an ounce of silver in 2001 could buy only one-sixth what it could 20 years earlier. If you think I am cheating by using these commodities over an awful time period, then consider the more recent experience of copper. It went from $1.03 a pound in June 1991, to $1.38 in June 1996 (its 15-year peak) to 66 cents in September 2001—less than half its price, adjusted for inflation, of 10 years earlier.

While it's true that the human mind can do wonders when applied to problems like extracting and refining gold in the least-costly way, the prices of precious-metals companies have, despite the 2001 blip, been plummeting. For the five years ending with the first half of 2001, Homestake, one of the best-run mining firms (and the object of a takeover bid in June 2001), fell 53 percent; ASA, Ltd., the South Africa-based gold-stock holding company, dropped 43 percent; and Placer Dome, the Vancouver-based gold, silver and copper company, fell 57 percent. By comparison, the typical U.S. stock roughly doubled over this period.

Still not convinced? Take a look at mutual funds, run by experts who are supposed to be adept at finding the best companies for their shareholders. Over the 10 years ending in mid-2001, the average precious-metals fund fell 5.5 percent annually—a performance that trailed the S&P 500 benchmark by an unbelievable 20 percentage points (a year!). Vanguard Gold and Precious Metals Fund, probably the best of the lot, returned an annual average of a little under 1 percent over the period. More precisely, an investment of $10,000 in the fund in 1991 became $10,800 in 2001. A modest 5 percent savings account, compounded annually, would have turned $10,000 into $16,300. And $10,000 in an S&P index fund would have become $40,500.

Even natural-resource funds (broadly defined to include ones that own oil retailers, aluminum producers and pipeline companies) trailed the S&P by at least four percentage points, on average, over the past five-, 10- and 15-year periods. I can tolerate good natural-resource companies in a portfolio, but they have to be exceptionally well-managed—like Alcoa under Paul O'Neill (later, Treasury Secretary), who led the world's largest aluminum producer to earnings of $1.5 billion in 2000, compared to $555 million in 1996. Over the five years through mid-2001, Alcoa stock jumped 140 percent, including dividends. But Alcoa is the exception. Profits for competitor Alcan have been flat, and the stock returned a pittance for the five years ending in June 2001; during that time, shares of Toronto-based Inco, Ltd., the world's largest nickel producer, fell by more than half while those of Phelps Dodge, the largest copper producer (with interests in chemicals and wire, too), dropped by one-third.

Worst of all is the ultimate commodity stock: Freeport-McMoRan Copper & Gold. Shares in this New Orleans-based company dropped from $36 in 1996 to a low of $7 in 2000 as sales fell slightly and profits dropped by two-thirds. For the first six months of 2001, Freeport rallied 63 percent to $14, but I don't feel bad about missing the run-up. In fact, I would be embarrassed to have participated. Cheap commodities stocks are not a bargain-hunter's paradise. Their prices have fallen for a reason: things mean less and less as people get smarter, trade increases and technology burgeons.

I am not saying that no one can make money in commodities or commodity stocks. After all, Warren Buffett apparently made a score in silver in 1997–98, when the price bounced from $4.38 an ounce to $6.69 to $4.92. I thought it was a silly use of Berkshire Hathaway's capital, but who am I to question the Master? Be warned, however: Don't try this at home. Timing commodity moves is nearly impossible for small investors and why even attempt it? History shows that a basket of solid U.S. companies returns an annual average of 11 percent a year. With precious metals, the long-term returns have been negative. Yes, there are positive stretches, but you will never be able to guess them with the slightest consistency.

Take 2001. Commodity stocks rallied for no good reason, except perhaps that they were so low and that some investors anticipated an economic revival later in the year. Commodities themselves have trended flat to down. Gold itself ended 1998 at $291 an ounce; 1999 at $284 an ounce; and 2000 at $271. That's exactly where it ended the first half of 2001, as well. Gold rose only slightly after the terrorist attacks in the U.S. in the fall of 2001. It's not the safe haven it once was.

The question that the precious-metals' and natural resources' investor must ask is this: Do you want to put your trust in things or brains? Things are fine in a period of rampant inflation or in an economy where brains aren't free to do their work because of excessive regulation, high taxes or cartels. But at least as far as the eye can see, brains have things beat by a mile.

CHAPTER THIRTY-SIX

DO DRUGS

IF YOU COULD INVEST in only one sector of the stock market, which would it be? I have a swift and emphatic answer: pharmaceuticals. Every stock portfolio should do drugs.

Developing and selling prescription pharmaceuticals is the best business in the world. It's the ultimate information-technology industry, driven by super-fast computers that have cracked the code of the human genome. But even before the big genetic breakthroughs, drug stocks were a great place to put your money. From 1967 through 2000, they rose seven times faster than the stock market as a whole.

In mid 2001, the five giants of the industry—U.S.-based Pfizer, Johnson & Johnson and Merck & Co., Swiss-based Novartis and British-based GlaxoSmithKline—had a combined market capitalization of more than $600 billion, beautiful balance sheets, and enormous flows of cash (over $20 billion annually). Even when times are tough for other stocks, pharmaceuticals tend to thrive. For example, in 2000, a year when markets around the world suffered double-digit declines, drug stocks rose 27 percent. During the recession years 1990 and 1991, Eli Lily, to choose one example, boosted earnings a total of 50 percent.

A big advantage for skittish investors is that prices of drug stocks aren't very volatile. "Beta," a popular measure of volatility, indicates the extremes of the ups and downs of a stock in comparison to the U.S. market as a whole. A beta of 1.00 means that a stock is just as volatile, or risky, as the benchmark S&P 500 index. But in 2001 Merck registered a beta of just 0.53, meaning that it was 47 percent less volatile than the market. Pfizer had a beta of 0.67; Johnson & Johnson, 0.61. These are strikingly low. Microsoft had a 2001 beta of 1.77—or 77 percent *more* volatile than the market; General Electric, 1.13.

The reason for the low volatility is not hard to fathom: Drug companies tend to increase their earnings at a consistent rate since demand for their products does not wax and wane with the economy. People can't skimp on their heart medicine, no matter what is happening with GDP. So, take a look at this gorgeous record of earnings per share for Merck from 1994 through 2000: $1.19, $1.35, $1.60, $1.92, $2.15, $2.45, $2.90. Earnings for 2001 were projected to be $3.20—another double-digit percentage increase despite a worldwide economic slowdown.

The sales numbers for drug companies are astonishing. Pfizer is famous for Viagra, the anti-impotence drug, but its biggest seller is actually Lipitor, which lowers cholesterol. In 2000, Lipitor sales rose 30 percent to an estimated $5 billion— twice the revenues of the entire Starbucks chain and roughly the same as the sales of the Washington Post Co. and Dow Jones & Co., publisher of the *Wall Street Journal,* combined. Norvasc (for cardiovascular illness) and Zoloft (an antidepressant) added another $5 billion, so that these three drugs alone accounted for more sales than Microsoft registered for all of its Windows operating systems, server applications and Internet products.

Drug companies not only pull in huge revenues, they also drop a big chunk of those sales down to the bottom line. In 2000, Pfizer earned 20 cents in profits, after taxes, on every dollar of revenue. (During the past decade, the most General Motors earned annually was 4 cents on the dollar; even Dow

Jones, in a profitable media niche, earned only 13 cents, a record, in 2000.) Why do drug companies perform so well? First, they enjoy a business with low marginal costs (it's not very expensive to roll another Prozac pill off the assembly line as opposed to, say, another Chevrolet) and broad moats, or barriers to competition, thanks to patents (see Chapter 8). On the other hand, pharmaceutical companies need to spend massive sums to develop new products. It costs an average of $350 million to bring a single drug to market and while that's a lot of dough, it's another impediment to upstart competitors.

But when a new drug does hit the market, it can produce fantastic revenues immediately. In its first full year, Vioxx, developed by Merck for osteoarthritis and acute pain, achieved $2.2 billion in sales.

What are the drawbacks of drug stocks? First, they are expensive compared with other stocks. In September 2001, for example, Pfizer was trading at a P/E of 36, or about 50 percent higher than the average S&P 500 stock, and that was a typical premium for the drug companies, at least since the mid 1990s. One of the worst reasons to postpone buying a good business is that the valuation of its shares is higher than that of a run-of-the-mill company. If you don't have pharmaceuticals in your portfolio, you should start adding them *now*, even if some analysts are saying they are too expensive. Philip Fisher, the author of the 1958 classic, *Common Stocks and Uncommon Profits* (see Chapter 7), put it well: "If the growth rate is so good that in another 10 years, the company might well have quadrupled, is it really of such concern whether at the moment the stock might or might not be 35 percent overpriced?"

As usual, Fisher was absolutely right. Again like all stocks, drug stocks tend to rise in price over the long term at the same rate as their earnings, and their earnings rise strongly and consistently. For example, Schering-Plough, maker of the allergy pill Claritin, has boosted its profits at an annual average rate of 18.5 percent for the past 10 years and was expected by the Value Line Investment Survey to keep increasing them at a 15.5 percent rate for 2001–06. If that pace continues, then Schering, a typical drug company, will more than quadruple its profits in the decade ahead. Even giant Glaxo, with nearly $30 billion in annual sales, was expected to double its earnings in about five years.

In addition, companies like Schering and Lily, maker of Prozac, the hugely popular anti-depressant, could be takeover candidates. The drug industry is consolidating. Merck bought Warner-Lambert, and Glaxo Wellcome merged with Smith-Kline Beecham. Pharmacia was created in 2000 from two firms, Pharmacia & Upjohn and Monsanto, best known for agricultural products. Novartis, maker of Voltaren, a popular arthritis drug, was formed in 1997 from the merger of two Swiss companies, Sandoz and Ciba-Geigy.

Novartis, a somewhat sleepy behemoth whose stock, nevertheless, rose 141 percent during the last five years of the 1990s, is a typical global drug company. The key to its success is not just what it is selling now but what it has in the pipeline, that is, in the final stages of approval by regulators. Pipeline drugs are usually revealed in annual reports of the companies themselves or research reports of analysts. In the case of Novartis, the hot pipeline item is the anti-leukemia drug Glivec. Meanwhile, Novartis has Diovan, a hypertension drug that is catching up to Merck's Cozaar and Hyzaar, which, with $1.7 billion in sales, are the industry leaders. (By the way, the two Merck drugs have been prescribed to over 10 million patients. That's how big the drug business is.) Novartis also has a cabinet-full of non-prescription favorites like ExLax, Maalox, and Theraflu.

Regulatory authorities in Europe and the U.S. have not tried to block such mergers of giants because the drug industry remains so fragmented. But, of course, politicians do get into the act in other ways, and their activity is the second drawback to buying drug stocks. In most of the world, pharmaceutical prices are strictly regulated by governments that foot the medical bills.

The U.S., which is by far the largest market for drugs, is different, though health insurance companies apply considerable pressure, and even President Bush was elected with a plan for the federal government to pay drug bills for seniors on Medicare. While such a subsidy might increase demand, drug companies fear it would lead to price controls, which afflict the medical-device industry, whose products like stents for propping open clogged arteries (like those of Bush's vice president, Dick Cheney) *are* covered by Medicare.

In addition, drug companies around the world are under attack for not providing, at lower cost, expensive drugs such as those that treat HIV and AIDS to poor countries in Africa and Latin America that can't afford them. The drug companies are not really worried about having to sell drugs cheaply to poverty-stricken sick people; in fact, they are eager to do so since marginal costs are low, and some sales are better than no sales. What worries the firms is the attack on their intellectual-property rights. The normal expiration of patent protections is bad enough (when Merck's Vasotec lost its marketing exclusivity in 2000, sales dropped by nearly half, and one reason Merck's P/E was a tame 21 in September 2001 was that it was losing patent protection on Prinivil, Pepcid, Mevacor and Primaxin in the year ahead), but if governments don't enforce patent laws, the drug companies become exposed to fierce competition—and, by the way, lose their incentive to innovate.

A still greater threat may be the availability of lower-cost drugs shipped from countries with price controls, like Canada or European nations, into the United States, the most lucrative market, made easily accessible by the Internet. (Even Glaxo gets 44 percent of its revenues from the U.S., more than from Europe, Africa and the Mideast combined.) Drug companies, however, have faced worse threats before and weathered them, and the election of a Republican president in November 2000 made their outlook brighter.

In general, superior investors view the continual political threats to the drug companies as a plus, not a minus. Without such worries, pharmaceutical stock prices would be considerably higher. Periodic scares allow investors to do drugs (in their portfolios, of course) at a bargain.

Investors looking for a more thrilling ride might want to turn to biotech stocks, which are much smaller, and thus riskier, than the more conventional pharmaceutical giants. As the Genentech annual report for 2000 warns: "The market prices for securities of biotechnology companies in general have been highly volatile and may continue to be highly volatile in the future." The largest biotech, Amgen, had sales of $3.4 billion in 2000, compared to $14 billion for American Home Products, a mid-sized company that sells over-the-counter favorites like Robitussin as well as prescription drugs. Some biotech firms have no approved drugs at all, but Genentech, a more established company, is marketing nine drugs for diseases such as non-Hodgkin's lymphoma, breast cancer and cystic fibrosis.

Many biotechs have worked out research deals with the bigger drug companies. When you own stocks like Merck, Bristol-Myers Squibb or Glaxo (maker of, among others, antidepressant Paxil, and HIV drug Ziagen), you are still taking advantage of the latest advances in genetic science. It's nearly impossible, however, for small investors to know which biotechs have drugs that are ready for prime time, so the best approach is to buy mutual funds or exchange-traded funds like Merrill Lynch's Biotech HOLDRs Trust, a broad portfolio that trades like an individual stock. With larger pharmaceuticals, you can do more picking and choosing. Another way to find good stocks is by checking the top holdings of good mutual funds. Investec Wired Index, one of my favorites, lists Aventis, S.A., a French pharmaceutical company that also makes herbicides and has a strong veterinary-drug line, as its second-largest holding and GlaxoSmithKline as its seventh. Or you can simply buy a specialized fund like Vanguard Health Care, eight of whose top 10 stocks are pharmaceuticals. But however you do it, do drugs.

IF YOU COULD BUY ONLY ONE STOCK

THE LAST CHAPTER answered the question for sectors, now, imagine you could buy only one stock to keep for the next 20 years. Which would it be? Again, the answer is not difficult: General Electric Co.

Why? General Electric is old, it's big, it's solid, it's well-run, and it's highly profitable.

The best gauge of a company's future is its past, and GE is probably the most successful firm in American history. It traces its beginnings to Thomas Alva Edison, whose Edison Electric Light Co., founded in 1878, was merged with Thomson-Houston Electric to create General Electric in 1892. As I noted earlier, GE is the only one of the 30 companies on the Dow Jones Industrial Average today to have been included in the first modern index in 1896.

After a few years in which usurpers like Cisco Systems held the crown, GE rebounded to become, once again, the king of the world's stock exchanges, with a market capitalization (that is, value according to investors) of $394 billion in September 2001, far ahead of number-two Microsoft at $298 billion and number-three ExxonMobil at $281 billion. In 2000, for the fourth straight year, GE was named *Fortune*'s "most admired company in America" and for the third straight year was recognized by the *Financial Times* as "the world's most respected company." *Business Week* ranked GE's board of directors number one, and the firm was first among the *Forbes* Super 100 companies.

GE in 2000 ranked fifth in revenues and third in profits among U.S. firms. In just three years, the company grew 50 percent. General Electric's return on invested capital is 27 percent. In other words, for every dollar plowed into the fertile fields of the company, an extra 27 cents springs up each year. For shareholders, between 1990 and 2000, GE stock produced an average annual return—price rise plus dividends—of 29 percent. In other words, an investor who put $10,000 into GE stock had $125,000 10 years later. (An investment in the basket of 500 stocks that comprise the benchmark Standard & Poor's index over this period rose to only $50,000.)

Other stocks, of course, have done even better. An investment of $10,000 in Home Depot in 1990 became $161,000 in 2000. Merrill Lynch rose to $311,000 and Dell Computer to an incredible $910,000. But these companies lack what GE has in abundance: variety. One share of GE alone provides nearly as much diversification, by industry sector, as a well-balanced stock portfolio. That's a major reason you can own just GE and feel more comfortable than with any other stock in the world.

GE's 340,000 employees in 100 countries work in such businesses as power systems (mainly making giant gas turbines, which generate electricity), aircraft engines and locomotives, plastics (like Lexan, used in CD-ROMs and DVDs), television (NBC in 2001 had seven of the top 10 prime-time shows for the key 18 to 49-year-old market; GE also owns CNBC, MSNBC and 13 broadcast stations in major markets), medical systems (like digital X-ray machines that detect breast cancer), capital services (global lending, with $370 billion in assets and earnings growing in double digits for past two decades), lighting and appliances. In fact, if they were separate businesses, 13 of GE's divisions would be large enough to make the *Fortune* 500 list. Jack Welch, who retired in September 2001 as GE's chief executive officer, required his subsidiaries to be number-one or number-two in their sector—and he got results.

Partly a result of this balance, GE tends to increase its profits with a consistency that few large companies can match. For example, the firm has boosted its earnings by at least 10 percent every year since 1992. Dividends have been paid every quarter since 1899 and have increased every year since 1975. They have been raised at a double-digit pace annually since 1991.

Those dividends are a big attraction to a one-stock-only buyer. They provide both stability and, if you need it, income. Think of it this way: An investment of $10,000 in GE stock in 1991 brought $340 in dividend checks that year. But by 2001, that initial investment was generating $1,280 in dividends—an annual return of nearly 13 percent in dividends alone. Welch, generally considered the top CEO in the world, stayed on in an effort to complete a $45 billion acquisition of Honeywell, a sort of junior-varsity version of GE itself, with a dominant role in aviation electronics, auto parts and home heating. But, in one of GE's rare failures, the merger was blocked by European antitrust regulators. If GE has any problem at all on the horizon, it is the same as Warren Buffett's with Berkshire Hathaway: trying to find investments large enough to matter. Honeywell was such an investment, and GE will have to look for others, or grow its own.

When Welch took over at GE, the company was much, much smaller. In 1981, his first year, the firm earned $1.5 billion on $25 billion in sales; in 2000, earnings were $13 billion on $130 billion in sales. GE pulled in more revenues than Merck, Sears Roebuck, Procter & Gamble and Gillette combined.

Welch appears to have a worthy successor in Jeffrey Immelt, who headed the company's Medical Systems division. Immelt, like other GE managers, has become adept at using the Internet for both buying and selling. Under his leadership, GE saved $1.6 billion by digitizing work processes and by conducting $14 billion in Web-based auctions with suppliers (a much higher volume than eBay), mainly using GE Global Exchange.

Meanwhile, according to an article in *Worth* magazine, GE was expected in 2001 to "sell at least $15 billion of its products and services over the Web. That's more than double the $7 billion it sold last year. By way of comparison, analysts project that Amazon.com's revenue will reach $3.4 billion in 2001, and Amazon is the largest Internet retailer. No wonder the trade publication *InternetWeek* named GE "business of the year" for 2000. Welch admits he was late to realize the importance of the Internet, not as an industry but as a tool. But he quickly caught on, and Immelt, whose Medical Systems division did more than one-fifth of its business on the Web, is pushing digital innovation even further.

As an investor, how do you analyze a company like GE? One place to start is the Value Line Investment Survey, available in most libraries and in a limited form online (Value Line gives full reports free on the 30 companies of the Dow: www.valueline.com). GE gets a top A++ rating from Value Line for financial strength and a perfect score (100) for earnings predictability and price growth persistence. By contrast, IBM, which also gets an A++ for financial strength, is rated only 35 on earnings and 70 on price growth. Value Line also forecasts that GE's earnings will grow for the next five years at a 14 percent average annual rate, a smidgen above the 13.5 percent rate for the previous five. In October 2001, GE was trading at a P/E of 27 and a P/B of 7. At its five-year high, GE's P/E was 49, and its P/B was 12.

No one knows how Immelt will perform or if a global economic slowdown will hurt GE (it could *help* by weakening competitors). But the company offers important lessons to investors. Share prices rose steadily from 1996 to 2000, climbing from $12 (adjusted for splits) to $60.50. Then the stock fell as the U.S. economy slowed, hitting $36 in the spring of 2001. A buying opportunity? It certainly looked that way for long-term investors. Within a month, the stock was back to $50. After the September

11 terror attacks, GE fell below $30, then jumped to $38 in a week.

GE usually trades at a price-to-earnings (P/E) ratio that is higher than the market as a whole—one-third higher in mid-2001 than the average S&P stock. But is GE one-third better than the average S&P company? Ask me a hard one.

Still, a company as big and diversified as GE is tied inextricably to the world economy. Value Line analyst John Kolter warns, "Because GE's employees can't control the economy, we see heightened downside risk should global growth slow. So, while our estimates reflect management's confidence, the risk seems greater than the potential rewards." That may be true in the short term. But in the long term, buying GE stock is the equivalent of partaking in the growth of the world economy, which is not a bad bet.

And GE should do *better* than the world economy. What's most impressive about General Electric is its general environment. Jack Welch likes to describe it as a "global learning company," which has adopted the best ideas from other firms "because 'we are boundaryless.'" As the annual report puts it, "Years ago Toyota taught us asset management. Wal-Mart introduced us to Quick Market Intelligence. AlliedSignal and Motorola got us started on our enormous Six Sigma initiative [a method for defining and improving quality]. More recently, Trilogy, Cisco and Oracle helped us begin the digitization of GE."

The company's true "core competency," says the report (available on GE's clear and inviting website—and a good site is a sign of imagination and excellence that offers a buying tip-off for potential investors), "is not manufacturing or services but the global recruiting and nurturing of the world's best people and the cultivation in them of an insatiable desire to learn." This is just the kind of attitude you want if you have to own just one stock for the next 20 years. Also, GE isn't slow and stodgy. Welch says he prizes informality. What does that mean? "At GE it's an atmosphere in which anyone can deliver a view, an idea, to anyone else, and it will be listened to and valued, regardless of the seniority of any party involved. Leaders today must be equally comfortable making a sales call or sitting in a boardroom. Informality is an operating philosophy as well as a cultural characteristic."

Of course, the truth is that you don't have to own just one stock. And you shouldn't. But every 30-stock portfolio should include General Electric.

CHAPTER THIRTY-EIGHT

THE INDUSTRY
TO BUY FOR THE
NEXT GENERATION

ONE WAY to make huge sums in the stock market is to figure out which industries and companies will be thriving 10, 20 or 30 years from now. That's not easy, of course, but consider the pay-off. Even as late as 1991, a prescient investor might have looked at the personal computer business and noted the favorable prospects of a certain Redmond, Wash., firm that produced systems software. At the time, Microsoft Corp. had sales of $2 billion and profits of $462 million, so it was no tiny company. But 10 years later, Microsoft's sales had risen 10-fold, its profits 20-fold, and its stock price—despite the Justice Department—30-fold.

But choosing stocks for the next generation is especially difficult. Choosing industries makes more sense. What are the likely success stories in the years ahead? With an aging population, health care, especially pharmaceuticals, looks especially attractive (see Chapter 36); energy should have a bright future; and some aspect of the Internet business will boom, though it's not clear whether the sweet spot will be software, hardware, telecommunications, or something that hasn't been invented yet. The problem is that all of these sectors are flush with excellent companies trading at relatively high prices. What about an industry that few investors are watching?

My candidate in this category is for-profit education. When I first became interested in the fledgling sector in 1995, I interviewed Michael Moe, who at the time headed the growth-company group at Lehman Brothers and was one of only a handful of analysts who followed education stocks. "The education market today reminds us of what the health care business looked like 10 to 15 years ago," Moe, who now has his own investment firm in San Francisco, told me.

In 2000, about $750 billion, or 8 percent of Gross Domestic Product, was spent on education in the U.S. alone, compared with $1.3 trillion on health care, but, most of the education money went to public kindergarten-through-12th-grade (K-12) schools, and much of the rest was spent on colleges and universities run by state and local governments or non-profit institutions. In 2001, the revenues of the major for-profit education firms (not including textbook companies) covered by the Value Line Investment Survey were only $4 billion, less than the sales for a single cholesterol-lowering drug.

But for contrarian investors, who like to travel places that few tourists have discovered, education has wonderful attractions. First, by any objective standard, the public schools have done a poor job. For example, from 1970 to 2000, spending per public-school student soared from $3,000 to $7,500 (in 1997–98 constant dollars), but test scores were flat or falling. Any private business that performed this way would have filed for Chapter 11 bankruptcy long ago. Government-run schools, however, have the advantage of being monopolies, or near-monopolies, supported by tax dollars.

Parents, business leaders and politicians are getting fed up, but the bad news is that they are still resistant to private solutions. The same reluctance, however, surfaced in health care when for-profit hospital chains sought to make the sector more efficient. People then would say, "You shouldn't make money off hospitals," just as they are now saying, "You shouldn't make money off a child's education." But, inevitably, it is the free market—the rough and tumble of competition and the joy of consumer choice—that will solve the education problem. And technology will help. Like the drug sector, education is a user of high-tech solutions developed by other, capital-intensive businesses. "The next killer application for the Internet is going to be education," is the way John Chambers, CEO of Cisco Systems, put it.

It's reassuring that Michael Milken, one of the most success-ful investors of the 1980s (he later spent time in prison for fed-eral securities violations), has recognized the potential of for-profit education. With his brother Lowell and Ron Packard, a former McKinsey executive, he started Knowledge Universe, a private holding company for several education firms, including a venture launched in 2001 called K12, headed by William Bennett, the former Education Secretary. K12 sells an online curriculum with families of home-schooled children (now 2 mil-lion strong) as its initial audience.

Will K12 succeed? There's no telling, but you can't buy the stock anyway. Even among listed companies, with for-profit edu-cation in its infancy, it's very difficult to pick winners and losers. As a result, the sector is perfect for a portfolio approach to invest-ing (a package of stocks in different education subsectors). The only drawback is that there are barely enough education stocks for a solid, diverse portfolio. In 2000, Merrill Lynch & Co., to which Michael Moe moved after leaving Lehman Brothers, put together the seminal volume on the subject, *The Knowledge Web*. It divided the field into four areas: services for K-12, for-profit uni-versities (online and off), corporate e-learning (a market that will grow from $1 billion in 1999 to an expected $11 billion in 2003), and human capital management (recruiting and developing talent—which is stretching the term "education," in my view).

Still in its venture stage, the K-12 sector is offering little more than red ink. There's a lot happening, but revenues aren't falling to the bottom line. The most conspicuous player is Edison Schools, founded in 1992 by the flamboyant entrepreneur Chris Whittle, who began with a plan for chain of mid-priced ($6,000 a year) private schools around the country. The plan changed, and Edison became a manager of public schools under contract mainly to big cities. Edison also launched charter schools, which are tax-funded but free of many of the regulatory and curriculum burdens of conventional public schools. By 2001, Edison was running 113 schools with 57,000 students and reaping $376 million in revenues but registering $38 million in losses. Profits were not expected until 2004 or so, and Edison stock, launched in 1999, was languishing in the fall of 2001 at the IPO price. It's not clear whether Edison has found a profitable model (the pioneer in this business, Education Alternatives, Inc., went through several iterations before going bankrupt), but it would be hard to leave it out of a for-profit education portfolio. Edison's problem at this point may be management talent. K12 (the company), by contrast, is chock full of it. Maybe a merger down the road?

The white-hot center of for-profit education, however, is worker-training. Leading firms are Education Management Corp., which runs media-arts, cooking and paralegal schools, and has been profitable ever since it went public in 1997, earning $28 million on $350 million in revenues in the most recent year; Learning Tree International, a smaller company that focuses on training information-technology professionals; ITT Educational Services, which serves 28,000 students in 70 technical institutes in 28 states; Career Education Corp., which owns the Katharine Gibbs Schools and InterContinental University and operates campuses in the U.S., Canada, Britain and the United Arab Emirates (exporting U.S. post-secondary education could turn out to be a huge business), earning $21 million in 2000 and $325 million in sales; and, most profitable of all, DeVry, Inc., with 50,000 students.

While DeVry is the largest company in the field, it's small by the standards of other industries, with annual revenues of $568 million, earnings of $58 million and a market cap of $2.2 billion, only slightly above small-cap status. But DeVry's earnings are projected to grow at 20 percent annually for at least the next five years. Run with an intense concentration on the bottom line,

DeVry has a huge advantage over government and non-profit schools that offer similar services, but it is able to take advantage of a government habit: raising price (in this case, tuition) by a little more than inflation, year after year. DeVry has a long history of asking industry recruiters what skills they want in their workers over the next few years and then tailoring their offerings to meet those demands. As a result, at Hughes Communications, the nation's largest satellite company, 22 of the 30 engineers reponsible for orbit maintenance are DeVry graduates.

Similar to DeVry but serving a more general audience of adults seeking bachelor's and graduate degrees is Apollo Group, whose stock I have owned for many years. Apollo, by mid-2001, had 111,000 students, about one-fifth of them enrolled in online programs. Apollo's primary brand name is University of Phoenix, with 56 campuses and 101 learning centers in 35 states and Canada. Like DeVry, Apollo is free of debt and well managed, and the stock has performed exceptionally since the company went public in December 1994, splitting six times and providing investors with a return of more than 4,000 percent in six years. But both DeVry and Apollo offer "a nice lesson in the benefits of value investing—buying stocks that are cheap relative to cash flow . . . and then holding them until they regain favor," according to Amey Stone in *Business Week Online*. In 1999, DeVry lost 40 percent of its value on concerns that enrollment was slowing (a false alarm) and Apollo fell nearly by half for no good reason at all. Then, the next year, in a process I described in Chapter 32, these value stocks turned into growth stocks.

Apollo is the best of breed in for-profit education. It was started in 1973 by John Sperling, a Ph.D. who was once a labor leader. Sperling told me a few years ago that he has his sights set on the K-12 sector, if he can figure out how to make money there. In the meantime, the company is doing very, very well. For 12 months ending in mid 2001, Apollo earned $84 million on $673 million in revenues, returning a hefty 27 percent on shareholders' equity. The stock, which went public in 1994 at a split-adjusted $1.09, was trading at $37 in September 2001. Growth is expected in same range as DeVry, which means sales could hit $5 billion within 10 years. With a market cap of $4.3 billion, Apollo is the biggest fish in what is now a small pond.

Other profitable education companies include Bright Horizons Family Solutions, which offers childcare and early education for employees at workplaces, with the firms it serves (like Cisco Systems) laying out the initial capital; Renaissance Learning, a leader in the highly fragmented K-12 software sector; and, perhaps most intriguing of all, Sylvan Learning Systems, which has diversified broadly. Sylvan, whose stock soared in the mid-1990s, then tanked due to growing pains in the late 1990s, now runs after-school tutoring centers, teacher training programs, and universities (plus a Swiss hotel management school) abroad. It has also entered the education-by-Internet business. Several smaller, publicly traded firms may have a bright future, but all of them are now losing money: Riverdeep Group, an Ireland-based company that sells K-12 software, and Saba, Digitalthink and Skillsoft, all of which have corporations manage their employee training.

Finally, some of the best education companies are subsidiaries of larger firms. The Washington Post Co. owns Stanley H. Kaplan Educational Centers, which prepares students for college-entrance and licensing exams. Pearson, plc, the British-based conglomerate that also owns the *Financial Times* and Penguin Books, has a huge and growing education business that includes Internet-distributed curriculum, teacher-training and textbooks. Selling textbooks, in fact, was for decades the only significant route to profits in K-12 education. Most textbook publishers—including Harcourt General, which was purchased by the Dutch firm Reed Elsevier, McGraw-Hill, which also own *Business Week,* and Houghton Mifflin, object of a takeover by the French firm Vivendi—sell to the general public as well. The most attractive of these companies for investors building education-stock portfolios may be Scholastic Corp., which sells children's books (the *Harry Potter* series), magazines, and multimedia services. Scholastic's sales exceed $2 billion (it sells 250 million books a year), but its market cap is only about one-third that of Apollo.

At this point in history, I can't imagine a diversified 20-stock core portfolio that does not include at least one education stock. Better yet, build a 10-stock sub-portfolio of education stocks alone. So far, no mutual fund or ETF offers an education portfolio, but that's fine. Take advantage of the early days while no one is paying attention.

BORING IS BEAUTIFUL

WHEN IT COMES TO STOCKS, boring can be better than exciting. Superior investors lean toward companies in mind-numbingly simple businesses that churn out cash for their investors year after year.

Consider Fastenal Co., a firm based in Winona, Minnesota, that sells "threaded fasteners" (a euphemism for screws) and other industrial and construction supplies in small stores in 48 states and Canada. The company has increased its profits every year since it went public in 1987, and, after taxes, it has earned at least 10 cents annually on every dollar in sales—an amazing rate for a retailer. (Home Depot, Inc., the powerhouse in this business, earns less than six cents on the dollar.)

An investment of $1,000 in Fastenal stock in 1990 was worth $20,000 in 10 years. Earnings increased at a 30 percent annual rate during the 1990s and, in 2001, the Value Line Investment Survey projected 18 percent yearly growth through 2006. Fastenal, whose outstanding stock in mid-2001 was worth $2.3 billion, is either a large small-cap stock or a small mid-cap. More important, it has no debt. If Fastenal were a high-tech company, it would probably trade at a price-to-earnings ratio of 50, but, since it's in the distinctly unfashionable business of selling nuts, bolts and janitorial supplies, its P/E has generally been in the mid-20s, extremely reasonable for a company growing so quickly. (In October 2001, the P/E was a mere 9.)

I became fascinated with Fastenal and other non-sexy stocks when, a few years ago, I stumbled onto a research service called LJR Great Lakes Review, run by a mild-mannered genius named Elliott Schlang in Cleveland. I wrote about Schlang in *Dow 36,000,* focusing on a boring stock called Tootsie Roll Industries, maker of those little chocolate logs. I fell in love with Tootsie Roll, and I like it even better now. Sales have increased for 24 consecutive years and profits for 19. Tootsie Roll has not missed paying a cash dividend since 1944, and it has a gorgeous balance sheet with (as of 2000) $132 million in cash and just $8 million in debt.

Like Fastenal, Tootsie Roll flies below Wall Street's radar screen, which means that you have to be patient. Every few years, investors wake up, realize what a great company it is, and bid up the stock price sharply.

Besides being in boring businesses, Fastenal and Tootsie Roll have other characteristics that produce big gains for investors over time:

- They have built strong brand names to distinguish themselves from their competitors. They're known for quality, not merely for low prices.

- They have consistently increased their earnings and sales, even in tough economic times (during the two recession years of 1990 and 1991, Fastenal increased its earnings per share by more than 60 percent).

- Top managers own a big chunk of the shares, giving them a major incentive to keep the value high, not for the short term (a problem for companies that issue stock options to executives) but for the long haul. Fastenal's officers and directors own 26 percent of the stock; Janus Capital, the mutual-fund house, 14 percent.

- They have strong balance sheets, with low or no debt.

- **They have low capital-spending requirements, so they generate lots of cash for their shareholders.**

- **They show every sign of being able to last another 50 years or more.**

And the good thing about boring stocks is that they abound. Consider Church & Dwight, the world's largest producer of sodium bicarbonate and maker of Arm & Hammer baking soda, toothpaste, gum and laundry detergent. From 1995 to 2000, the company boosted its earnings from 26 cents a share to $1.23. It has a powerful brand name, a high return on equity (that is, profits as a percentage of the shareholders' investment) and strong cash flow. Or what about La-Z-Boy, one of Schlang's favorites, with the best-recognized brand name in the furniture industry? In a rocky business, La-Z-Boy has managed to increase its dividend for the past 20 years in a row and its earnings for the past 12. It has relatively low debt, and sales and profits that are both rising at double-digit rates. Another consistent, boring performer is Alberto-Culver, maker of VO5 and other hair products, with the Lavin family owning about one-fifth of the stock. Shares quadrupled in price during the 1990s, and dividends rose from 9 cents a share to 29 cents, but, for a company with consistent 10 percent annual growth, the P/E remains modest.

Many boring companies are small- and mid-caps. Analysts just can't be bothered with them, which is fine for long-term investors. Redchip Review, a small-cap advisory service, cites stocks like Cascade Bancorp, a fast-growing bank headquartered in Bend, Ore. (a boring but beautiful place with "bore" in its name), whose shares tripled in price between mid-1996 and mid-2001 but was still trading at a low P/E and paying a decent dividend. Regional banking is one of the best boring businesses of all time. In an age of mega-banks, regionals still retain loyal customers who are more interested in quality and comfort than in price.

Another small ($400 million market cap), well-run, unnoticed company is Thomas Industries, who makes (no, not English

Muffins) compressors and vacuum pumps. Earnings have risen every year from 1992 to 2000, growing from 13 cents to $1.86. Debt is minuscule. Danaher Corp., which makes mechanics' hand tools, leak-detection sensors and other unsexy items, is an $8 billion mid-cap with a 10-year average annual earnings growth rate of 13 percent and a modest P/E that's generally in the mid-20s. Profits have risen impressively and annually since 1991, and one-third of the stock is owned by officers and directors. When the going gets tough, it's nice to have stocks like Thomas and Danaher in your portfolio. From mid-2000 to mid-2001, Thomas's price rose by one-half; Danaher's, by one-quarter. Meanwhile, the S&P was *losing* nearly one-fifth of its value.

Boring can be big as well. I would put Walgreen Co. (market cap in September 2001: $35 billion), the magnificently unflashy drug chain that doubles its earnings every five years or so, in that category. And what about United Parcel Service (market cap: $60 billion), the world's largest air-and-ground package delivery carrier, with operations in 200 countries through 150,000 trucks and 570 airplanes? UPS stock languished in the two years after the company went public in 1999, but to long-term investors that's all to the good. Revenues have risen nearly 50 percent, to well over $30 billion, in five years. And the uniforms on the company's 344,000 employees are perfect for lovers of the boring: unobtrusive brown.

CHAPTER FORTY

SMALL-CAPS ARE
BIG WINNERS

EVERY PORTFOLIO HAS TO HAVE small-cap stocks, but, from time to time, investors need to be reminded of that fact. Every few years, they become convinced that small-caps are dead. The reasons vary. Take your pick: Big companies with strong brand names, aided by the ubiquity of the Internet, will squash firms no one has heard of. Small stocks aren't liquid enough, so big institutions shun them. As the economy grows more global, small companies without the resources to sell their products or outsource their production abroad will suffer. I could go on.

You can always think up reasons why small companies are at a disadvantage to large (or vice versa: e.g., large companies aren't as nimble in a New Economy where quick decisions are everything), but history shows that, across a wide variety of conditions, both little and big can do well. What is important to understand, however, is that small-caps and large-caps behave differently in the market. As a result, whenever investors begin grousing about small-caps, the Secret Code interprets the whining as a good buy signal. It means that small-cap prices are having one of their regular swoons, but they will quickly wake up.

For reasons not entirely clear, small-caps and large-caps seem to move in cycles; first, one dominates, then the other. For example, small-caps beat large-caps in every year from 1974 to 1983; then, large-caps beat small-caps in six of the next seven years; then, small-caps beat large-caps for the next four years in a row; then, large-caps began the reign that so many investors found discouraging, whipping small-caps from 1995 to 1998 by an annual average of 14 percentage points. But things changed quickly: Small-caps beat large-caps in 1999 and 2000 and were ahead by 10 percentage points through mid-2001.

In 1998, large-caps gained 29 percent while small-caps fell 7 percent, a nearly unprecedented difference. The common explanation was illiquidity. Since they are not traded in such heavy volume as, say, General Electric or Coca-Cola, small-cap stocks are harder to sell in large lots. So, when big institutions like mutual funds (which own a bigger and bigger chunk of the total stock market) decide to dump small-caps, they have to lower the prices to find buyers, less often a necessity with large-caps.

Of course, liquidity works both ways. When institutions buy small-caps, they push prices up more than they would with large-caps. Institutions often behave like sheep, nearly all of them moving first in one direction, then the other. So when they sour on small-caps, the prices go down a lot; when they change their minds (usually when small-caps become irresistibly cheap), the prices go up a lot.

This is another way of saying that small-caps are more volatile than large-caps. For example, a study by Ibbotson Associates divided all listed U.S. stocks into 10 equal groups, or deciles, according to the size of their market caps. The study found that, between 1926 and 2000, stocks in the two smallest-cap deciles were twice as volatile, or risky, as stocks in the two largest-cap deciles. The small-caps had a standard deviation of 42 percent, meaning that, in two-thirds of all years, they produced returns roughly between minus-30 percent and plus-54 percent. Whew! By another measurement of risk, the largest stocks had a beta of 0.98, meaning they were 2 percent less volatile than the market as a whole, but the smallest stocks had a beta of 1.38, meaning they were 38 percent more volatile than the market.

There's a rule in investing that higher risk means higher returns. If you agree to buy a riskier asset, then your chances of a big loss in any year are greater, but you are compensated with bigger gains over time. That's true as well with small-cap stocks. From 1926 to 2000, they returned an annual average of 12.4 percent, compared with 11 percent for large-caps. That apparently small difference mounts up. If you had put $1,000 into the largest-cap decile of stocks in 1926, you would have $1.6 million at the end of 2000; but if you had put $1,000 into the smallest-cap decile, you would have had $10.3 million.

Another rule is that, if you hold a basket of stocks long enough, the risk will dissipate. That's true in spades with small-caps. Over the past three-quarters of a century, the worst single year for small-caps was a loss of 58 percent (in 1937), compared with a loss of 43 percent in the worst year for large caps. But the worst 20-year period for small-caps produced an average annual *gain* of 5.7 percent, compared with a gain of 3.1 percent for large-caps.

Three points, then, about small-caps:

- **They're more risky than large-caps, but they return more, too.**
- **Since their performance diverges, year to year, from that of large-caps, they provide excellent balance for a portfolio. In other words, large- and small-caps lack correlation, so, if you own both, your yearly returns are smoothed out.**
- **Although small-caps move in cycles, you should not be tempted to guess when a new cycle will begin or the current cycle will end. Very simply, small-caps should be a permanent part of your portfolio.**

Another part of the small-cap phenomenon is that the sector does especially well as the U.S. economy emerges from recessions. As a letter to clients of T. Rowe Price put it, "While the overall market has rebounded as economic conditions improved . . . small-company stocks have enjoyed especially vigorous recoveries." In the 12 months following each of the nine post–World

War II recessions, small-cap stocks rose an average of 38 percent, and they beat large-caps in every one of the nine recoveries.

But the bad news about small-cap stocks is that they are not as easy to choose as brand-name large-caps. It may be harder to understand their niche businesses, and they are followed by fewer analysts, so professional help is more difficult to find. As a result, I prefer holding small-caps in mutual funds with good track records like Meridian Value, Wasatch Micro-Cap and Core Growth, AIM Small-Cap Growth, Armada Small-Cap Value and State Street Research Aurora. As for balancing a portfolio, the Armada fund, for example, gained 33 percent in 2000, a year when large-cap fund managers were happy to escape with 10 percent losses.

Believe me, you won't recognize many of the companies that these funds have managed to find. Armada's widely diversified portfolio is led by stocks such as Cooper Cos., a fast-growing maker of contact lenses and devices for gynecologic surgery; Gables Residential Trust, an Atlanta-based apartment REIT; and Arch Coal, which mines and transports bituminous. Or try these even smaller firms from the top of Wasatch Micro's list: Corvel Corp. (market cap: $260 million), which monitors service given to insurance claimants; Resources Connection ($590 million), which provides businesses with financial and technical workers on a project basis; and National Dentex ($75 million), maker of dentures, crowns and bridges, whose price rose by one-third for the year ending June 30, 2001, but was only trading at the time at a P/E of 13. Another approach is to own larger small-caps. Fidelity Low-Priced Stock fund, which has performed brilliantly, owns some fine companies in the $2 billion market-cap range: Outback Steakhouse at a P/E of 15 in September 2001; Ross Stores, a well-run retailer at a P/S of 0.8; and homebuilder D. R. Horton at a P/E of 8.

The truth is, every portfolio needs small-caps, and, even though they run in cycles, it's never a good idea to time your purchases in an effort to catch an investing wave. Instead, hold between 10 percent and 25 percent of your portfolio in smaller-company stocks for the long term, riding out the inevitable ups and downs but enjoying, in the end, returns greater than the market as a whole typically produces while, at the same time, balancing your large-caps. Quite a deal.

TECHNOLOGY IS A SECTOR, NOT A RETIREMENT PLAN

IN THE SPRING OF 2000, high-tech stocks, which had been riding high for five years, suddenly collapsed. The catalyst may have been a decision by the Justice Department to push for a breakup of the largest and most successful of the technology companies, Microsoft, which had soared from $14 (adjusted for splits) in May 1996 to $119 three and a half years later, but plummeted by year's end to $43. Or, the crash could merely have been the result of lots of investors realizing at the same time that many of the high-tech companies on which they had pinned their hopes were not going to make it as businesses.

The Nasdaq Composite Index, which in the past had simply been an index of smaller companies but had come to be dominated by tech stocks, fell by two-thirds over 12 months. In the past, Internet stocks had been indulged. They weren't making profits, but investors were content to wait. But in the spring of 2000, with an economic slowdown looming, investors lost patience. A typical e-commerce stock, Priceline.com (which I picked on earlier in this book, but which deserves it), eventually dropped from $162 to $1.06. CNET Networks, which provides content for other sites and offers advice to consumers buying tech equipment on its own, fell from $79.90 to $3.46. CMGI, a holding company for other Internet firms, soared from $1.70 in 1998 to $163.50 in the spring of 2000, then back down to $1.70 again. There was blood on the Street.

Many small investors were devastated by these declines. They had loaded up on high-flying high-tech stocks, letting them dominate their portfolios. Some had bought on margin, borrowing so that they could buy twice as many shares as their capital would normally allow. If the price of a stock doubled, they would make four times their money. If the price fell by half (as that of many tech stocks did), they were wiped out. These margin buyers could not wait out the decline; they had to put up more cash or be sold out of their positions. (Don't buy on margin; see Chapter 19.)

Unfortunately, the lesson many investors learned from their tech experience was to get out of the stock market entirely. In early 2001, I appeared on ABC's *Nightline* with Ted Koppel to talk about something that practically broke my heart. In 1999, a *Nightline* crew had visited Providence, R.I., to see how the boom in the stock market had touched average folks. Everyone, from the mayor's errand runner to a lobsterman to a doctor, seemed to be heavily invested in high-tech stocks. Now, admittedly, this was no scientific sample, and no one explicitly stated how much money he had in the market, but it was a compelling story of Main Street going to Wall Street and getting fleeced. Nearly two years later, reporter John Donvan went back to Providence to visit these same investors. The results were sad, indeed.

In 1999, Donvan interviewed a waitress named Rosie Cioe, who told him, "I have doubled my initial investment . . . in less than a year."

At the time, said Donvan, Rosie could really see that day coming when she would be wealthy enough to hang up the apron for good.

Alas, on his follow-up visit, he found that Rosie's "entire paper profits from investing were wiped out last year." She had bought stocks like Dell Computer and America Online. Now, where does she put her money?

"In the bank in a short-term CD," she replied.

"This is back to grandma-type investing, then?" asked Donvan.

"Well," Rosie said, "grandma had some good ideas."

Undoubtedly, grandma did. But bailing out of the stock market when the prices of good companies like Dell and AOL have fallen is not one of them. (Dell fell from $55 to a low of $16; AOL, which merged with Time Warner in January 2001, peaked at $96, fell to $27.)

The real lesson of the high-tech debacle is that diversification is a necessity. Technology is a sector, not a retirement plan. And, despite what you hear, it is not that different from any other sector: By itself, over the short term, it is highly volatile, but so are the oil-service sector and the health-provider sector and practically any industry you can name.

In May 2001, I reviewed the performance of various sectors, using Dow Jones statistics, over the previous 12 months. During this period, the Dow Jones Industrial Average itself (30 stocks that were picked to reflect the entire U.S. economy) was not particularly volatile. Its high was 11,311; its low was 9389, or just 17 percent below the peak. (Think of an individual stock that fluctuates during the course of a year between $50 and $60 a share and you have the picture.)

But now consider the volatility of individual sectors. For high-tech communications equipment (the tech sector that saw the biggest price swings), the index high was 2515; the low, 560. So the low was 78 percent below the high. *That's* volatile! But look at coal stocks: index high, 123; low, 30. The low in this case was 76 percent below the high. For the industrial equipment sector, the difference between high and low was 63 percent; for securities brokers, 55 percent; entertainment stocks, 43 percent; water utilities, 48 percent; clothing and fabrics, 46 percent. I don't need to belabor the point, which is simply that tech is not the *only* risky sector. Most sectors are risky when compared with the market as a whole. Superior investors should not avoid sectors or, worse, like Rosie, avoid the stock market. Instead, they should own stocks in many different sectors, balancing risk through diversification.

But isn't there something different about technology?

Yes, and the difference begins with economics.

In the late 1990s, technology accounted for two-thirds of the growth of the U.S. economy. It was the main source of an increase in productivity from 1.7 percent in the 1980s and early 1990s to 2.7 percent in the late 1990s: an astounding rise that, if sustained, means that the U.S. economy will grow at about 3.5 percent a year, well above historic averages. At that rate, real per-capita wealth in the nation will rise by a factor of eight in about 60 years. Imagine the typical family being eight times as rich: a 16,000 square-foot house instead of 2,000; 16 cars instead of two, etc., etc.

Productivity is a measure of the output we get from a given input. A rise in productivity of 2.7 percent means that, for $1,000 invested, we get 1,000 pounds of finished kryptonite, or some such, the first year, but, from the same labor and capital, 1,027 pounds the next. What does the Internet have to do with all this? The special quality of fast, networked computers is that they speed information simultaneously to all parts of a business. Better information frequently means more efficient performance. Also, as Alan Greenspan, the Federal Reserve chairman has pointed out, information technology reduces uncertainty, so businesses don't have to keep as many employees on hand or build big inventories. Eliminating these kinds of redundancies means that businesses can get the same output for lower inputs which is the same thing as saying more output for the same input. Either way, productivity rises.

There's another, positive way to look at the tech revolution. Work published in 1999 by a highly regarded economist, Boyan Jovanovic, shows that the world is in the midst of a "technology wave," indicating that the stock market, especially the tech sector, still has a long way to go.

Jovanovic also found that companies that were formed in the last great technology wave, which he calls "Jazz Age vintage," have been remarkably resilient, and equivalent stocks in our own high-tech age may show the same characteristics. For example, critics of tech stocks today frequently cite the collapse of Radio Corporation of America (RCA), which went public in 1920 at $1.50 a share, rose to $114 in 1929 and plummeted to $2.50 by 1932, a pattern reminiscent of CNET, which once had a market cap of $15 billion. But, in fact, RCA reached twice its peak 1929 value when it was bought out by General Electric in 1986 (and that doesn't count the dividends earned by shareholders along the way). Similarly, Procter & Gamble, another Jazz Age stock, dropped from $95 in 1929 to $20.50 in 1933 but had risen by 11,000 percent by 2000. In other words, "new economy" stocks, of the Jazz Age or our age, aren't necessarily flashes in the pan, though, of course, they rise and fall in the short term based on the moods of Mr. Market and on the effects of short-term outside events like oil-price shocks, Fed interest-rate hikes, high-profile antitrust suits and disputed elections.

Here is how Jovanovic sees the tech cycle. First, a new technology comes along and signals the end of the old era. During the Jazz Age, it was electrification (as well as mass consumerism boosted by advertising); now, it's computers and the Internet. "The signal is bad news for the stock market incumbents," he wrote in a summary of his work in the National Bureau of Economic Research [NBER] Reporter. Those old-economy stocks drop sharply because, while such large firms "are good at routine innovation and good at improving methods they use and products they sell . . . in small ways, a step at a time . . . in times of change, [they are] held down by ignorance, outdated training, and the vested interests of . . . employees."

But what about the small, innovative companies that are introducing the new technologies? Eventually, these firms push up the stock market, but in the early stages of the tech revolution, they aren't even listed on the exchanges. "Inventions such as computers tend to be developed in small, privately held companies," Jovanovic writes. "These inventions do not add any value to the stock market until the small companies go public or are acquired."

So only after a wave of IPOs and mergers does the market rise again and, according to Jovanovic's model, keeps rising until the next new technology (which, by the way, he guesses will arive, "if history were to repeat itself," around 2040).

Jovanovic is no eccentric. He is a professor of economics at New York University, a visiting professor at the University of Chicago and a research associate at the highly regarded NBER. He has published several academic papers on technology and the market, and, while they are available on his website (www. econ.nyu.edu/user/jovanovi), they are filled with difficult math and are not very accessible to the public. He says that his "findings do not support the conventional view of the 1920s as an era of misguided optimism that ended with a crash and depression." Yes, some stocks became overvalued, but that "overvaluation was concentrated among the then-old economy" firms. "The firms that went public between 1918 and 1934 did much better than the adjacent vintages."

Similarly, he writes in the NBER Reporter, the tech wave really began with the disruptive technology invented by Intel in 1972: its second computer chip. But, "while the information technology revolution was gathering momentum in the 1970s, stock prices fell; some companies went out of business" because they could not keep up, just as in the 1930s. But then in the 1980s, "IT developers started going public [Microsoft's IPO came only in 1986] . . . Wall Street surged."

Of course, tech stocks fell sharply, beginning in 2000, and, perhaps by old-economy standards, valuations still seem high. But, if Jovanovic is right, that economy is rapidly being displaced. Under such a scenario, it is not hard to see why tech remains an excellent bet.

I don't necessarily agree with the entire Jovanovic thesis, but I am convinced that the high-tech revolution is for real and that it is as important as any economic change in history, on a par with the industrial revolution of the 19th century. But that still doesn't mean that you should load up your portfolio with high-tech stocks.

In his book, *The Intelligent Investor,* written more than a half-century ago, Benjamin Graham pointed out that it wasn't difficult to predict that in a decade or two, tens of millions of Americans would be flying around on commercial aircraft. But did that make airline stocks a great buy? Not at all. Airlines might have to plow their profits into new and better airplanes to keep up with the competition. The airline sector could end up being a bloodbath, with companies offering lower fares and better service, driving each other out of business. The brand names of airlines could become meaningless. Flying could become a commodity business, with price the only differentiating factor.

That nightmare—for investors, though not for consumers—did indeed become reality. The most famous brand names of the early days of flying, like Pan American and Eastern, are gone, and TWA, bankrupt and then bought out, is a ghost of its glorious youth. The same could happen with technology. Kevin Hassett and I wrote in our 1999 book *Dow 36,000:*

"We advise caution when it comes to Internet companies. A company can generate a consistent and growing stream of cash for many years only if it has protection against copycat competitors. The Internet makes entry extraordinarily easy. While an online retailer does not need an investment in bricks and mortar to sell books or computer equipment, neither does the *next* online retailer. And since shopping is easy on the Net (you don't have to walk down the street, or even pick up the phone, to compare prices), margins are probably going to be squeezed lower and lower. It will be hard to make profits that grow and last."

That was a good prediction, not just for e-commerce but for software, hardware, and telecommunications. Once, for example, Lotus 1-2-3 held a virtual monopoly with its fast, easy-to-use spreadsheet, but Microsoft came along with better software in Excel, and Lotus disappeared overnight as a spreadsheet power-house. Leading hardware maker Gateway was hurt badly by price-cutting online competitors like Dell, and, having estab-lished itself as a brand-name seller of books, Amazon.com has had a difficult time breaking into electronics retailing, which is widespread on the Internet. With practically no barriers to entry as protection, every e-commerce company is fully exposed to a hurricane of competition.

Of course, many high-tech companies have continued to thrive, including the behemoths like IBM. But the biggest win-ners in technology could turn out to be the firms that use the stuff, companies like Automatic Data Processing and Paychex, Inc., which both provide payroll and tax-processing services to corporations, or pharmaceutical houses that use high-speed computers in their research, or retailers like Wal-Mart and the Home Depot, which track their inventories and sales with the best technology.

Does that mean you should eschew tech entirely? Of course not. The best advice is that the proportion of tech in your port-folio should be close to the proportion of tech in the market as a whole. Unfortunately, the tech's share has changed a great deal in recent years. When tech was flying high in 1999, it repre-sented about one-third of the market capitalization of the S&P 500, the benchmark index. But little over a year later, it repre-sented only about one-fifth of the S&P. And by some calcula-tions, tech's share of GDP is less than 10 percent. So which proportion is it?

My own rule is that tech should comprise about one-fourth of your portfolio. Never more than one-third and never less than one-tenth. I would not obsess over this number. In other words, don't feel you have to reallocate your portfolio every few months as tech prices go up and down. But definitely keep an eye on the percentages. Many investors could have spared themselves grief and losses if they had paid attention to the soaring proportions of tech stocks in their portfolios and had trimmed them back.

Tech should play a key role in any portfolio for the 21st century because, very simply, tech is where the growth is. But it should not be the entire portfolio, or most of it, or even half of it. When you let tech rule, you can come to the same grief as Rosie Cioe of Providence.

PART 6 ∘

BONDS AND CASH

CHAPTER FORTY-TWO

BONDS ARE FOR THE SHORT-TERM AND MEDIUM-TERM ONLY

THIS BOOK is mostly about stocks. Do I have something against the alternative, bonds? Well, yes. As Peter Lynch once put it, "Gentlemen who prefer bonds don't know what they're missing." Over the long term, bonds simply don't give investors a high enough return for the risks they take.

What risks? When you buy a bond issued by the United States Treasury, you have an iron-clad commitment from the government that you will be paid back, every penny, and sent interest checks along the way. Where's the risk?

When you give the government $1,000 for, say, 10 years, the $1,000 that it gives you back at the end of that decade may not buy very much. It is almost certain that it won't buy as much as $1,000 did 10 years earlier. The reason, of course, is inflation. Over the past 75 years, inflation has averaged 3.1 percent annually. It reached a maximum of 18.2 percent in 1946 and an average of 6.4 percent in the worst 20-year stretch, 1966–85.

If inflation continues at the same rate as the last half of the 20th century (4.1 percent annually), then, in 10 years, it will cost $149 to buy what $100 buys today. Another way of saying this is that, in a decade, today's dollar will be worth just 67 cents ($1 / 1.49 = $0.67). If inflation is 5 percent, then, in 10 years, today's dollar will be worth just 61 cents. It's been a lot worse: From 1973 to 1982, the value of a dollar fell by more than half.

The interest that a bond pays an investor is supposed to compensate for the losses from inflation, but, of course, no one ever knows what inflation will be in the future. That's the risk that bondholders take. For example, at the beginning of 1977, a $10,000 Treasury note maturing at the end of 1981 was paying 7 percent interest, which is about one-fourth higher than the historic average for such securities, but over the next five years inflation totaled 60 percent, so that it cost $16,000 to buy what $10,000 could buy in 1977. Over the five years, interest payments totaled only $3,500. An investor in bonds over that period was a loser to the tune of more than $2,000.

What history shows is that, when you look at both the returns of bonds and their riskiness, then, over long periods, they are a poor investment compared with stocks. For example, the Ibbotson Associates data show that, from 1926 to 2000, long-term government bonds returned 5.3 percent a year while large-company stocks returned 11.0 percent a year. For the long term (10 years or more), with inflation taken into account, bonds and stocks carry about the same risk. So stocks are obviously a better buy. But not for the short term! If you can put your money away for no more than five years, then bonds are precisely the ticket. You run some risks, but the risks of stocks are so much greater that the higher returns don't offer enough compensation.

A bond is an I.O.U., a piece of paper you receive in return for lending your money to a company or a government agency. When you buy a bond, you become a creditor, or lender. The borrower, the U.S. Treasury, for example, takes $1,000 from you and promises to pay the money back at the end of a set period, with the final date called "maturity." In the meantime, the lender (you, the investor) gets interest from the Treasury. The nature of a bond is that it is a "fixed-income" investment. In return for the use of your money, the Treasury pays you a set rate of interest until maturity. (There is one big exception to this rule for Treasuries, and I will get to it in Chapter 46.)

There are two kinds of risk you take with bonds. The first is "credit risk," that is, the chance that the lender won't pay you back. With a Treasury bond, the credit risk is essentially zero. The taxing power of the U.S. government insures that you will be repaid. With a corporate bond, the credit risk is higher; just how high depends on the company that is borrowing your money. Some corporations go bankrupt, after all, and can't meet their debts. Corporate bonds, naturally, pay interest rates higher than Treasury bonds in order to compensate investors for this higher risk. For example, in mid-2001, a Caterpillar, Inc., bond, maturing in 2007 and trading on the New York Exchange, was yielding 6 percent at the same time a Treasury note, also maturing in 2007, was yielding 5.1 percent. Some bonds, called "high-yield" or "junk" bonds, carry especially high rates because the borrower is new or shaky: Lyondell Petrochemical bonds, with six years to maturity, were yielding 9.5 percent in July 2001.

In between Treasuries and corporates, when it comes to credit risk, are federal agencies such as the Tennessee Valley Authority and the Farm Credit Financial Assistance Corporation ("Farmer Mac"). The chance that they will default (miss payments of interest or principal) is almost nil, but, in theory at least, their debt is riskier than the debt of the Treasury, and their bonds pay slightly higher interest, typically a quarter to a half point for medium-term maturities. The debt of so-called government-sponsored enterprises, such as Fannie Mae, a private company that provides money for banks and mortgage companies to lend out for home-buying, is more ambiguous. The government gives an "implicit," though not absolute, guarantee that it will back Fannie's debt in case the company gets into trouble, which it never has. Fannie's longer-term bonds were yielding about three-quarters of a percentage point more than Treasuries in

September 2001. Then, there are bonds issued by state and local government agencies, debt that goes under the rubric "municipal bonds." Muni bonds vary widely in credit quality (see Chapter 44).

The second kind of risk is imposed by inflation. It has two effects: First, as I noted earlier, it depletes the buying power of the principal you get back at maturity; second, it can lower the value of your bond if you want to sell it before it matures. This is not an easy concept, but you need to understand it before you invest in bonds.

The simple way to invest in a bond is just to buy it when it is issued and hold it to maturity. You put down $1,000; you get back $1,000, plus interest at a fixed rate (the bond's "coupon") along the way. What adds complications is that the value, that is, the price in the market, of a bond rises and falls daily. If you are a long-term holder, you can ignore this volatility and be assured that you will get your money back, unless of course, the lender defaults.

Why do the prices of bonds bounce around? Two reasons: First, the creditworthiness of the bond's issuer changes (that is, if business turns bad, a corporation will be more likely to default). Second, interest rates fluctuate.

When a bond is issued, it will be priced at about 100, or 100 percent of its face value. Let's say it's a Treasury bond with a face value of $10,000, a coupon of 6 percent, and a maturity that is 10 years away. A few months after the bond is issued, the price might drop to 95 (or $9,500 for a $10,000 bond); a year later, the price might soar to 110 (or $11,000). Why?

At 6 percent interest, the $10,000 bond pays an investor $600 a year. But now assume that, a year after the bond is issued, the general level of interest rates rises, and new bonds are being issued by the Treasury with a similar maturity date but with a coupon of 7 percent, or a payment of $700 a year. Bonds are traded in an open market, just like stocks. If you decide to sell, no one will give you $10,000 for a bond that pays $600 annually if there are new bonds being sold at $10,000 that pay $700 annually. To sell your bond, then, you will have to take a discount. You might get only $9,500 (a price of 90). Of course, the same process works in reverse. If rates fall, then your bond will be worth *more* since it pays out more interest than a new bond with, say, a 5 percent coupon, would. Its price might rise to 110.

It is this inverse relationship between bond prices and bond interest rates (or yields) that confuses many investors. Just remember: When rates rise, bond prices fall; when rates fall, bond prices rise.

By the way, an extreme example of what can happen when an issuer's credit quality declines can be found in the junk bonds of a telecom infrastructure company called Level 3 Communications. When the firm first issued its debt a few years earlier, the bonds carried a coupon of 9.1 percent. But Level 3's fortunes declined quickly as demand for its fiber-optic network fell off, and losses mounted to $1.5 billion in 2000 and an estimated $2.8 billion in 2001. Investors could smell default, and the price of the bonds dropped to a mere 41 by July 2001. If, nevertheless, you bought bonds with $10,000 in face value for $4,100, held them to maturity and got your promised interest and principal, your return would be nearly 30 percent annually.

Credit risk is always a threat with corporate and muni bonds, but there are ways to dampen the often-severe ups and downs that interest-rate risk imposes on all bonds, even Treasuries. First, hold the bond to maturity. Buy at 100; sell at 100. (Since most people buy bonds in the open market, rather than when issued, they are more likely to be buying at 98 or 103 and selling at 100 but it's roughly the same thing.) Second, buy only short-term, or medium-term bonds. It stands to reason that the farther off a bond's maturity, the riskier the investment. At 6 percent interest, a $10,000 bond pays $600 a year. Over 30 years, that's $18,000. If rates suddenly rise to 8 percent, then new bonds will pay $800 a year in interest. Over 30 years, that's $24,000, a difference of $6,000. But if these bonds mature in only five years, then the difference will amount to just $1,000. And, at the end of five years, if rates are still high, the proceeds from the 6 percent bond can be invested in a new 8 percent bond. The lesson, then, is to stay short.

But can't you make big profits by anticipating the movements of interest rates? Buy a 6 percent bond at 100 and watch it soar to 140 when rates fall to 4.5 percent? In theory, yes. In practice, gambling on bonds is a dumb thing for small investors to try; it is at least as difficult (that is to say, impossible) to guess the course of interest rates as it is to guess the course of stock prices.

Back in September 1996, *Money* magazine was screaming on its cover, "Invest Safely and Make 20% or More." Yeah, I'll admit it: I bought a copy. Incredibly enough, the story turned out to be about bonds. Now, there is no way you can make an annual 20 percent "safely" with bonds (or with stocks, for that matter). Even unsafely, the only way to do it is: 1) Buy the bonds of some woebegone country like Haiti or Afghanistan and pray you get paid back, or 2) buy a long-term Treasury bond, hope that interest rates will plummet and sell it at a profit. *Money* magazine was suggesting the latter course.

But interest rates move in a random walk, just as stock prices do. In fact, when *Money* magazine made its ridiculous 20-percent claim, long-term government bonds were yielding 7.0 percent; six months later, they were yielding 7.2 percent. No 20 percent profit there.

The right way to invest in bonds is to forget about predicting interest rates and forget about making 20 percent. Bonds are not for speculation. They are for one of three uses:

- **To generate reliable income for paying living expenses.**

- **To provide a modest, non-risky return for a relatively short period. For instance, if you have a child beginning college in three years and have saved up $60,000 for that purpose, then put the money into bonds, not stocks, which are too volatile over such a brief time.**

- **To serve as ballast in a diversified portfolio. Short- and medium-term bonds produce lower returns at lower risk than stocks. For older investors, especially, it makes sense to inject a dose in bonds (20 percent to 50 percent, depending on how old you are) to reduce the overall riskiness of your holdings.**

In general, however, bonds are not long-term investments. Examining every 20-year period since 1926, Ibbotson researchers found that the worst period for stocks (1929–48) produced an average annual return of 3.1 percent; t he worst 20-year period for bonds (1950–69) produced an average annual return of only 0.7 percent. The best 20 years for stocks (1980–99) scored a 17.9 percent annual return; best for bonds (1981–2000), 12.0 percent.

In other words, stocks are better on the upside (as you would expect), but better on the downside as well. And remember that, on average, stocks returned more than twice as much as bonds.

Yes, bonds have their place in a portfolio, but it is a very specific, very narrow place. And that place is only for certain kinds of bonds, usually the ones that mature within just five years.

CHAPTER FORTY-THREE

BUILD A LADDER FOR YOUR BONDS, AND HOLD THEM TO MATURITY

NOT ONLY do investors own too many bonds, they own them in the wrong way. Typically, someone with a five-year time horizon will buy a single five-year bond, or perhaps a stake in an intermediate bond fund. But owning just one or two bonds needlessly increases your risk, and buying a bond fund puts you at the mercy of the fund's manager, who may be making wild bets on interest rates.

Remember that the bond portion of your portfolio is where you want to *lower* your risk. It's for your short- and medium-term money—the down payment for a house you want to buy in the next few years or the funds you are saving for your 14-year-old's college education.

Reducing the credit risk of bonds is no secret: own Treasuries, not corporates (see Chapter 45). But reducing the interest-rate risk is tougher. The answer is to build a ladder by purchasing bonds that mature in successive years, so that you keep replacing them. Say you have $50,000 to invest. Instead of putting all your money into a single series of bonds that matures in five years, you put $10,000 into bonds that mature after one year, $10,000 into bonds that mature after two years, and so on.

At the end of year one, the shortest-maturity bonds come due. Take the $10,000 in proceeds and invest the money in new five-year bonds that will mature in year six. Continue the process. Your portfolio always contains five bonds, maturing one year after another.

One of the smartest investment advisors I know, H. Garrett Thornburg Jr., left Bear, Stearns & Co., the big New York firm, and moved in 1982 to Santa Fe, N.M., where he started his own company that manages money for pension funds and wealthy individuals. For the public, Thornburg also manages bond funds that use the laddering technique. "Consider an environment of increasing interest rates," says a Thornburg investor guide. That's a bond investor's worst nightmare. If you buy a five-year bond with an interest rate of 5 percent and rates soar to 8 percent, then you either have to sell at a loss or forgo an attractive flow of income. But with laddering, "as the shortest bonds in the portfolio mature, we have the opportunity to reinvest the proceeds at the new higher yields in longer maturities."

In other words, the proceeds from the year-one bonds get rolled into new year-six bonds that pay 8 percent interest. The result, says Thornburg, is that his bond funds get "90 percent to 95 percent of the income of long-term bonds, but with less than half the volatility and a very stable income."

The only drawback to laddered-bond funds like Thornburg's is the hefty expenses they charge. But it's easy enough to build a bond ladder yourself. For example, in mid-2001, through a broker or banker, your could have bought a bond maturing in June 2002, paying 4.0 percent interest; one maturing in June 2003, at 4.4 percent; May 2004 (bonds aren't always available in every monthly maturity), at 4.8 percent; May 2005, at 5.0 percent; and May 2006, at 5.2 percent. Typically, the longer the maturity, the higher the interest rate. Investing $50,000 in such a portfolio, you would receive $2,340 in interest the first year, and, if rates rose, you would be getting more, as you swapped your bonds yielding 4.0 percent and 4.4 percent for bonds paying higher rates.

You aren't going to get rich by laddering, but that's not the point. A ladder gives you safety, and safety is the bondholder's main objective.

The safest way to invest in bonds is to take advantage of their edge over stocks: Bonds mature, and stocks don't. At a certain date, every bond requires the borrower to pay the lender the face amount of the bond. If you bought a bond when it was issued for $1,000, then you will get $1,000 (assuming the borrower hasn't gone broke). Stocks offer no such guarantee. Buy a stock at $50 a share, and there is no promise that the price will ever see $50 again. (There are, however, special investments that package stocks and bonds together, so that an investor can put, say, $10,000 into the S&P 500 index and be guaranteed by a firm like Merrill Lynch that he will receive the $10,000 back at the end of five years or benefit from the price rise in the S&P, whichever is greater. These investments go by different names, but MITTS, for "market-index target-term securities," is the most familiar. MITTS are, essentially, bonds that pay interest based on the performance of the S&P.)

The Secret Code on bonds is simple: hold them to maturity. Exploit the promise; don't play games. Many investors will gamble with bonds. They guess that interest rates will fall and that their 7 percent, 10-year Treasury will soar in value from $10,000 to $15,000. That's a risky, foolish gamble, and frankly the payoff is not very high. I would much rather take risks with stocks.

Say you have saved $20,000 for a trip around the world that you plan to take at retirement, three years from now. The best place for that money is in bonds that mature in three years, or in a laddered three-year bond portfolio. But with just three years to go, a single Treasury bond will do nicely. Another choice is the American Century Benham Targeted Maturity series, which offers portfolios of bonds maturing in or around a single year. Benham has such funds with targets in 2005, 2010, 2015 and so on.

Holding bonds to maturity, you might say, is the mature way to invest with bonds.

MUNICIPAL BONDS CAN BE BARGAINS

AT FIRST BLUSH, municipal bonds look like a kindly oversight by the tax man. Affectionately called "munis," they are I.O.U.s issued by state or local agencies, just like the I.O.U.s issued by the U.S. government, federal agencies or businesses. But munis enjoy a special tax status. On U.S. Treasury bonds, income from interest payments is taxed by the feds but not by the states. On corporate bonds, interest income is taxed by both federal and state governments. On municipal bonds, interest is not taxed by the feds and, in some cases, not by state or local governments either.

Thanks to this tax break, almost always, high-quality municipal bonds will pay interest that's less than the interest on Treasury bonds; nevertheless, many investors in high or even medium tax brackets can end up putting more money in their pockets with munis than with taxable Treasuries. Munis can be magnificent bargains, but you have to be careful.

First, unlike Treasuries, munis can carry significant credit risk. Between 1980 and 1994, a total of 1,333 out of 130,092 muni issues defaulted. Most of these were small, but compared to a rate of zero for federal securities issues, even a rate of 1 percent is scary, especially because the bond part of your portfolio is supposed to be the non-risky part. So it's important to look for quality, that is, bonds that are rated AA or AAA or are insured by private agencies such as giant MBIA, Inc., against loss. Also, recognize that general-obligation (or G.O.) munis are backed by the taxing power of the state that issues them while revenue bonds generate their interest and principal repayments from a special source of income, such as bridge tolls or university dormitory fees. So G.O.s tend to be safer than revenue securities.

But it is not difficult to find munis that are about as risky (as far as credit is concerned) as Treasuries, which is to say not risky at all. After you have found such bonds, the arithmetic for discovering whether you should own munis or Treasuries works like this:

Take the interest rate on a high-quality muni and divide it by 1 minus your marginal tax rate (the federal income-tax rate on the next dollar you earn) expressed as a decimal. As a result of the 2001 tax cuts, rates are changing in complicated ways, but assume that your marginal rate is 30 percent. In mid-2001, a five-year AAA-rated insured revenue bond was trading at 3.9 percent. Divide 0.039 by [1-0.30] and you get 0.0557, or about 5.6 percent. That's the "tax-equivalent" yield or the yield on a taxable Treasury that would provide the same income, after taxes, as the muni. At the time, five-year Treasuries were yielding 5.2 percent, so the muni appears to be a better buy. Longer-term munis were an even better deal (though, in general, I don't believe in using bonds for the longer-term part of your portfolio). A California state G.O., due in 2031, was yielding 5.4 percent for a tax-equivalent yield, for someone in a 36 percent bracket, of 8.4 percent. (The Bond Market Association has a calculator on its website at www.investinginbonds.com to make computations easier.)

Unfortunately, the decision to buy munis is not so simple as it seems. Don't forget that Treasury interest is not taxed by state governments, but muni interest may be. Most states, however, don't tax the interest on their *own* muni bonds, and many cities have the same policy. New York City bonds, for example, are "triple tax-exempt" for New York City residents: no federal, state or city taxes. Since New Yorkers may face marginal tax rates of 50 percent, a muni yielding 5 percent is equivalent to a corporate yielding 10 percent. The District of Columbia and a few states don't tax the interest on any out-of-state bonds. (Some special munis, however, are subject to the federal Alternative Minimum Tax, or AMT. That is, if you have too many deductions, the interest on these bonds—usually for public-private-partnership ventures like stadium construction—may be taxable. Be on the lookout for them.)

Also, beware that some muni bonds, unlike Treasury bonds, can be "called." If interest rates drop, the state agency has the choice of repaying its lenders and issuing new bonds. It has, in effect, a "call" option on its own debt, the way that you have a call option on your mortgage that lets you re-finance if rates drop far enough to cover your closing costs for a new loan. Most muni call features go into effect after a minimum waiting period, frequently two years or more, so you can escape calls on short-term bonds, and the borrowing agency often pays a premium when it calls its bonds. Certainly, you get your money back when your bonds are called, but you usually can't reinvest the funds in similar bonds at as high a rate as you previously enjoyed. Low rates, after all, explain why the agency called the bonds in the first place.

Another problem with munis is that their revenue sources may not be easy to analyze (they could be riskier, in a credit sense, than they first seem). Also, there are 50,000 separate local taxing jurisdictions with 1.5 million individual muni issues outstanding (it would take 90 pages in a newspaper to list them all), and many are small and not very liquid (that is, buyers may be scarce). Total muni volume is about $7 billion a day compared with about $100 billion a day on the stock exchanges.

In addition, prices aren't very transparent, and brokers often charge stiff commissions or make a bundle on large spreads between the "ask" price paid by the seller and the "bid" price paid by the buyer. Diversification with munis is a must, but for modest investors buying small amounts of several issues can be expensive and time-consuming. The obvious answer is a muni-bond fund, but, when you buy one you put yourself at the mercy of a manager who may want to place big bets on the direction of interest rates and could also run up capital-gains tax liabilities (a big and ugly surprise for investors who think they are escaping federal taxes when they buy munis is that the exemption applies only to interest, not to the gains that accrue when a bond is sold for more than its purchase price). A better solution may be a unit investment trust, or UIT. That's a broad pool of bonds, of which an investor owns a specific percentage, or unit. It's similar to a mutual fund except that the pool, or portfolio, does not change during the life of the trust except as bonds mature. The drawback to UITs is the traditionally high up-front fees that packagers charge.

In short, munis are not easy to buy. But for investors in high tax brackets, they can be very attractive. The best answer is to find a broker you can trust or look for a good intermediate fund (Sheldon Jacobs, editor of the No-Load Fund Investor, recommends Vanguard California Insured Intermediate for California residents and Vanguard Intermediate Tax-Exempt and Fidelity Spartan Intermediate Muni Income for a mix of state bonds) or a well-priced UIT. It's worth the effort.

CHAPTER FORTY-FIVE

FORGET CORPORATE BONDS

OF ALL THE CHOICES in the investment universe, corporate bonds are the worst.

Corporate bonds, as the name implies, are I.O.U.s issued by large companies. The coupon, or stated interest rate, varies according to the economic climate, the company's balance sheet and business prospects, the terms (is the bond backed by any kind of security? can it be called?) and the maturity. Corporates are traded mainly on the New York Exchange, and, in a typical year, traders will rack up $3 trillion worth of transactions. Prices of corporates are quoted in percentages, just like Treasuries and munis (100 representing the full face value of the bond), and the price is used to compute a "current yield," that is, the percentage of your investment you will get back this year in interest.

Those yields can vary widely. One typical day in mid-2001, an AT&T bond maturing in 2029 and carrying a 6.5 percent coupon was trading at about 84, for a current yield of 7.7 percent (6.5 / 0.84 = 7.7); meanwhile, a Bethlehem Steel bond with a coupon of 8.45 percent, maturing in 2005, was trading at 76, for a current yield of 11.1 percent. Do you want to spend your precious investment time analyzing such debt issues? I don't.

The truth is, I detest corporate bonds and urge you to do the same. Is it a prejudice? Yes, partly. I'll admit that, well chosen, a diversified portfolio of corporates can provide a nice (taxable) flow of income. But, on the whole, corporates are bad news in principle and in practice. As for principle, listen again to Peter Lynch:

"When you buy a bond, you're only making a loan, but when you invest in a stock, you're buying a piece of a company. If the company prospers, you share in the prosperity. If it pays a dividend, you'll receive it, and if it raises the dividend, you'll reap the benefit. Hundreds of successful companies have a habit of raising their dividends year after year. This is a bonus for owning stocks that makes them all the more valuable. They never raise the interest rate on a bond!"

Take a modest example: IBM. The giant computer company a while ago issued bonds that mature in 2025 and carry a 7 percent coupon. In other words, for a $10,000 investment, you get $700 a year and the promise that you will have your $10,000 returned a quarter of the way through the 21st century. Compare that return to the dividends on IBM stock. In 1995, when the company floated the bond issue, the stock was paying a 25-cent dividend on shares that cost $20. That's not much of a yield, only a little over 1 percent. Buy 500 shares of IBM for $10,000, and you got $125 in dividends in 1995. But by 2001, the dividend had risen to 60 cents, or $300 a year. Meanwhile, IBM stock had jumped to $100, so your $10,000 was worth $50,000 while the bonds are still worth $10,000.

But stick to dividends vs. interest. Value Line projects IBM will double its dividends every six years. At that rate, by the time the bond matures, the dividend per share will be $9.60, or $4,800 on your original investment of $10,000. Meanwhile, the interest payment in that year will be the same old $700.

In other words, with corporates you sacrifice the upside, which can be considerable. Forget dividends. A stock can double, triple, quadruple over the life of a bond. The bond's advantage is a limited downside, but, when you compare the two assets, you have to admit that the bondholder gets a raw deal. An investor takes risks with both stocks and bonds, and the risks are nearly the same over time, but bonds have a much smaller payoff. Yes, by law, if a company goes bankrupt, the bondholders stand in line in front of the stockholders, who will probably get nothing at all. But very few companies that you ought to be buying—the companies that comprise, for instance, the Standard & Poor's 500-Stock Index (roughly the 500 largest U.S. firms) or the Dow itself—will go bankrupt. And, for bonds, the chance of default is definitely out there. In 2000, a total of 125 American companies defaulted on $29 billion worth of bonds; the year before, 99 companies failed to meet their obligations on $24 billion worth.

With bonds issued by the U.S. Treasury or by agencies like the Federal Home Loan Bank System or the Tennessee Valley Authority or by government-sponsored enterprises with an implicit federal guarantee such as Fannie Mae and Freddie Mac, there is zero credit risk (or as close to zero as you can examine with a microscope). Since 1926, long-term government bonds have returned an annual average of 5.3 percent, and long-term corporate bonds (Salomon Brothers Long-Term High-Grade Corporate Bond Index) have returned 5.7 percent. Is four-tenths of a percentage point enough extra return for you to take on the extra risk of corporates? Certainly not for superior investors. For that reason, I much prefer Treasuries and agencies.

In addition, corporate bonds are difficult for the small investor to analyze. Services, including Moody's, Standard & Poor's and Fitch IBCA bestow ratings on bond issues, but you'll have to take their word (or group of letters) for it. No sensible investor would buy stocks simply on a soundness rating, but with corporate bonds, you have little choice. Still, if you insist on buying corporates, stick to top-rated issues: AAA or AA for S&P and Fitch, Aaa or Aa for Moody's (full Moody's ratings can be found at www.moodys.com). In 2000, the average Aaa bond yielded 7.6 percent while the average Baa bond, the lowest "investment-grade" securities, yielded 8.4 percent.

Bonds rated below BBB for S&P and Fitch, or below Baa for Moody's are termed "speculative" grade, that is, high-yield or junk bonds. In the early 1980s, mainly through the research and promotion of investment banker Michael Milken, investors learned that junk bonds were not as risky as had previously been thought; that is, the extra returns for high-yield bonds more than compensated investors for the extra risk, compared with a standard corporate bond. But that irrational spread appears no longer to operate. Junk bonds are fine in the hands of experts, but small investors should ignore them (though, to tell the truth, I am tempted by that Level 3 bond in the last chapter with a current yield of 29.8 percent).

Small investors should ignore corporates, too. Over the past three-quarters of a century, the average long-term corporate bond has returned 2.5 percent after inflation, compared with nearly 8 percent for stocks. Even intermediate-term Treasuries returned 2.2 percent. You have enough on your mind as an investor. Forget corporates. They aren't worth the risk or the time.

HOT TIPS: BUY THE ONE INVESTMENT GUARANTEED TO BEAT INFLATION

BONDS, REMEMBER, ARE RISKY in two ways: the creditor might default, and the principal might fall so far behind inflation that the interest won't compensate for the loss. In 1997, the Clinton Administration, in what may have been its greatest long-term accomplishment, introduced bonds that eliminate both those risks. They are called Treasury inflation-protected securities, or TIPS. Since they're Treasury bonds, the full faith and credit of the U.S. government stands behind them, eliminating credit risk. And their value rises to keep up with a rising cost of living, eliminating inflation risk. TIPS still have some drawbacks, but, on the whole, they are extremely attractive investments.

Economists of varying ideological persuasions had been pushing the idea of inflation-indexed bonds for a half-century. Conservative Nobel laureate Milton Friedman, writing in 1971, saw them as a way to end "the disgraceful shell game" by which the government borrowed from investors and repaid them in dollars whose value was eroded by inflation that the government itself helped induce. Friedman knew what he was talking about. If you had invested in long-term government bonds at the end of 1971, over the next three years they would have lost one-seventh of their value because of inflation. Meanwhile, liberal Nobel laureate James Tobin was arguing that inflation-indexed bonds would help "savers of limited means and knowledge, [who] should not be forced to gamble either on the price level or on the stock market." (I don't agree with him about the stock market, but his point on bonds is right on the money.)

Inflation-linked bonds were introduced in Britain in 1981, and they became popular as well in Canada, New Zealand, Australia, Israel and Sweden. Finally, under the leadership of Treasury officials Bob Rubin and Lawrence Summers, they made their U.S. debut with an issue of 10-year bonds maturing in January 2007. The bonds carried a "real" coupon of 3.375 percent, meaning that the Treasury guaranteed that interest yield annually. Each year, the principal amount, which started at $1,000, would be increased by the percentage rise in the Consumer Price Index (CPI), the benchmark inflation measure. Boosting the principal rather than paying out extra current interest makes TIPS more complicated than they should be. But the effect is the same: think of TIPS as regular Treasury bonds whose interest annually rises with inflation.

As a hedge against rising prices, "TIPS are . . . much better than gold," says Greg Jensen, senior research associate at Bridgewater Associates, a bond and currency firm that specializes in global inflation-indexed bonds. Gold, which was probably the best protection against inflation before TIPS, can fluctuate for all sorts of reasons, including the vagaries of supply and demand of the precious metal itself (see Chapter 35). It doesn't track overall inflation very well. But TIPS do. That's why they were invented.

It was easy during the late 1990s to forget the virulence of inflation, but from 1970 to 2000 the average annual rise in the CPI was 5 percent. At that rate, the purchasing power of a dollar declines to 48 cents in 15 years and to 24 cents in 30 years. In mid-2001, a 10-year Treasury bond was yielding 5.4 percent while a 10-year TIPS was yielding 3.4 percent. The difference between the two, 2 percent, represents the inflation expectation for the next decade. If you think inflation had a good chance of exceeding 2 percent, then TIPS were a good buy. If inflation averages 5 percent, for example, then a 10-year TIPS will yield 8.4 percent while a conventional 10-year Treasury will yield just 5.4 percent.

No one knows for sure where inflation will go, but since 1960 there has never been a 10-year stretch (out of 32 such intervals) in which the CPI has averaged an annual increase of less than 2.5 percent. So a TIPS that will pay off with 2 percent inflation or higher seems a good bet. In fact, TIPS appear too good to be true. There must be a catch, and there are, in fact, three catches:

First, while the real coupon is set when each TIPS series is issued, the price of an inflation-protected security can fluctuate, just like any bond or stock. In the first few years, demand was low (perhaps because inflation did not appear worrisome), so prices of TIPS fell, and investors who wanted to sell had to take losses—to their surprise and chagrin.

Second, TIPS are not very liquid. Four years after being issued, they still hadn't really caught on with the public and were mainly used by institutions for sophisticated hedging. Not many of the bonds are traded regularly and, as a result, prices can be volatile. This means that, if you want to sell TIPS before maturity, you might not get as much as you think you deserve.

Third, even if you do hold to maturity (as I always advise), TIPS have a nasty tax feature. On a current basis (that is, twice a year), the bonds pay only real interest, which, naturally, is taxable. The bonds, as noted earlier, don't pay out the CPI increase as interest but rather as principal, which means you get the inflation bonus at the back end. For example, an investor who bought the first five-year TIPS note for $10,000 when it was issued in mid-1997 will be paid about $11,500 when it matures, meanwhile receiving $362.50 a year in real interest. The nasty part is that taxes, at the ordinary income rate, are due annually on the amount ($300 or so a year if inflation stays in the 3 percent range) that is added to principal—even though the investor doesn't get the cash until maturity! (This same tax wrinkle applies to zero-coupon bonds, which investors buy at a discount and receive, at maturity, the full face value.) As a result, it makes sense to hold TIPS, like zeroes, in tax-deferred accounts such as IRAs and 401(k) plans.

Still, the drawbacks are more than outweighed by the unique insurance policy. Inflation can be a killer, and there is no better way to shield part of your portfolio against it than TIPS. Gold is not the answer. Charles Rother, president of American Strategic Capital, conducted an analysis of how different investments responded in periods of moderate inflation (CPI increases between 2 percent and 5.9 percent) over the last half of the 20th century. He found that the S&P 500 index trumped all asset classes with an annual return of 14.8 percent. But if inflation-indexed bonds had existed throughout the period, they would have placed second with average annual returns of 7.1 percent. Gold averaged only 3.8 percent. In periods of rapid inflation (more than 6 percent annually), gold topped the list at 13.4 percent a year, but TIPS were close behind at 11.3 percent. The S&P returned 4.1 percent while corporate bonds, my least favorite investment (see the preceding chapter) *fell* 0.1 percent annually. Yes, gold can help in extreme climates, but TIPS work rain or shine.

Four years after TIPS were introduced, there were eight separate issues from which to choose, with maturities ranging from 2002 to 2029. Several mutual funds have sprung up, devoting their portfolios to TIPS, including PIMCO Real Return Bond fund and Vanguard Inflation-Protection Securities Fund. Or you can buy TIPS from your broker or banker, or straight from the U.S. Treasury (www.treasurydirect.gov) when they are issued. My guess is that the popularity of TIPS will rise, and their real interest rates will fall. But, at any rate, it is hard to imagine a Secret Code portfolio without them.

CHAPTER FORTY-SEVEN

STASH YOUR CASH

CASH ISN'T AN INVESTMENT ITSELF, but it has to be part of your investment strategy. "Cash," in financial jargon, is actually a very short-term loan that you, the lender, can call in whenever you want with no penalty. Cash comes in different forms: a checking account (where you are lending money to a bank and can take it back whenever you write a check), savings account, certificate of deposit (a loan with a fixed term, usually from three months to five years, again from you to a bank), Treasury bill (a government security with maturity within three to 12 months), or money-market fund (a mutual fund that invests only in bonds, CDs and commercial paper that mature in a few months). By the way, commercial paper is a loan that big investors make directly to a big corporation.

The main reason you need cash is for normal living costs and emergencies. The rule of thumb, a reasonable one, is to keep two months' expenses on hand. Cash is also nice to have hanging around, so you can take advantage of a sudden investment opportunity. But my advice is to have as little of it as possible. Cash tends to keep up with inflation, but not much more.

From 1926 to 2000, the average annual interest paid on the shortest-term Treasury bills, probably the best proxy for cash, was 3.8 percent. The average inflation rate was 3.1 percent. But, since interest is taxed at the ordinary-income rate, for a typical investor the after-tax return is no greater than 2.7 percent, so, against inflation, you're usually losing ground. In fact, according to research by Ibbotson Associates, T-bills earned less than the inflation rate, on a before-tax basis, in one-third of the years since 1926.

Of all the places to stash your cash, which is best? The differences are tiny. For example, in June 2001, a three-month T-bill was yielding 3.6 percent. The average money-market fund was yielding 3.8 percent, which was also the rate on a three-month certficate of deposit. T-bills are, of course, backed by the U.S. government, and bank CDs are usually insured by a federal agency up to $100,000. Most money-market funds carry no insurance, but that's really not a big problem; no public money fund has ever failed to meet its obligations (a scary prospect that financial experts call "breaking the buck" since $1 is the net asset value of a share in all money-market funds). Still, I would stay away from funds that yield much more than average because that's usually a sign they are investing in a lot of commercial paper rather than government securities. Cash is supposed to be the least risky part of your portfolio, so don't mess with it.

You may, however, be able to find attractive CDs, issued by banks that can then put your money to use in profitable loans. *Barron's* lists high-yielding CDs every week. For example, in June 2001, Capital One FSB of Richmond was offering six-month certificates yielding 4.9 percent for minimum deposits of $10,000. That was 1.3 percentage points higher than the T-bill rate. With all such CDs, however, make sure that the bank has federally backed insurance on your deposit and that you can withdraw your money before maturity with no penalty.

The only other question with cash is taxes. At a time when taxable money-market funds were yielding an average of 3.8 percent, funds that invest only in tax-exempt municipal securities were yielding an average of 2.6 percent. Which to choose? Use the formula in Chapter 44: divide the tax-exempt yield by 1 minus your tax rate (in decimals) to get the tax-equivalent yield. If you're in a 36 percent bracket, a 2.6 percent tax-exempt yield is the same as a 4.1 percent taxable yield (as far as federal taxes only are concerned). Since both returns fluctuate day to day, these sorts of differences are rarely worth the arbitrage. Choose either.

My own cash stashes of choice are high-interest checking accounts, CDs and, for cash in brokerage accounts, tax-exempt money-market funds. But the main message for the superior investor is this: Almost all interest-bearing cash vehicles are about the same. Don't waste brainpower deciding which you pick.

CONCLUSION

NOW THAT YOU HAVE FINISHED this book, read it again.

But read it differently. Dip into it as you need advice about electronically traded funds, inflation-indexed bonds, gold or drug stocks or any of the dozens of discrete investing topics the book addresses. *The Secret Code for the Superior Investor* is meant to be kept around—and used. It should become as dog-eared and soup-smeared as my first edition of *Mastering the Art of French Cooking*.

However, before you read this book a second time, review what it said the first time. By now, I hope, the principles have become a catechism: buy and hold; diversify; find stocks with moats; avoid the ravages of inflation, expenses and taxes; ignore the media din; buy bonds for the short-term, stocks for the long-term. And investing, you will remember, comes in three stages: first, set a strategy; second, pick your specific assets; and, third, behave like a disciplined investor. Let's review.

Strategy: Know who you are and what you want. That's the first step. You need to understand your limitations—that neither you, nor any other investor, can guess the direction of stock prices in the short term; that you will be scared to death when stocks fall and far too elated when they rise; and that you should be very happy just meeting the market's average return over the past three-quarters of a century: an 11 percent annual increase, which means that the value of your portfolio doubles in less than seven years.

You also have to realize what investing can do (practically insure considerable gains over long periods) and what it cannot (make you a big winner over short periods). You also need to decide on your own goals: If you're young and saving for retirement, you can afford to invest heavily in stocks; if you need funds in the next few years, then stick to bonds, which return less but are also less risky in the short term.

Allocate your assets according to your time horizon, and stick to that allocation. Don't switch from stocks into bonds because the market has dropped and you've become frightened (though you should start switching in that direction as you get older and come closer to cashing in part of your portfolio). In fact, like a Shakespearian character, try to observe your own reactions, step outside yourself. If you see yourself panicking, that is almost certainly a sign to buy stocks, not sell them.

There is good reason to believe that the stock market is undergoing a long-term period of revaluation, in which investors are bidding up shares to their rational and proper levels. That period began in 1982 with the Dow Jones Industrial Average at 777, as my colleague Kevin Hassett and I argued in our 1999 book, *Dow 36,000*. When the process will be over, no one can say, but this is a wonderful juncture in history for being in the stock market. Still, stocks are always extremely volatile in the short term, and there will inevitably be corrections and bear markets along the way. Speculators who jump in and out of the market are *playing*, the same way gamblers play in Las Vegas. Playing is fine, in its place, but don't confuse it with the serious and profitable long-term process called investing.

Assets: The three key assets for investors are stocks (the right investments for the long term), bonds (if you can put your money away only for one to five years) and cash (for your emergency stash, in Treasury bills, money market funds and bank certificates of deposit). These elements combine in a portfolio, whose most important feature is diversification. And, within your main portfolio are separate portfolios for stocks, bonds and cash.

Owning only a few stocks is highly risky. Owning about 30 allows winners to balance losers—so that you'll get performance close to that of the market as a whole, which is a reasonable objective. This does not mean you should avoid playing favorites. Among my own are drug stocks like Pfizer and Johnson & Johnson, for-profit education stocks like Apollo Group and DeVry, and boringly profitable stocks like Fastenal (screws) and Tootsie Roll (candy).

But with all stocks, it is the business that counts—wherever that business is based, in Helsinki or Hell's Kitchen. Examine sales, income, cash flow and balance sheets. Check whether the company has been boosting its profits nicely for the past decade (a sign that it has a "moat" to protect it from competitors) and whether it's likely to continue prospering 50 years from now. Where to find great companies? Check the holdings of the best mutual fund managers, read newspapers, business magazines and research reports, keep your eyes open at work, at the mall and when you travel, the way that Peter Lynch, the best fund manager of our time, did so well.

A stock portfolio can comprise either a few dozen individual companies or a small number of mutual funds, electronically traded funds (like Spiders, which mimic the benchmark S&P 500) or packages of stocks that are put together by investment firms but that you manage yourself. Mutual funds are wonderful innovations, but they can have drawbacks: unexpected tax bills, high expenses and surprisingly poor performance. The best idea is to use a mix. That's what I do.

For bonds, superior investors choose a laddered portfolio of separate securities that mature in succeeding years. That way, you're protected against rising interest rates since you can put the proceeds from a bond that matures into a new bond at a higher rate. Treasury bonds and other bonds guaranteed by the federal government carry the best risk-reward ratio. Don't bother with bonds issued by corporations, but, if you are in a high tax bracket, give close attention to municipal bonds, whose interest is tax-exempt. And don't forget TIPS—Treasury bonds whose interest rates are linked to increases in inflation. They offer the best way to insure against a rising cost of living.

Discipline: What you do after you have assembled your portfolio is the most important part of investing. The best advice is simple: Don't trade. Buy bonds and hold them to maturity. Buy stocks and keep them through bull markets and bear. Yes, there are times to sell, but they are rare. You should sell only when something significant has happened to change the nature of the business in which you are a partner. Don't sell because the stock has risen a lot or fallen a lot, or because you think the economy is slowing down.

It is hard to stay disciplined when the media are continually offering distractions, but try to resist. Avoid the ticker-tape shows, don't read the stock tables every day or even every week. Pay no heed to the Fed or the economy as a whole. In the short term, you can't predict what they will do; in the long term, it doesn't matter since the U.S. economy has been remarkably consistent.

And, if you are like most investors, you will need professional help—not necessarily to pick your stocks and bonds, but to hold your hand and stop you from doing something rash (like selling your best assets) when the inevitable downturn strikes.

Remember to think of yourself as a partaker, sharing in the rising fortunes of exceptional businesses, rather than as an outsmarter, thinking you're so clever you can beat the system with inside advice and superior brainpower. The superior investor has modesty and integrity.

Now, you're ready to take on the financial world. You know the basic code, and the *real* secret is that the rest is simply common sense and good judgment.

INDEX

After-tax returns, 135
Airlines sector, 73
American Depository Receipts, 235
Analysts, 13
Annual return, 9–10
Apollo Group, 261–262
Arnof, Ian, 208–210
Ask price, 146, 301–302
Asset allocation funds, 45
Assets, 115–119, 316–318
Average annual return
growth and value stocks, 220
standard deviation and, 87

Backtesting, 184
Balanced funds, 45
Balance sheet, 105, 115–119
Bank accounts, 39
Bankruptcy, risk of, 86
Bears, 54, 58–59, 154, 191–193
Berkshire Hathaway, Inc., 94–95, 159
Beta, 35, 87, 246, 270–271
Bid price, 146, 301–302
Biogen, 107–108, 110–112, 113–114,
    116
Biotech stocks, 250
Bond funds, 147
Bonds, 38, 45, 292–293. *See also*
    specific types

holding to maturity, 295–297
inflation and, 27, 141
investment time horizon and, 33–34
as I.O.U., 288–289
issuing agencies, 289–290
prices of, 290–291
ratings of, 300
risk of, 35
for short- and medium-term, 23–26,
    287–293
vs. stocks, 17–18, 297
taxation of, 134
Book value, 117
"Branded wallflower" stock, 222
Brand names, 266
Broad Market Social Index, 214
Brokers, compensation to, 146–147
Browne, Christopher and William,
    162
**Buffett, Warren, 5, 20, 68, 69, 74, 94,
    128, 179**
commodity stocks and, 243
on inactivity, 168, 199
stealing stock ideas from, 159
Business, quality of, 12–13
Buy-and-hold investing, 49–52, 69,
    129
Buying, during bear markets,
    191–193

"Call" option, on muni bonds, 301
Campbell, John Y., 54, 89, 90
Capital gains, 110, 134, 135
Capital investment, 110
Capitalization, 127
Capital requirements, 99–100
Carret, Philip, 67, 70–71
Cash, 8, 25–26, 311–313
   forms of, 311
   from investment, 109–110
   investment time horizon and, 34
   as reserve, 39
   risk and, 35–36
Cash flow, 99
   statement of, 105, 110–114
Certificates of deposit (CDs), 39,
   312
Children, investment and, 175–178
Cisco Systems, 150–151, 196–197
Clinton, Bill and Hillary, Whitewater
   Development and, 63–64
Closed-end funds, 42–43
CNBC, financial reporting on, 164
Coca-Cola, 75, 177
Commodity stocks. *See also* Precious
   metals
   trading in, 241, 243–244
Common Stocks and Uncommon Profits
   (Fisher), 69, 200, 247
Consumer Price Index (CPI), 142,
   308
Corporate bonds, 295, 303–306
Corporate Responsibility Newswire,
   213
Costs, of investing, 143–148
Countries, investing in, 231–238
Credit risk, bonds and, 290–292,
   299–300
Cycles
   of growth and value stocks, 220
   in tech stocks, 279–280

"Dating" funds, 154–155
Davis, Christopher, 157–158
Debt, 115–119
Defense, through management,
   76–77
Defined Asset (Equity Investment)
   fund, 42
Dell Computer, 100, 108–109, 113,
   117–118, 203, 229
Depreciation, 110

Developing nations, corporate
   governance in, 236–237
DeVry, 260–261, 262
Diamonds, 44
Discipline, 318
Discount rate, 82
Diversification, 51, 85–91, 129,
   176–177, 252
   benefits of, 89
   international, 231–238
   with munis, 302
   in portfolio, 38–45
   tech stocks and, 277
Dividends, 9–10, 34, 99, 137,
   169–174, 253
   as cash, 110
Dogs of the Dow, 185–187
Domini 400, 211, 214
Douglas, Leslie, "Douglas Theory"
   and, 184–185
Dow, Charles Henry, 127
Dow 36,000 (Glassman and Hassett),
   15, 57–58, 60, 200, 266, 281,
   316
Dow Jones Industrial Average, 54,
   58–59, 86
   "Dogs of the Dow" and, 185
   investing in, 125–131
   investment truths of, 128–129
   problems with, 130
   stability of, 192–193
   tech stocks in, 126–127
Dow Jones Sustainability Group
   Index, 211–212
Dreman, David, 102
Drugs. *See* Pharmaceutical stocks

Earnings. *See also* Price-to-earnings
   (P/E) ratios
   average rate of, 103–104
   companies with moats and, 77
   growth of, 60
   increasing, 266
   net income as, 107
   profits and, 56
   reality of, 98–99
Earnings per share (EPS), 95–96, 107
E-commerce, 275–276, 281. *See also*
   High-tech stocks; Technology
Economy
   international, 233–234
   role in investing, 60, 81–84

slowdown in, 60–61
technology and, 278
warfare in, 74–75
Education, for-profit, 258–263
Education account, 177–178
Environment. *See* Socially responsible
    investing
E/P ratio, 97, 98
EPS. *See* Earnings per share (EPS)
Equity Investment fund, 42
Ethics. *See* Socially responsible
    investing
Exchange-traded funds (ETFs),
    43–45, 146
Expenses, 106–107, 143–148
of mutual funds, 26

Fannie Mae, 76, 289–290, 305
Fastenal Co., 265–266
Federal Home Loan Bank System,
    305
Federal Reserve Board, 22–23,
    81–84
Regulation T, 149–150
Fed funds rate, 82
Feinberg, Kenneth, 157–158
Fidelity Dividend Growth, 172
Financial journalism, 163–168
Financial statements, 105–114
First Commerce, 207–210
Fisher, Philip A., 20, 67, 68–70, 200,
    201, 247
Fixed-income investments, bonds as,
    34, 288–289
FOLIOS, 41–42
Foolish Four strategy, 186
Forecasting, 84
Foreign stocks, 38–39, 231–238
For-profit education, 258–263
401(k) plans, 136–137
Franklin Templeton funds, 72
Freddie Mac, 76, 305
Free cash flow, 99
Friedman, Milton, 307–308
"Fun-and-games account," 179–182
Future, 257–263

Gains, from boring stocks, 265–268
Gardner, David and Tom, 186
General Electric Co. (GE), 251–256
Generally accepted accounting
    principles, 105

Global companies. *See* International
    investing
Goals, 31–32
Going public, volatility and, 90
Gold. *See* Precious metals
Government bonds. *See also* Treasury
    bonds
inflation and, 307–308
Graham, Benjamin, 5, 19–20, 59, 67,
    161–162, 193, 195, 200, 281
Greenspan, Alan, 54, 278
Gross Domestic Product, education
    and, 258
Growth, 72, 96, 252
Growth stocks, vs. value stocks,
    217–223

Hassett, Kevin, 57, 281, 316
Health care, 258–259
Hedge, TIPS and, 308
High-tech stocks, 59, 61, 85–86, 115,
    275–283. *See also* Technology
High-yield (junk) bonds, 289

Idiosyncratic risk, 88, 89
Immelt, Jeffrey, 253–254
Income, estimate over working life, 32
Income-producing stocks, 38, 44
Income statement, 105
Indexed bonds, inflation and, 308
Indexes. *See* specific indexes
Index funds, 44, 145
Individual Retirement Account (IRA),
    133, 136–137, 178
Individual stocks, as sub-portfolio,
    39–40
Inflation, 27, 138–142
bond risks and, 290–291
bonds and, 287–288, 310
cash and, 312
Fed and, 84
government bonds and, 307–308
investment and, 307–310
TIPS and, 308–309
Information technology, 278, 280
Initial Public Offering (IPO), 43, 90
Integrity of management, 69
Interest
on bonds, 288
cash and, 312
municipal bonds and, 299
rates, 81–83, 292

Intermediate funds, 302
International investing, 231–238
Internet
companies, 281–282
pharmaceutical sales via, 249
stock research on, 146
Investec Wired Index Fund, 130
Investment(s). *See also* specific types
assets, 8
basic truths about, 84
cash and, 311–313
costs of, 143–148
in countries, 231–238
goals for, 31–32
history of, 61
minors and, 175–178
in people, 207–210
problems with systems, 183–187
socially responsible, 211–215
three rules of, 72
Investors, as partners, 67–68

January Effect, 53–54
Janus Twenty mutual fund,
85–86
Journalism, financial, 163–168
Jovanovic, Boyan, 278–280
Junk bonds. *See* High-yield (junk)
bonds

Keynes, John Maynard, 90–91
K12, 259

Laddered-bond funds, 296–297
Large-cap stocks, 38, 270
Levitt, Arthur, Jr., 75, 144–145
Liabilities, 116–117
Life plan, 32
Lipper, 212, 219
Liquidity, of small-cap stocks, 270
Load funds, 143–144
Loans
fed funds rate and, 82
margin buying and, 149–152
Long run, 21
Long-term investment
bonds and, 293
taxation and, 136–137
Losses, using, 135
Low-Price Action List, 196
Low-Tax Retirement Account,
constructing, 32

Lynch, Peter, 23–24, 90, 171, 203,
225, 287

Madrick, Jeffrey, 123, 124
Magellan Fund, 225. *See also* Lynch,
Peter
Malkiel, Burton, 7, 89, 155, 165–166
Management, 252–256
defense through, 76–77
integrity of, 69
share ownership by, 266–267
Margin of safety, 68
Margins, buying on, 149–152
Market, matching risks and returns
of, 87–88
"Market Call," 166–167
Market capitalization, 251, 282
Market timing, 121–124, 181
"dating" funds and, 154–155
Maturity of bonds, 288, 295–297
Media
agenda of, 21–22
firms, 158
Medicare, pharmaceuticals and,
248–249
Medium-term, bonds for, 287–293
Merck & Co., 76, 97–98, 151, 214
Merrill Lynch & Co., 172–173, 222
Microsoft, 101, 171, 214
Mid-cap companies, 267
Milken brothers, 259
Mining companies, investing in,
239–244
Minors, investing and, 175–178
Moats, 75–77
Moe, Michael, 258, 259
Momentum buys, 180–181
"Moneyline," 164–165
Money-market funds, 39
Money supply, 81–82
Monopoly, 76
Morgan Stanley Capital International
(MSCI) World index, 235
Morningstar, 145. *See also* specific
issues
growth vs. value and, 219
website, 146, 147, 158
Motley Fool, 186
Movement of stocks, 123–124
Municipal bonds (munis), 134–135,
290, 299–302
Mutual funds. *See also* specific funds

cost calculator for, 144–145
Dow-like, 129
expenses of, 26
expenses ratio for, 144
fee/return comparison of, 145
FOLIOS as, 41–42
loads of, 143–144
managers of, 225–226
mix of stocks, bonds, and cash in, 45
precious-metals funds and, 242–243
selecting, 41
socially responsible investing and,
    211–212
stealing ideas of managers, 157–162
as sub-portfolio, 40–41
value-stock, 221

Nasdaq Composite Index, 44, 54,
    125–131, 275
Natural-resource stocks, precious
    metals stocks and, 239–244
Net asset value (NAV), 43
Net income, 107, 109
New Economy stocks, 130
Newspapers, financial journalism and,
    163–168
Nondiversifiable risk, 15
No-sell strategy, 199–200

Objectives, 32
Oil shock, 60–61
One-stock portfolio, 251–256
Open Market Committee, of Fed, 81,
    82
Outsmarters, 6
vs. partakers, 63–65
Outstanding Investor Digest, 70

Partakers, 7, 63–65
PEG ratio, 97
Penney, JC, 74
People, investing in, 207–210
P/E ratios. See Price-to-earnings (P/E)
    ratios
Perry, H. Bradlee, 21, 84
Pharmaceutical stocks, 245–250
Pilgrim Corporate Leaders, 129
Portfolios, 13–15, 37–45
small-caps as percentage of, 273
tech stocks in, 282–283
TIPS in, 310
Precious metals, 239–244, 310

Pre-tax returns, 135
Priceline.com, 119, 202
Price movements, Fed and, 82
Prices
inflation and, 139
of muni bonds, 301–302
of stock, 93–94
Price-to-book (P/B) ratio, 101, 117,
    218
Price-to-earnings (P/E) ratios, 55,
    93–104, 255
Price to sales (P/S) ratio, 102–103
Price weighting, of Dow, 127
Procter & Gamble, 77, 85, 201
Productivity, tech stocks and, 278
Profits. See also Dividends
earnings as, 107
interest rates and, 83
of pharmaceuticals, 246–247
stream of, 56
Protection, moat as, 75–77
Prudent Bear Fund, 154, 155

Quality, gains and, 266
Quantum Fund, 68

Random walk, 155, 165–166, 292
Rapier, Tom, 207–209
Ratings, of bond issues, 305–306
Rational behavior, 59–60
Ratios, 93–104. See also specific ratios
Real estate investment trusts (REITs),
    38, 172
Real returns, 35–36
Recessions
oil shocks and, 61
small-cap stocks after, 271–272
stock market fall preceding, 191–192
"Reciprocal 100" companies, 235
Regulation, of pharmaceutical
    companies, 248–249
Regulation T, 149–150
Reinvestment, of dividends, 176
REITs. See Real estate investment
    trusts (REITs)
Reporting, to SEC, 157
Resources, itemizing, 32
Retailing sector, 74
Retirement investments, 133, 136
goals and account for, 32
inflation and, 140
Returns, 9–10, 34

average annual, 121–122
real, 35
risk and, 271
Revenue, 105–106
Risk, 32, 34–35, 86–88. *See also* Credit
  risk; Volatility
of bonds, 35, 287–289
consistent growth and, 96
credit risk, 290–292
diversification and, 85
margin buying and, 152
returns and, 271
standard deviation and, 18, 86–87
of stocks, 35
systematic (nondiversifiable), 15
Risk aversion, 8
Risk premium, for stocks, 58
Roll Call, 74–75
Roth IRAs, for children, 178
Rule of 72, 10

Safety margin, 68
Sapir, Michael, 154
Savings, estimating, 32
Scheiber, Anne, 49–52
Secret Code
five basic lessons of, 50–52
principles of, 5–27
Sectors. *See also* specific sectors
for future, 257–263
technology as, 275–283
Securities and Exchange
  Commission, reporting to, 157
Selected American, 157–158
Self-knowledge, 6–8
Selling
reasons for, 199–204
after stocks have risen, 202–203
Selling short, 153–156
Sell-target, 203
Shareholder equity. *See* Book value
Shares, top management ownership
  of, 266–267
Shiller, Robert, 54, 59
Shorting a stock, 153–156
Short-term
bonds as investments, 23–26
bonds for, 287–293
cash as debt, 25–26
stock ownership in, 18–21
stock prices in, 200
Siegel, Jeremy, 17, 36, 57

Silver stocks. *See* Precious metals
Simons, Gail, 155–156
Small-cap stocks, 38, 44, 267, 268,
  269–273
Socially responsible investing,
  211–215
Socrates (research service), 213–214
Spiders, 44, 146
Splits, 94
Standard deviation, 18
margin buying and, 151–152
risk measurement with, 86–87
of small-cap stocks, 270
Standard & Poor's 500-Stock Index,
  9, 53, 125–126, 145, 160
stability of, 192–193
Start-up companies, 75–76
Stein Roe Young Investors Fund, 177
Stock
one stock worth owning, 251–256
price of, 93–94
shorting of, 153–156
Stock analysts, stealing stock ideas
  from, 159–160
Stock funds, 144, 147, 234. *See also*
  specific funds
Stock movements, journalists on,
  163–168
Stock-picking systems, 183–187
Stock prices, 7, 57–58, 60, 83
Stocks. *See also* Dividends
vs. bonds, 297
buying, 50–51
costs of, 53–61
in "fun-and-games account,"
  181–182
individual as sub-portfolio, 39–40
individual vs. portfolios, 13–15
inflation and, 27, 141
investment time horizon and, 33, 36
long-run performance of, 192–193
movement of, 123
personal experience and, 226–230
in portfolio, 38
pricing of, 57–58
selecting own, 88
splits in, 94
taxation of, 134
trading of, 18–21
wish list of, 195–197
"Stop-loss," 202
Strategy, 315–316

Sub-portfolios, 39–45
Sullivan, Dan, 227–228
Systematic risk, 15
Systemic risk, 88

Taxation, 133–137
bracket and, 32
cash and, 312–313
minimizing, 51
of municipal bonds, 299–301
stocks vs. bonds and, 26–27
TIPS and, 309–310
Tax-deferred investments, 32, 136
Technology, 14. *See also* High-tech
    stocks
bear markets and, 192
portfolio investing and, 44
as sector, 275–283
volatility of, 277–278
Television, financial journalism and,
    163–168
Templeton, John, 67, 71–72
TheStreet.com, 150
Time, 9–11, 17
Time horizon, 8
for bond ownership, 295
for small-cap stocks, 271
stocks and, 33–36
Timing of market, 121–124
TIPS. *See* Treasury inflation-protected
    securities (TIPS)
Tobias, Andrew, 148
Tobin, James, 308
Tootsie Roll Industries, 200–201,
    266
Torray Fund, 158
Total return, 123
T. Rowe Price, 172, 236, 271
Trading, of stocks, 18–21
Train, John, 68, 70
Transaction costs, 19, 160–161
Treasury, TIPS from, 310
Treasury bills, 39, 141–142
cash and, 312
Treasury bonds, 142, 287, 288–289,
    295

Treasury Inflation-Protected
    Securities (TIPS), 27, 307–310
Treasury securities, interest rates and,
    81–82
Trusts, unit investment, 42
Tweedy, Forrest Berwind, 161–162

Uniform Gifts to Minors Act, 177
U.S. stocks, vs. non-U.S. stocks, 231
U.S. Tax Code, 133–137
U.S. Treasury Bonds, 133
Unit investment trust (UIT), 42, 302

Valuation, 55
Value investor, Graham as, 68
Value Line Investment Survey, 41,
    95, 118, 158, 161, 172, 254
Value stocks, vs. growth stocks,
    217–223
Vanguard Funds, 145–146
Volatility, 15, 16–17. *See also* Risk
increasing, 89
of Nasdaq, 126
risk as, 86–87
of sectors, 277–278
of small-cap stocks, 270–271

Walgreen Co., 196, 268
Wallman, Steve, 41, 42
Washington Post Co., 93, 94, 100,
    163, 167–168
Weiss, Michael J., 226–227
Welch, Jack, 252–253, 255
What Works on Wall Street (O'Shaugh-
    nessy), 102
Whittle, Chris, 259–260
Wilshire 5000, 145
Wish list, of stocks, 195–197
Worldwide stock funds, 234
Wrigley Company, 172, 177

Yields. *See also* Dividends
of corporate bonds, 303–304
tax-equivalent, 300

Zero-coupon bonds, 31

JAMES K. GLASSMAN is a fellow at the American Enterprise Institute and writes a weekly investing column for the *Washington Post*. He was the coauthor (with Kevin Hassett) of *Dow 36,000*, the bestselling book on stock valuation. He is host of the popular website www.TechCentralStation.com and has been the financial columnist for *Reader's Digest* and the *International Herald Tribune*. He lives in Falls Village, Connecticut, and New York City.